# The Sex Factor

# The Sex Factor

How Women Made the West Rich

Victoria Bateman

polity

The right of Victoria Bateman to be identified as Author of this Work has been asserted in accordance with the UK Copyright, Designs and Patents Act 1988.

First published in 2019 by Polity Press

Polity Press
65 Bridge Street
Cambridge CB2 1UR, UK

Polity Press
101 Station Landing
Suite 300
Medford, MA 02155, USA

ISBN-13: 978-1-5095-2676-5
ISBN-13: 978-1-5095-2677-2 (pb)

A catalogue record for this book is available from the British Library.

Library of Congress Cataloging-in-Publication Data

Names: Bateman, Victoria N. (Victoria Naomi), 1979- author.
Title: The sex factor : how women made the West rich / Victoria Bateman.
Description: Medford, MA : Polity Press, [2019] | Includes bibliographical references and index.
Identifiers: LCCN 2018043360 (print) | LCCN 2018044879 (ebook) | ISBN 9781509526802 (Epub) | ISBN 9781509526765 (hardback) | ISBN 9781509526772 (pbk.)
Subjects: LCSH: Women–Social conditions. | Women–Employment. | Wages–Women. | Sex role–Economic aspects. | Feminism–History.
Classification: LCC HQ1121 (ebook) | LCC HQ1121 .B338 2019 (print) | DDC 305.4–dc23
LC record available at https://lccn.loc.gov/2018043360

Typeset in 10.5 on 12 pt Sabon
by Toppan Best-set Premedia Limited
Printed and bound in the UK by TJ International Ltd

For further information on Polity, visit our website:
politybooks.com

# Contents

# Table and Figures

# Acknowledgements

Whilst much of my academic life is spent writing in isolation, with a laptop in front of me and a cup of tea to one side, the connections that inspired the words on the pages of this book span the world and life not only within but beyond academia. I have found myself part of a stimulating online global community of academics, including Dr Judy Stephenson, Professor Mark Koyama, Dr Alice Evans, Dr Carolina Alves, Dr Vincent Gelaso and the anonymous economic historian Pseudoerasmus (to name just a few). I have also learnt a lot from – and been touched by – the support I have received through social media from sex workers and sex worker groups when advocating for policy change and de-stigmatization. I have had the pleasure of hosting Professor Julie Nelson and Professor Yana Rodgers, from the United States, and author Kat Banyard at special seminars in Cambridge, and I am grateful that my college is always happy to facilitate such events, along with our annual Women in Economics Day, for which I am indebted to Lucy Ward. I would like to thank the many people I've been fortunate to engage with in policy and journalistic circles, along with the Office for National Statistics and the British Civil Service's Exploring Economics group, Gender Equality Network and Women in Economics Network, all of which have graciously hosted my talks. My artistic work and experiences have greatly shaped my thinking about society and the economy, and for that I am forever grateful to Anthony Connolly RP, Jenna Young, Tamsin Sancha, Shelly Bancroft, Leena McCall and Mark Longworth. I have learnt a lot about attitudes towards women and their bodies through my artistic endeavours, attitudes that I see as central to restrictions on women's freedom – and, with it, economic prosperity – across the world. Although academic life is more commonly associated with the spoken and written word, I have found art to be a powerful means of engaging with the world beyond the ivory towers, one that is two-way and bottom-up (as opposed to one-way and top-down).

I am very fortunate to be able to call the Cambridge community home. It is a community that I have found to be unceasingly liberal, open-minded and supportive. Cambridge was the first place I could escape (and question) convention. My College has never insisted that I toe the usual academic line or restrict myself to the standard modes of academic engagement, and I never take the space and freedom that it offers me for granted. I am particularly grateful to Dr Ruth Scurr, Dr Clive Lawson, Professor Sir Alan Fersht, Dr David Secher, Dr Arif Ahmed, Dr Karenjit Clare, Dr Bronwen Everill, The Reverend Dr Cally Hammond and Dr Amy Ludlow, along with many other Cambridge colleagues outside of Caius, and those further afield: Professor Avner Offer, Professor Michelle Baddeley, Professor Deborah Oxley, Professor Bob Allen and Dr Marina Della Giusta. It has been a pleasure to work with George Owers at Polity Books, and I thank him, Gail Ferguson, Julia Davies and all the Polity team for their help, professionalism and expertise, along with three expert anonymous referees.

This book is dedicated not only to my female relatives, past and present, who have all lived much more difficult lives than my own, and without whom I would not be here today, but also to my husband of fourteen years, James. James and I first met in the winter of 1997 at our Cambridge University interviews. I could not do what I do without his unfailing love and support. James understands me more than anyone ever could and always supports me in whatever I choose to do. He keeps me as close to sanity as is possible, gives me strength and lets me fly.

# Introduction

Not much more than a year ago, in March 2018, in the British coastal resort of Brighton, I was on a secret mission – one that I'd been planning for a while. I left my dark and dingy hotel room, took the lift downstairs to the conference suite and walked into the gala reception of the Royal Economic Society annual conference (a gathering of some five hundred economists) wearing nothing but shoes, gloves, a necklace – and, of course, a smile.

I didn't choose to appear naked at such an event because it was unseasonably warm (it certainly wasn't), nor due to a lack of suitable outfits in my wardrobe (I have a sizeable collection at home), but because economics has a sex problem. If economists were going to stand up and listen, I knew it would require something more than a short conference speech of the kind I was scheduled to deliver the following day.

Whilst naked protest isn't the usual approach employed by an academic, I do not – as you might have guessed – subscribe to the view that words are the only suitable means of communication. It is, after all, more than five hundred years since Johannes Gutenberg invented the printing press. Just because the written and spoken word is the usual means of academic communication, it doesn't mean that we should restrict ourselves to them at all times. When I think about what has most powerfully affected my own thinking as an economist, on everything from poverty and prosperity to capitalism and the state, it is something else entirely: it is art. Whether it be painting, sculpture, theatre or film, art has power, a power that goes beyond words. As a great believer in the power of art, I thought that an artistic statement of the kind long used by feminist performance artists would be a creative addition for a meeting of economists.

My aim was simple: to punch feminism into the centre of economics or at least into the centre of the largest annual gathering of economists here in the United Kingdom. As a feminist and an economist, I'm regularly asked 'What do feminism and economics have in common?' The answer is simple: not nearly enough. Despite the many courageous efforts of feminists over the last century or more, feminism seems to have passed economics by. Unlike virtually every other academic discipline, mainstream economics just carries on as normal. As if the feminist revolution never happened. As if women didn't exist. And as if we were still living in a bygone age.

In almost every area of study, economics overlooks sex, gender and women's freedom, including the vital importance of women's freedom over their bodies. As I wandered around the event, chatting and sipping champagne, these issues were an elephant in the room that no single economist could ignore.

It was my body and my choice, and, to quote the famous feminist mantra, personal is political. Nothing – not even the naked body – should be too personal for economists to consider. It is in the most personal aspects of our lives, including those that revolve around women's bodies, that economic outcomes, such as poverty and inequality, are determined. It is in this sense that economics has a sex problem – at least until it takes women's bodies seriously.

In the nineteenth century, economists created an artificial barrier between the public and the private spheres of life. The public sphere – life in the market and in politics – was deemed important enough for economists to study. By contrast, what went on in private – in the home, the family and community – was deemed irrelevant; it was seen as too female and too soft. Even when economists ventured into the personal sphere – as Nobel prizewinning economist Gary Becker famously did[1] – it seemed more like a vanity project, one that served to teach non-economists that economics could explain everything else in the world and that society could be reduced down to basic economics. It was certainly not an interdisciplinary project, one of bringing together great minds from different subjects in order to create a whole that was more than the sum of its parts. It was economics (wrongly in my opinion) trying to prove itself to be the 'king' of the social sciences.

The artificial wall between the public and the private spheres is long overdue a wrecking ball. After all, how can we understand poverty and inequality without opening the black box that is the home and the surrounding community? It is here, outside of the market, that we can find the roots of many of today's economic problems. The economy simply cannot be understood without also thinking about society, along with psychology, history and philosophy. Yet, disappointingly, whilst the vast majority of other social scientists agree with the statement that 'in general, interdisciplinary knowledge is better than knowledge obtained by a single discipline', 57 per cent of economists actively disagree with it.[2] Perhaps they have something to fear.

Whilst seeing, as I did, hundreds of economists standing around at a conference sipping champagne might create an illusion that all is well, economics is in fact in one of the most tumultuous periods ever, rebuilding its reputation after the crash of 2008. And ten years on, out there in the real world, the economy stands in a precarious position, facing de-globalization, secular stagnation and the political and social unrest caused by inequality, austerity and deindustrialization. On a good day, I like to think that economics is moving forward – that it is, at least in some areas, undergoing something of a revolution. But not all revolutions have positive results. If economics is to fully get to grips with the latest set of economic challenges, it needs to draw upon new ideas and new voices, embracing experiences that differ from the norm. That includes feminism. Economics needs to embrace the sex factor.

As I will argue in this book, women's freedom – and that includes their bodily autonomy – is central to answering many of the big questions economists face: Why is the West rich? Why is poverty so stubborn? What are the costs and benefits of free markets? How can economies develop capable and democratic states? And why has inequality increased? As we will see, the economists' sex problem has even affected their ability to explain boom and bust.

Whilst some are already starting to draw connections between gender and economic outcomes, and a pioneering school of feminist economics has been taking root since the 1990s, centred on the International Association for Feminist Economics (IAFFE), economists still pay far too little attention to gender, as feminist economists themselves note. Although mainstream economics has attempted to incorporate gender in regard to labour markets and wages, though certainly not to the satisfaction of feminist thinkers,[3] sex and gender are largely ignored in theories of economic growth, boom and bust, and inequality, whilst the standard assumptions, measures and methods employed by economists are (wrongly) assumed to be gender neutral.[4]

This failure may in part reflect the fact that women in economics are themselves quite rare, as was indeed apparent at the Royal Economic Society annual conference. There has only ever been one female economics Nobel prizewinner (Elinor Ostrom), and in the United Kingdom and the United States male students outnumber female students by between two and three to one. No wonder feminism has, unlike most other academic disciplines, largely passed economics by,[5] or that there is mounting evidence of sexism within economics.[6] But it would of course be wrong to assume that every female economist has her eyes open to gender and that every male economist is anti-feminist. As Julie Nelson notes, what needs challenging about economics goes much deeper than a lack of women: the very methodology of economics needs reform. This methodology holds on tight as, unlike most other disciplines, what defines economics is not so much its subject matter as its methodological approach to the world.[7] It is an approach that embraces gender bias at its very roots in what is seen as 'good practice and scientific detachment'.[8] Economics has for too long revered independence and denigrated human connections. It has treated emotion as irrational and not worthy of incorporation into economic models. The very things that make human life differ from the robotic assumptions that economists like to make – fertility, family and society – have all been neglected. This doesn't mean replacing economists' standard assumptions that we are all independent, self-interested and rational with an opposite set of assumptions: that we are dependent, altruistic and emotional. Instead, it means getting to grips with the everyday tensions that can arise between these two polar extremes, and how those tensions, and the way they are resolved, help explain economic outcomes.

I myself used to think that economics was gender neutral. It is only with time, and after years of thinking and research, that I've been able to identify for myself numerous areas of economics in which economists' neglect of sex and gender has come at great cost: the cost of truly understanding and confronting the problems our economy faces. And this, therefore, forms the subject matter of this book.

In part I, I begin by outlining the standard narrative of how the West grew rich, condensing the latest thinking down to five key take-away lessons – lessons that are relevant to rich and poor countries alike but which, as we will see, also contain significant holes. In the process, I will show how women have been airbrushed from history, and with it from our thinking about the causes of economic prosperity. Little wonder, therefore, that we still find it difficult to answer the question: 'How did the West get rich?' Whilst women are commonly seen as passive beneficiaries of the process of economic growth, I instead treat them as active agents. Drawing on history, I go on to argue that women made the West rich: that feminism began before, not after, the seeds of prosperity were sown. To understand why so many countries are poor, we need to delve into the home – into the 'private' world beyond politics and the marketplace.

Part II turns from prosperity to inequality. Having seen its importance for prosperity, chapter 3 considers whether we can rely on women's freedom to naturally improve over time – or whether it can also, sadly, retreat. As we will see, much like income inequality, gender inequality moves in a wave-like fashion. It has, in fact, got worse (rather than better) for much of history, and 'economic growth' in the form of technological change cannot be guaranteed to move it in the right direction.

Chapter 4 argues that without greater progress in regard to gender equality, it will be impossible to address the recent rise in income inequality. Gender equality is necessary for both increasing the size of the economic pie and ensuring that it is more equitably distributed. I outline the all too often neglected links between income inequality and gender inequality and offer a new explanation for the rise in inequality in the West: a global sex problem resulting from women across the world having too little control over their bodies. The implication is clear: inequality in the West cannot be addressed until women's bodily freedom is placed on the right trajectory. At present, access to birth control cannot be guaranteed.[9] Globally, almost one in two pregnancies are unintended[10] and more than 200 million women who would like to avoid pregnancy lack access to modern birth control methods.[11]

My consideration of inequality concludes in the final chapter by highlighting a neglected form of inequality, one that is focused on inequalities *between* women: between those who monetize their bodies and those who monetize their brains. It is an inequality which not only divides feminists but which, as we'll see, some feminists are actively contributing towards through their policy recommendations in regard to sex work. Whilst it means confronting a major social taboo, no one who takes social justice seriously should be ignoring sex workers. The ultimate question is this: If we can make money from our brain, why shouldn't we also be able to make money from our bodies? Isn't it hypocritical and intellectually elitist to suggest otherwise? Sex work is the perfect example of how social attitudes, even when well intentioned, can seriously harm the most vulnerable women.

Part III of the book moves on to consider the most defining political debate that has hung over economics since the time of Adam Smith: markets versus state. I look at whether gender equality and the equitable prosperity it helps to deliver are best served by the market or by the state. In the first chapter, you can find both a feminist attack – but also a feminist defence – of the market. As we will see, wherever you find yourself on the political spectrum, feminist thinking has a lot to offer and in a way that can transform policy on the ground, improving the everyday lives of women and, at the same time, boosting the economy. As we will also see, whilst feminists may disagree on the optimal combination of market and state, they are united in the suggestion that we need to bring a third sphere to bear on the debate: that life exists outside of the market and beyond the purview of the state, and that this literal 'economic no man's land', for better or worse, holds the keys to understanding and improving economic outcomes. In the second of the part's two chapters, I turn to the state and highlight the way in which women's freedom helped to positively shape the western state, making it more democratic and more capable, ultimately enabling a more conducive (albeit not perfect) relationship between the market and the state and, with it, greater prosperity. Needless to say, further such gains still remain up for grabs, something we must remember in light of the recent growth slowdown in the West. If economies at home or abroad want to get the best of both worlds – of both market and state – women's freedom can take them a long way.

The final part of the book (part IV) asks: Why have economists neglected women (and their bodies) for so long? What is it about economics that leads economists to ignore sex and gender and, more generally, to dehumanize the economy? It goes to the root of the matter by looking at the common assumptions made by economists: that we are all rational, self-interested and calculating beings; that we are all, in other words, robots. Sex and gender do not exist. This part begins by considering how economics came to make those assumptions, and then goes on to see why these assumptions face increasing criticism for their lack of 'humanity', as popularized by behavioural economics. I argue that economists' failure to incorporate real human characteristics has left them not only incapable of properly explaining everyday economic phenomena such as poverty and boom and bust but is itself indicative of a sex problem within economics – that a ghost of machismo hangs over the discipline that has made economics reluctant to change. The final chapter shows that behavioural economics both goes too far and not far enough. It argues that we need to incorporate three additional elements – the body, family and society – within the core of economic thinking. Doing so is not 'soft', as the ghost of machismo would have us believe. It is vital.

Throughout the book, I will be drawing on (a lot of) history. History is crucial to understanding the economy, albeit that is something not always appreciated by economists themselves. You will therefore find included in this book a brief history of prosperity, a history of gender inequality, a history of the state and a history of the individual. We will span vast periods of time – from the Stone Age to the Industrial Revolution. You might want to fasten your seat belt!

Whilst I am proud to declare myself a feminist, I should note that nothing divides feminists more than capitalism, though sex work comes a close second. Both debates are tackled in the course of this book, and I will refrain from sitting on the fence. As someone who has seen the dark side of society – its tendency to enforce conformity and to punish those who deviate from the norm – I will not be suggesting, as Marxist feminists do, that we should be disposing of the market. Markets, as I will argue, have provided women with a release from society and have in fact been central to building women's freedom. That does not, however, mean that markets are perfect, as we will see. But it does mean that the state and society can sometimes deliver far worse outcomes. That is no more clearly the case than in regard to sex work: the way in which society stigmatizes sex workers; and the state chooses to enact laws that make life more difficult for women who choose to monetize their bodies, unlike those who monetize their brains. Women's bodies are the battleground we face today, a battleground that does not disappear by covering them up and ignoring them. And it's why I have absolutely no shame when it comes to protesting naked.

Join me in this book as I knit together my two great passions: economics and feminism, hopefully in a way that brings new light to bear on each.

# Part I

## Prosperity

# Introduction

Perhaps the most fundamental question economists face is why are some countries rich and so many others still poor? Why is average yearly income in the United States (measured in international dollars) close to $59,532 a year but not so far away, in Guatemala, average yearly income is only $8,150, whilst in Pakistan and Sudan it is even lower, at $5,527 and $4,904 respectively? The differences are stark.[1] What would take a year for someone to earn in Pakistan could be earned in not much more than a month in the United States. Whilst money certainly isn't enough to make us happy, the fact that so many people risk their lives attempting to cross the Mexican border or clambering on board boats owned by unscrupulous people traffickers destined for the European coastline is clear enough evidence that the gap in prosperity matters.

It seems that the greatest determinant of whether we live a long and comfortable life or a short disease-ridden one threatened by hunger, is little more than where we are born. As the economist Branko Milanovic shows, at least 66 per cent of the differences in people's income worldwide is explained by the country in which they live.[2] It is often not our capabilities, work ethic or drive that has the greatest effect on our standard of living but where, by the luck of the draw, we first entered the world. Those of us born in countries like the United States and Britain have literally hit the jackpot.

Looking to history helps us understand how we got to where we are today, and, when doing so, one particular event has long stood out: the Industrial Revolution. The Industrial Revolution took place in Britain in the late eighteenth and early nineteenth centuries, spreading to continental Europe and the United States in the course of the nineteenth century. Ever since, western incomes have travelled along an upward trajectory, albeit with some bumps along the way. The result was a big divergence in economic fortunes between 'the West and the rest'.

At the centre of Britain's Industrial Revolution was the area in which I grew up in cold and wet northern England: Manchester. Whilst Manchester is perhaps best known internationally for football (admittedly, my family were keen Manchester United fans and, as a result, I was dressed in red rather than baby pink as a child), it is in fact the Industrial Revolution for which it truly deserves fame. This was a time at which the city became known as 'Cottonopolis', and my grandparents and their grandparents before them all earned a living working in cotton mills in or on the outskirts of Manchester. When I was growing up in the 1980s, my grandmother bombarded me with stories of an age that was by then rapidly vanishing – and, of course, of the difficult lives of my female ancestors. Deindustrialization was setting in and Manchester had long passed its peak – industrialization and cotton manufacture had spread overseas, so that many of the cotton mills in which my family had worked had fallen silent. However, the evidence of earlier success was clearly visible in the landscape, which was scattered with imposing red-bricked mills, with chimneys that reached high into the sky, most of them in a dilapidated state of disrepair, with smashed windows and crumbling brickwork and the occasional sound of children 'exploring' the derelict stairwells. Some of these industrial mausoleums found a new use as warehouses and, by the time the 1990s were in full swing, as blocks of New York-style loft apartments (with prices well out of the reach of the former cotton workers). With the factory doors firmly closed, some of my aunts and uncles moved to work at the other end of the 'cloth trade', on the production floors or in the design studios of expanding British fashion labels or in small couture houses. Britain's early industrialization was clear in every aspect of my early life, as it is in the fashion conscious and stylishly dressed Britain of today.

Why Britain successfully industrialized, and, with it, how Europe and indeed the West became global economic leaders, were questions I could not help but ponder from a young age. However, when I took to the books to find the answers, I found accounts almost purely of men – of the famous male engineers, entrepreneurs, scientists and inventors whose statues, cast in bronze, basked in sunshine in the centres of our big cities (including my home town). It left me wondering: where were the women who, I knew from my own family stories, had, for example, filled the cotton mills and who were so clearly central to the development of the Industrial Revolution? And what about the generations of women before them who, unlike those in many poor countries today, seem to have had a much greater degree of freedom than popular narratives would have us believe? Why was all the focus on men's lives when what seemed to me to be the greatest difference between 'the West and the rest' was women's lives – women's freedom?

The answer is, of course, that women's freedom is all too often seen as a by-product of growth, rather than as an underlying driver. We assume that history is made by men and that what's going on in women's lives is just a sideshow: that men create prosperity and women simply benefit from it. Not so in this book.

In the first of the two chapters that follow, I bring together the work of many different economic historians to present a summary of thinking about how the West grew rich. We will see what this research has to offer but also identify a number of holes – holes that are a direct result of leaving women out of the picture. We will see that whilst big debates now rage about the causes of the Industrial Revolution, the different sides are united in one vital respect: their neglect of women. As things stand, we cannot explain 'how the West grew rich' – and it's in no small part because we are ignoring the elephant in the room. In the second chapter, I therefore delve into the lesser-told story of the Industrial Revolution – the story of how women made the West rich, and not just during the Industrial Revolution itself but by sowing the seeds of growth many centuries beforehand.

I should say from the start that this is *not* a story of a small handful of female scientists and entrepreneurs who defied expectations and broke the mould[3]; it is a story of the everyday woman. That includes women like my great-great-great-grandmothers. As we will see, through the decisions they were able to make about work, family and fertility, the average woman was just as instrumental to the creation of economic prosperity as were the more famous male figures known to us today. Understanding this secret story of how the West grew rich is crucial to understanding why so many countries remain poor today – and what needs to change.

# 1

## Censored: How the West (Supposedly) Got Ahead

In the words of the Nobel prizewinning economist Robert Lucas, 'once you start thinking about growth, it's hard to think about anything else.' The unassuming little number that represents the economy's rate of economic growth could not be more powerful. Whilst a growth rate of just 2–3% a year might seem marginal, compounded over decades it has the power to transform economies and improve lives. With a starting income of just US$1,000, a growth rate of 1% a year would see that income rise to more than US$1,600 after fifty years. However, edge that growth rate up to 3%, and in fifty years' time you would instead be four times richer. Increase it even further to 5% a year, and your income would be more than ten times the initial figure. If we can unlock the black box that holds the recipe of economic growth, we have the keys to bring about untold improvements to the lives of millions of people across the world today. The stakes are high.

Unsurprisingly, economic growth has mesmerized economists (and it certainly has always had my attention). Open any economics 'growth theory' textbook and you will find a whirlwind depiction of all of the time and energy that goes into modelling the process of growth, together with proofs of which factors do (or do not) matter. However, as I found out in my student days, much of this work is mathematical, with little connection to the world today – or to our longer-run history. Whilst technically it is impressive, it is lacking in context. Assumptions are made that can lead us to ignore important causes of growth, and some causes of growth are simply left out because they cannot be easily quantified. History can tell us so much more.

Hence, in this chapter, I want to consider the whole ocean of existing historical evidence in an effort to shed light on the process of economic growth. As we will see, the creation of prosperity is much more complex – but also much more interesting – than any mathematical model could ever capture. However, big gaps in our knowledge remain, gaps that, as we will see, are the result of a gender blindness in the way economists approach the past.

## A Potted History of Growth from the Stone Age to the Present

Economic history used to be simple. Until relatively recently, we used to look back at the past and make two grand and sweeping assumptions: that nothing much of interest happened until the British Industrial Revolution, and that the West has always been best.[1] However, as historians have opened their eyes – as economic history has 'gone global' and as we have penetrated further back in time – we have learnt to become much more humble. We have been forced to admit that western dominance has in fact been the exception and not the rule. Only in the last two hundred years has the West firmly managed to climb the global ladder. Before this time, all the interesting action was taking place outside. And not just for a short while – for millennia.

The reality is that for thousands of years, all of the major technological advances took place outside Europe. Whether it's the first time we began to settle down in one place and farm the land, the invention of the first manufacturing technologies, the construction of the first urban settlements or the first time we put pen to paper (or, rather, stylus to clay tablet), it was civilizations outside of the West that dazzled. Whilst they were becoming 'civilized', many Europeans were still running around practically barefoot, chasing wild animals.

Three regions stand out: the part of the Middle East historically known as Mesopotamia, between the Tigris and Euphrates rivers (an area sometimes referred to as the fertile crescent); the Yellow River Valley in China; and the Indus Valley, which is in modern-day Pakistan and India. In each of these regions, farming became established between 10,000–6,500 BC, with Africa's southern Eastern Sahara not far behind.[2] It took up to another two thousand years for this 'Neolithic' revolution to reach the western outskirts of Europe.

With farming came manufacturing. Before humans first settled down, we were regularly on the move, following the migration patterns of animals. Possessing anything other than the most basic goods would have made life cumbersome. With the birth of farming, we 'put down roots', which meant we could become ever more acquisitive. We could, quite simply, own 'stuff'. Hence it is in the areas where agriculture first developed – outside of Europe – where we also find the first manufacturing activity, including the production of textiles, pottery and metal ware. That included bronze.

The Bronze Age, which dates to around 3,500 BC, stimulated long-distance trade between the East and the West. Europe became the natural resource heap for merchants from the Middle East and beyond. Copper and tin mines – the two substances needed to produce bronze – sprung up in some of the furthest (and coldest) reaches of the continent, including Cornwall and Wales. Britain's (and indeed Europe's) first international economic transactions were, to say the least, primitive.

Where farming and manufacturing first developed, urban settlements also began to sprout. Jericho is one of the first such towns, dating to around 7,000 BC. Also located in the Middle East was what is often thought to be the first human civilization, Sumeria, with its historic city of Ur. A united Egypt had formed by 3,000 BC, and the Purple People of the Lebanese Coast operated trading routes between the two regions. Known to us today as the Phoenicians, they pioneered developments in shipping and commerce that later diffused to the ancient Greeks.

With urban developments and trade came a need for the written word – and for arithmetic. Administration of towns would have been near impossible without it, as was trade beyond anything other than meagre levels. As with the earlier technological revolutions, this revolution also first took place in the Middle East, Pakistan and China. The revolution in writing in turn enabled the development of intellectual thought, whilst the development of mathematics enabled the design and construction of buildings and, ultimately, laid the foundations for modern science.

The fact that, despite its many centuries of 'underdevelopment', the West managed not only to catch up with but overtake the rest of the world is nothing short of astonishing. Although historians have in the past emphasized the achievements of ancient Greece and Rome, we now know just how much they had to thank the earlier civilizations for their success. The roots of ancient Greece are to be found in small groups of traders who rose to challenge the Phoenicians. They adopted the writing and commercial techniques of not only the Purple People but also the Lydians and the Babylonians, including coinage, the joint stock company, banking, insurance and the alphabet. In many respects, Europe first began to make its mark not as an innovator but as an assimilator. By the time the Romans were marching across Europe and, as former master of my own Cambridge college Joseph Needham revealed decades ago, China was still well ahead. And, rather than being the poorest part of the world, Africa was instead pretty average, globally speaking, albeit with 'significant heterogeneity'.[3] Europe was firmly on the back – not front – foot.

As the Roman Empire fell into decline, Europe entered a period which has traditionally been known as the Dark Ages. Recent history has shed more light on this period of darkness, but it was nonetheless an unsettling time for the continent. Europe became highly fragmented and had to begin the process of rebuilding trade and political institutions from the bottom up, rather than relying on a strong top-down state. By medieval times, Italy had become Europe's seat of prosperity, and much of its wealth was built on the back of connections to the still much more prosperous East.

For other Europeans, Italy provided the only seemingly attainable model of growth. Looking on in envy, they reasoned that, if they were to compete with cities such as Venice, they needed to forge their own connections eastwards, breaking the Italian monopoly on long-distance trade. The royal courts of Spain and Portugal, and later England, sent out explorers and navigators to open the door to the East, hoping for a piece of the action. Vasco da Gama sailed under the southern cape of Africa and out into the Indian Ocean, establishing new trade routes for Portugal. Christopher Columbus took a different tack. Thinking outside of the box, he sailed westwards, hoping to find a back door to China. Without knowing it, he stumbled on the Americas.

What followed was one of the darkest periods of Europe's engagement with the world: the exploitation and elimination of indigenous peoples, and the slave trade – the buying and selling of individual human life as if it were little different to the tobacco, sugar and raw cotton that those very same lives were being bought and sold to produce. And not just on a small scale but on a massive scale: the total number of Africans shipped to the Americas stands at between 11 and 12.5 million.[4]

It was, of course, through the riches they acquired in the Americas that Europeans were able to get their hands on more and more of the sophisticated manufactured goods of the Far East, including silks and porcelains, along with exotic spices. Europeans now had something real to trade with the East, something for which the East had a great appetite: silver. From Europe's point of view, this was the first era of globalization. The growth of world trade in the first half of the sixteenth century (at 2.4% p.a.) was not far from that in the twentieth century (3.44% p.a.).[5]

Ultimately, though, it wasn't Spain or Portugal – the first big traders and of course colonialists – that went on to industrialize and provoke sustained economic growth. Neither was it Holland that played host to the first Industrial Revolution, a country that had carved out a place for itself not only in international trade but as the merchant serving the rest of Europe, connecting the Baltic Sea with the Mediterranean. 'Why the West?' cannot be answered by simply pointing to European trading and political activities abroad, however destructive and violent those activities were for the people involved.[6] Otherwise, the Industrial Revolution would have occurred more widely – and earlier in time. No one, but no one, would have predicted that Britain, not Italy, Spain or Holland, would move centre stage.

By the time the British Industrial Revolution was operating at full steam in the late eighteenth and early nineteenth centuries, the tables finally began to turn between East and West.[7] Whilst the West progressed, the East regressed. Other 'reversals of fortune' came alongside: between the Mediterranean and north-western Europe, between Africa and the Americas, and between the northern and southern Americas. Whether by the same or by very different forces, the whole globe was being reshaped.

When seen in this longer-term and more global perspective, understanding why Europe was home to an industrial revolution that ushered in sustained economic growth – sustained for a sufficiently long enough period of time and at a sufficiently high enough level to bring about a rapid transformation of our standard of living in the last two hundred years – becomes even more difficult to explain. And, in light of the re-emergence of the Far East and the recent slowdown in economic growth in the West, it is an ever more pressing question. Does the West really have what it takes to continue its advance? The answers to such questions will hang crucially on what we identify as being the causes of the rise of the West, causes that could either have been fortuitous and superficial or deep and long lasting. Not to mention benign or malign.

## Five Lessons

Economic historians are still getting to grips with the past, and debates on the causes of economic growth continue, but there are five important takeaway lessons that I myself draw from existing research on the rise of the West. Although condensing down an immense literature to just five key findings is inevitably gung-ho, it nevertheless helps us to see the wood for the trees, to see where we are at. Each of the five lessons has something important to offer us – something that helps us answer the question of 'how the West got rich'. However, taken together, these lessons also reveal something else: the sidelining of women throughout our thinking about how we got to where we are today. Women's freedom is the elephant in the room. It is, quite simply, and as we will see in the chapter that follows, impossible to properly understand 'why the West?' – and why Britain first – without zooming in on women's freedom.

### History Lesson 1: markets are necessary but not sufficient for economic prosperity

Since Adam Smith published his *Wealth of Nations* in 1776, economists have been obsessed with markets, so much so that at the time of writing his face appears on the reverse side of the British £20 note. The market-based approach has attracted extensive criticism, particularly in light of the global financial crisis.[8] At its root, the market view of growth is one that places faith in us as individuals. It is bottom-up as opposed to top-down: rather than seeing growth as something created by the actions of the state, it places emphasis on our own individual efforts. It favours giving individuals freedom to engage with one another, to start new businesses, to search out new technologies and to create new products. It values the diversity offered by millions of different people, each with their own thoughts and ideas, seeing all of these numerous individual efforts as the cause of human progress. It also points to the way in which markets provide opportunities for people to escape alternative systems, such as serfdom, enslavement and patriarchal family forms that lock women inside the home.

But whether or not one buys into markets, history suggests that they are simply not enough by themselves. Looking at evidence from as far back as ancient Babylonia and through to medieval, early-modern and modern Europe, my own research, along with that of other economic historians, has built a picture of the evolution of markets across the long span of human history.[9] If the market-based view of growth is correct, the picture revealed should be straightforward: that markets were poorly developed until the eve of the rise of the West. Instead, we find that markets were certainly not a 'modern' invention, and neither were they a purely 'western' one.[10] Active markets in history can be found in the Middle East and Asia, and in parts of Africa.[11] The extent of trade and market activity over the last two centuries has been on a different scale to that beforehand, but it has been as much a product of economic growth as it was a driver – the result of using new technologies, from the steam engine to the computer, which made the world smaller and flatter.

In sum, although markets are a common ingredient of successful economies, the fact that they have existed for much longer than has modern-day prosperity strongly suggests that they are not enough to create sustained economic growth.[12] Something else was needed to light the fire. Key to identifying precisely 'what' may be looking not at who used markets but who did not: who, in other words, was excluded. Some chose to exclude themselves, viewing markets as beneath them, which, as Deirdre McCloskey argues, is not conducive to the creation of prosperity.[13] Others were involuntarily excluded. And that, of course, often included a mere half of the population: women. As we will see in the next chapter, the benefits of including women in market activity are substantial – and go above and beyond the benefits of market involvement for men. One of the things that most stands out about the part of Europe in which the Industrial Revolution began was that women faced relatively fewer restrictions on their engagement with the market compared with not only other parts of Europe but also much of the rest of the world.[14]

### History Lesson 2: institutions matter

Markets do not exist in a vacuum; to bring out their best, they require supportive institutions. The economist Douglas North won a Nobel prize for bringing 'institutions' to the party, particularly institutions that uphold property rights, such as democracy and a competent legal framework.[15] After all, without secure rights of ownership we have little incentive to work hard, to be entrepreneurial and to invest in the future: if the monarch or the mafia continually threaten to strip you of your wealth, it reduces your drive to create. And if institutions result in perverse incentives, such as incentives to prey on the efforts of others rather than to be creative, or act to exclude them, then our interactions with one another are unlikely to be productive from the point of view of the economy. That's why legal and political institutions matter for the creation of economic prosperity. Markets can only direct us along the right path – the path to prosperity – if they are underpinned by the right kind of institutions.

But whilst institutions no doubt matter (after all, who wants bad ones), economists' treatment of them can sometimes seem rather selective and superficial, selective because we seem to have 'mined' history for examples that best support our idea of what a 'good' institution is. In the case of political institutions, the British Glorious Revolution of 1688 has, for example, received a wealth of attention.[16] Occurring a good century before the relatively better-known French Revolution, the Glorious Revolution shifted power away from an unelected monarch to an elected parliament, and the timing seems to work well for making the argument that democratic institutions gave birth to the British Industrial Revolution in the following century. However, it would be untrue to suppose that there was no democracy in Britain beforehand; medieval parliaments had, for example, been very active until the Tudors and Stuarts began to stamp on them.[17] The Glorious Revolution was, in part, about parliament reasserting control.

In addition to rather selectively looking for favourable institutional turns in the history of the now prosperous economies, looking for historically 'bad' institutions in any modern-day poor country has similarly become a common pastime. Unsurprisingly, as the Bible tells us, 'keep on seeking, and you will find'. Bad institutions are top billing when it comes to research on, for example, the relative decline of the Middle East (with Islamic law being a key target), Africa (both before and after colonization) and China (after the Mongol invasion).[18] However, in such historical excursions, examples of where 'good' institutions existed and yet economic growth has not been sustained – or where 'bad' institutions existed and yet prosperity still managed to take hold – can easily be ignored or excused. The Dutch Republic was, for example, relatively democratic, and yet its economy did not play host to the first industrial revolution. And, though institutions are commonly seen as a factor that has held back Africa,[19] it is important to note that parts of Africa were in fact home to what economists consider 'good institutions'; the idea that Africa was filled with despots is, to say the least, an exaggeration, one propagated by European explorers, colonialists and missionaries.[20] Furthermore, China, an economy that has witnessed a more recent growth miracle, does not exactly fit the bill in terms of having the types of institutions that western economists see as favourable to growth. There is, inevitably, an extent to which good institutions may instead *follow* growth. Indeed, it may be possible to grow through one or two good policies – such as support for widespread education and skills – with improvements in institutions following later on, as a by-product of growth.[21]

Not only can economists' consideration of institutions sometimes be selective, it can also be superficial. 'Institutions' has become a catch-all term that captures more or less anything and everything that affects the incentives we face in our daily lives: incentives to (so long as institutions are 'right') behave in a way that, whether directly or indirectly, results in the best possible outcome for the economy. As Sheilagh Ogilvie and A. W. Carus have pointed out, this catch-all focus has resulted in economists being quite 'vague' and doing little more than stating the obvious.[22] They note the tendency to see 'institutions' in a black-and-white fashion, ignoring their complexity, the way in which they can have both negative and positive effects and how they interact with one another. There can also be a presumption that 'whatever is, is right'; that if an institution exists it must be because it was some 'optimal solution' to the problems that society faced. Economists, after all, like to think in terms of optimality.

Since institutions can have many faces, the very same institution could be argued to be either favourable or unfavourable – depending on whether one is looking at a rich or a poor country.

Last but by no means least, although 'formal' institutions have received considerable attention, 'informal' ones have received far less. They have long been lumped into the catch-all term 'culture' and left for sociologists to explore on the assumption that good or bad culture is merely the product of a good or bad economy. Indeed, whilst esteemed sociologists have long pointed to the way in which culture affects the economy, economists have often lambasted such arguments as being woolly, soft and superficial.[23] Where culture has received more serious consideration, it has been by forcing it into the economic straitjacket: its repackaging in the form of what economists have come to call 'social capital'.

Recently, however, economists have begun to take culture more seriously, particularly given that research now suggests that formal institutions are insufficient to explain economic outcomes (rather like markets).[24] This includes evidence of the way in which the same ethnic groups have been found to perform relatively well in whatever country they are located in (and so whatever institutions they are subjected to),[25] and that the same formal institutions can produce different effects in different places.[26] Culture seems to matter.

Culture can be defined in a number of different ways (indeed, one study cites 164 different definitions[27]), but we can think about it as 'information capable of affecting individuals' behaviour that they acquire from other members of their species through teaching, imitation, and other forms of social transmission.'[28] It can include attitudes to risk, to family, to strangers and to rule breaking, such as whether accepting bribes is deemed acceptable. Crucially, and as Deirdre McCloskey argues, culture can also include attitudes to markets, entrepreneurship and production: whether trade, work and rolling up your sleeves to produce are deemed acceptable – something we too often take for granted today but wasn't always the case in years gone by.[29] Culture is also, to say the least, key to bringing women into our story. Culture is, of course, extremely difficult to measure, which may help explain why economists, who tend to favour quantitative techniques, have neglected it. However, economic historians are currently working on novel ways to measure culture, including by finding ways of comparing and quantifying aspects of folklore – the beliefs, stories and customs passed down from one generation to the next.[30] In the next chapter, we will span the world to document historic attitudes and practices relating to women.

Culture can affect prosperity independently of formal institutions, but it can also affect the evolution and success of those formal institutions.[31] As we will argue in part III, family systems that are more supportive of women's freedom can go a long way to explaining the emergence of 'good' institutions. Where families involve extended kinship structures, who provide for themselves and who closely monitor their members' actions, they can be inimical to the emergence of generalized trust and cooperation between *non-family* members. This both restricts the development of a deep and broad market and the emergence of a supportive state, whilst favouring nepotistic practices.[32] Although it is rarely noted, these family systems are also exactly the ones that are most inimical to women's freedom – that constrain women's ability to live independent lives, that rely on them to provide caring activity, and that connect family honour with female modesty, sometimes with violent implications.[33] They also, as we will see, start to crumble as women find opportunities outside in the marketplace.

Bringing women into the story also allows us to understand why transplanting democracy doesn't always deliver the expected benefits. As we will see, patriarchal cultures are much more supportive of autocracy than they are of democracy. By contrast, cultures in which women are viewed as equal – and where, in parallel, 'fathers' have less power over the young – socialize all young people to speak up rather than shut up, to challenge people in authority and to hold them to account.

Women's freedom is at the roots of the type of cultural practices that deliver and sustain institutions that support prosperity. As the famous feminist saying goes, *personal is political*. Economists have, sadly, been too reluctant to integrate the private sphere of life with the public sphere.[34]

## History Lesson 3: freedom is needed outside (as well as inside) the marketplace

Although when it comes to economic growth it is common to give much of the credit to the market, the fundamental driver of economic advance – continued scientific and technological progress – requires freedoms that go well beyond it.

According to Joel Mokyr, it is not the market alone that explains the increased scientific and technological activity in Europe, something that spurred the Industrial Revolution and sustained economic growth; it was the Enlightenment.[35] The Enlightenment, which began in the late seventeenth century but gathered steam in the eighteenth century, involved a whole new way of looking at the world: one that was scientific. It involved a shift away from seeing the world as driven by fate, magic and heavenly forces to instead seeing events around us as the result of scientific law – law that was for us to explore, to understand and to harness in the process of taking charge of 'nature' in an effort to better human lives. Rather than feeling that individual human life was out of our hands – that our fate was something over which we had little individual control – it introduced the modern-day notion that we have the power to bring about improvement by taking charge of nature. Not only did we have that power, but there was a sense that improvement was something that we should value. Progress, to paraphrase Mokyr, became both possible and desirable.

Rather than investing time and money in fasting, praying and purchasing religious relics, Europeans began investing those scarce resources in other ways: in innovation, investment and working longer and more intensively.[36] Deference to authority was replaced with values that are crucial to fostering scientific improvement: openness and tolerance to new ideas; valuing merit over status; and free speech.

Of course, one of the major risks of arguing that the Enlightenment caused the rise of the West is that it implies that other parts of the world were 'unenlightened'. Rather than taking such a route, Mokyr's more recent work points not to a lack of intellectual capacity outside of Europe but to the way in which powerful political actors in China and the Middle East responded by suppressing it.[37] The implication is that, for the good of scientific advance, no one state should be large enough to turn off the lights of growth; that Europe's historic division into multiple states, between which intellectuals could move to escape repression, was crucial to sustaining scientific advance.[38]

Interestingly, in some ways the Enlightenment involved the exact opposite of 'capitalist' or 'market' values. It created a more cooperative and collaborative research spirit, one in which ideas were openly and freely distributed. And, unlike those involved in the marketplace, what drives scientists is, in general, something other than money: curiosity, intellectual discovery, peer recognition and the desire to reduce human suffering.

Now when economists think about freedom, their focus has traditionally been on the market: freedom for merchants and entrepreneurs. Following Mokyr, they now also emphasize the importance of freedom for intellectuals (basically, for people like themselves). However, we still need to think about freedom much more broadly, as Deirdre McCloskey[39] has suggested in her *Bourgeois Trilogy* of books: the freedom to make the most of our lives no matter where we are born, to whom we are born or into what gender we are born.

To be free to make the most of our lives, we need to be free to stand up and stand out. In general, any society that enforces conformity limits the individual experimentation required for progress. In Africa, the slave trade became a tool to enforce conformity, with those seen as 'troublemakers' being the first to be sold into the hands of slave traders.[40]Accusations of witchcraft could easily hang over any individual who stood out – including those who succeeded. If you did well, such as by trying a new seed that resulted in a bumper harvest, you risked being accused of being a witch.[41] That's quite a disincentive to individual effort and experimentation. According to Jean-Philippe Platteau, witchcraft accusations are still a problem in many rural parts of Africa today – if anything, increasingly so as economic opportunities create disparities between households. Of course, witchcraft accusations were also common in sixteenth- and seventeenth-century Europe, when more than 100,000 people were tried, 40–60,000 of whom were executed, and 80 per cent of whom were women.[42] Interestingly, however, relatively fewer trials took place in England, which was to become the home of the Industrial Revolution.[43] Cultures that are tolerant of individual difference are also those supportive of growth.

Not only is the Enlightenment story one which tends to focus on freedoms for intellectual elites as opposed to freedoms more generally, it is also a largely male story. Of course, as time went on, Mary Wollstonecraft and others argued that women were equally as capable of 'reason' but, with the very notion of freedom having developed at a time when women were second-class citizens and when birth-control technology was, compared to today, largely non-existent, the central importance of women's bodily freedom was left off the freedom agenda. Women's freedoms came to be seen as a duplicate of men's, ignoring the fact that there is one vital difference between the two: that a woman can never be free unless she has control over her fertility.

Indeed, at the very same time that the Enlightenment was beginning to take hold in Europe, restrictions on women's fertility and sexuality, including penalties for abortion, non-marital births and sex work, were deepening in many parts of Europe.[44] As Merry E. Wiesner-Hanks points out, European authorities at this time executed more women for infanticide than any other crime (apart, that is, for witchcraft); restricted the hiring of unmarried mothers; built asylums to house and imprison not only sex workers but also women who had had sex before marriage ('fornicators'), and even those simply deemed pretty enough that they risked falling into prostitution or fornication. It was not unknown for authorities to instruct midwives to examine the breasts of all local young single women in their neighborhood in the event that a baby was found abandoned, and one eighteenth-century German doctor went as far as to suggest that all unmarried women should bathe publicly once a month to 'prove' that they were virgins – that through such bathing any traces of non-marital births could be detected and punished. Indeed, as Merry E. Wiesner-Hanks goes on to note, '[i]mprisoning women for sexual crimes marks the first time that prison was used as punishment in Europe rather than simply as a place to hold people until their trial or before deportation.'[45] Women's freedom to take charge of their own bodies (not only of their brains) seemed to escape the 'freedom' agenda, which continues to leave women's bodily autonomy at risk today, including through lack of access to birth control (the 'global gag rule'), abortion and sex worker rights (under attack from the Nordic model).

As we will see in the final part of this book, the Enlightenment seriously affected the way in which economics itself developed: it pushed it in a direction that sidelined women. As Anne McClintock points out, metaphors of sexual dominance of men over women were central to the Enlightenment movement: nature was represented as female, as something that sat waiting to be dominated and tamed by male reason; so too with the exploration of foreign lands, European contact being commonly represented as a strong, white, armoured European chancing upon an 'easy' naked women basking sensually in the tropical sunshine, waiting not only for his seed but also to be 'civilized' by his application of reason.[46]

The Enlightenment explanation for the rise of the West might be increasingly popular, but it is also one which, through the groups it excluded, helps us identify what was limiting growth as much as what was driving it. The rise of the West might have been even stronger and faster had women's freedom been included rather than excluded. It's not surprising, therefore, that industrialization began first in the part of Europe where, relatively speaking, women had greater freedoms (and those freedoms had suffered less of a retreat).

### History Lesson 4: high wages (not low wages) are good for growth

Since Karl Marx's time, it has been popular to argue that growth is built on the back of low-wage labourers, exploited by capitalists who extract 'surplus value' to fund investment and expansion. Marx had argued that the Industrial Revolution was a result of British peasants being dispossessed of their land rights in the 'enclosure movement', during which commonly owned land was privatized, which created a 'working class' ripe to be exploited by factory owners. Recently, there has also been a revival of interest in the way in which cheap slave labour contributed to the British Industrial Revolution and the rise of Europe.[47]

However, an economy might only grow so far by relying on cheap labour. That's the lesson of Robert C. Allen's research, which suggests that industrialization and sustained economic growth began not in a part of the world where workers were super-cheap, but in a part of the globe where they were relatively expensive.[48] Allen argues that the Britain that gave birth to the Industrial Revolution was, in fact, a high-wage economy, and that these relatively high wages meant that businesses had to search for and develop machines that could mechanize production, saving on labour costs. According to Allen, high wages incentivized the movement of scientific ideas out of the 'ivory towers' (the intellectual domain considered by Mokyr) into the 'real' world: onto the factory floor, where productivity consequently rose and economic growth could, as a result, be generated. By the late nineteenth and early twentieth centuries, the centre of industrialization shifted towards the United States, where wages were even higher than in Britain. The result was an even more machine-intensive growth path, one of mass production, and a virtuous circle between rising wages and rising productivity.

However, whilst Allen considers the consequences of high wages for growth, what we also need is a complete explanation for the origin of high wages. Although Allen has himself explained high wages as being the consequence of increasing *demand* for labour, it is essential to also think about the *supply* of labour. And that requires us to bring reproduction, and with it women's freedom, into the story.

Although the argument that high wages are good for growth challenges models of development based on cheap labour, Allen's work has recently been the subject of intense debate. Three main objections have been raised. The first suggests that Allen overestimated British wages.[49] The second revises upwards estimated wages in some other parts of Europe.[50] The third, originating in the work of Jane Humphries, argues that high wages were not available to women and children[51] nor, we might add, poorly paid immigrant labour, including that from Ireland. The high-wage story of the Industrial Revolution is, much like the Enlightenment story, a largely male story (and a white male one at that).

However, proving that cheap labour existed in Britain is one thing. Proving that it helped rather than hindered the Industrial Revolution is very different. Correlation does not mean causation. The Industrial Revolution might have been even faster had wages been higher. Cheap labour could have slowed things down, reducing the need to innovate, as we will see later on in this book.[52] If that's the case, then cheap labour is doubly tragic: it certainly doesn't help the workers themselves, and neither does it help the economy. It is a lose–lose. We can debate the extent to which wages were high in Britain, and the extent to which they were likely hangs on what is going on in women's lives, but it is trickier to deny the notion that low wages can be bad for long-term growth. As we will see, women's freedoms were better in Britain than in most other parts of the world; had they been closer to where they are today, growth could have been even more spectacular.

### History Lesson 5: understanding why growth stops

It is not enough to understand why growth gets going in the first place; we also have to understand why it comes to a stop.[53] As we saw at the start of this chapter, there were a number of noticeable expansionary episodes in the many millennia before the Industrial Revolution. Dynamism was clearly capable of taking hold – and in quite a few different periods of history.[54] History also reveals a series of unexpected 'reversals of fortune': between the Mediterranean and north-western Europe (after 1350)[55]; between West Africa and the Americas (after 1500) [56]; within the Americas between the south and the north[57]; between Asia and Europe (some time before 1800)[58]; and between Latin America and Asia in the mid-twentieth century.[59] Despite numerous sparks, no other civilization succeeded in maintaining economic growth for long enough or at a sufficiently high level to transform the standard of living to the extent that happened in the West.

History provides us with at least three reasons for why economic expansion can fizzle out: population growth; environmental ruin; and politics. All have implications for whether we can expect the western growth spurt to continue. And if we open our eyes to gender, all serve to highlight the vital role of women's freedom.

### 1  *Population*

On the eve of the Industrial Revolution, ironically just as Britain was beginning its miraculous rise, the economist Thomas Malthus was feeling pessimistic. Malthus took a famously dismal view of the economy's ability to sustain growth. He argued that population had a propensity to expand in a rapid 'geometric' fashion, outstripping the earth's ability to provide food and raw materials, which increased at a slower – 'arithmetic' – rate. Wherever the economy started to expand, such as due to a new technology, Malthus believed it was ultimately doomed. As incomes began to improve, the death rate would, he argued, naturally decline. That together with high fertility (he was, after all writing at a time before modern-day contraceptives) meant population growth would increase. Under the pressure of population, food and raw material prices would rise, reducing the 'real' value of people's income, and making production more costly. As a result, the economy would soon end up back at the old standard of living, just with a bigger population than before.[60] Technological superiority did not show up in people's income but in population density. Malthus was so convinced by his model that he had very little patience with attempts by government – or revolutionaries – to help the poor. He believed that the redistribution of income, as was the aim of the French Revolutionaries of the time, would simply lead to larger numbers of people, rather than serving to improve the lot of each one.

Now, of course, the key feature of the last two hundred years has been the coincidence of both rising populations and rising incomes, indicating an escape from the Malthusian trap. The way economists have typically explained this escape is to point to sustained techno-logical change (endogenously driven by an increasingly skilled work-force),[61] followed by falling fertility, itself argued to be a result of technological change, incentivizing parents to shift away from having lots of poorly educated children to having just a few that they could better afford to invest in.[62] Quality replaced quantity. The divergence between 'the West and the rest' is subsequently explained by their resultant interactions in the trading domain. As the West industrial-ized, 'the rest' began to specialize in exporting primary products, which meant less of a demand for skilled workers and so a lack of transition from 'quantity to quality' in regard to childbearing deci-sions. Whilst the West therefore experienced the benefits of growth in terms of rising incomes per capita, the rest of the world experienced it in terms of an expanding population, which held down their stan-dard of living.[63]

In these modern-day Malthusian-style models (known to economists as unified growth theory), fertility is modelled as a straightforward economic calculation. The problem is that it cannot – and should not – be thought of independently of women's freedom to take charge of their bodies. Economists explain changes in fertility across long spans of time as if they were purely a result of choice: of women initially choosing to have lots of children and then, as we reach the late nineteenth and twentieth centuries, and at least in the West, choosing to have fewer children – in response to growth.[64] Birth control is taken for granted – as if it has existed in a reliable enough form for centuries.[65] Women are *assumed* to have been making a free choice, when for most of history pregnancy was not always a choice. It was often an inevitability. The shift to a world in which women do have control over their bodies deserves recognition for its contribution to lifting prosperity – and the lack of that bodily autonomy is equally vital to explaining why many poorer countries are still desperately poor. Given economists' failure to acknowledge the importance of women's bodily autonomy, it is hardly surprising that, despite increased attention given to how to help the global poor, international funding for birth control for the world's poorest women has been on a declining trend.[66] Indeed, more than 200 million women across the globe who would like to avoid pregnancy still lack access to birth control.[67]

## 2   *Environment*

Population growth wasn't the only obstacle to continued economic expansion in the past. So too was the environment. Some environmental episodes appear to be entirely external to the process of growth – a matter of bad luck – but others are a direct consequence. Jared Diamond's magisterial economic history of the world points to the relationship between changing geography and the economy, including the shifting fortunes of the Middle East. Bruce Campbell has recently made connections between the performance of the medieval economy and environmental conditions.[68] Moving forward in time, the Little Ice Age has been blamed for the long seventeenth-century crisis in Europe, a period in which there were serious upheavals politically, socially and economically. As current environmental conditions deteriorate, we need to take seriously the possibility of a negative feedback process through which environmental damage makes growth ever more difficult to sustain. As the Stern Review concluded: 'The evidence shows that ignoring climate change will eventually damage economic growth ... Tackling climate change is the pro-growth strategy for the longer term ... The earlier effective action is taken, the less costly it will be.'[69]

Needless to say, there are clear links between Malthus's population concerns and today's environmental ones. Whilst many economists feel confident that Malthus is dead and buried, the environmental toll of the human race suggests that such thinking is at best hopeful and at worst arrogant.[70] For those who are concerned, clean technology has been the focal point. However, evidence suggests that women's freedom over their bodies can be just as, or even more, cost effective. Project Drawdown – a coalition of scientists, scholars and others interested in the planet – ranks 80 separate solutions to global warming.[71] Family planning and the education of girls are ranked in the top ten, ahead of solar farms and wind turbines. Women's bodily autonomy is vital to making growth sustainable.

Gender also feeds into another, albeit indirect and more subtle, cause of environmental decay: how we choose to measure the economy and how that in turn affects what governments choose to prioritize. Where activities that result in the degradation of the natural environment actually benefit measured gross domestic product (GDP), the damage involved can easily be overlooked and even encouraged. When only the physical production of goods and services is included in how we measure the economy, activities that contribute to our well-being, and that have a much lower cost for the planet, can easily be ignored, along with the potential trade-offs between the two, trade-offs which, when not properly considered, can result not only in the depletion of the natural environment but also in the depletion of daily human energy and the *va-va-voom* needed to both look after ('provide') and create ('reproduce') human life.[72] According to Bina Agarwal, '[t]here are important connections between the domination and oppression of women and the domination and exploitation of nature.'[73] Both the environment along with reproductive and caring labour share common features: they are taken for granted, are historically ignored by national accounting and are undervalued. And, as a result, both are inevitably at risk of depletion, reducing our ability to sustain life on earth.[74] Where the environment and non-market work *are* captured in how we measure the economy, politicians and policy makers are much more likely to stand up and pay attention to any warning signs. Feminist economists therefore recommend that our traditional focus on economic growth be replaced with a broader measure of the economy that incorporates both well-being and sustainability, and they have developed concepts accordingly such as 'social provisioning' and 'social reproduction'.[75]

A number of alternatives to GDP are now available which take into account both the environment and non-market activities that generate well-being, such as household labour. They include the Index of Sustainable Economic Welfare, which builds on the early work of economists William Nordhaus and James Tobin, along with the Genuine Progress Indicator (GPI).[76] In fact, alternatives to GDP seem to be ever expanding, with different countries, economic organizations and think tanks developing their own measures, often in competition with one another. There are also a number of different ways of valuing caring activities and a significant debate about the best means to do so.[77] The problem is, therefore, that despite growing recognition of the importance of well-being and sustainability, as set out in the Sustainable Development Goals (SDGs), there is, as yet, no common agreement on an alternative measure to GDP, which means that it remains the most popular headline measure for any economy.

Gender matters not only for understanding the causes of environmental damage, but also for the consequences. As Agarwal notes, 'it is women of poor, rural households who are most adversely affected and who have participated actively in ecology movements.'[78] As Senay Habtezion notes, women 'are highly dependent on local natural resources for their livelihood. Women charged with securing water, food and fuel for cooking and heating face the greatest challenges', and yet they are often locked out of policy making, and 'socio-cultural norms can limit women from acquiring the information and skills necessary to escape or avoid hazards (e.g. swimming and climbing trees to escape rising water levels). Similarly, dress codes imposed on women can restrict their mobility in times of disaster, as can their responsibility for small children who cannot swim or run.'[79]

Making growth sustainable is not possible in a world where women lack basic freedoms.

## 3   Politics

In addition to population and the environment, a further explanation for 'growth stops' is political. In particular, it is argued that the reversal of fortunes between the northern and southern Americas, and the stagnation of Africa after 1650,[80] was a result of the adverse effects on institutions of European political interferences.[81] In regard to the Americas, economists have argued that Europeans set up extractive institutions – ones that resulted in a high degree of persistent inequality – in parts of the continent which were initially relatively prosperous: where there were obvious resources to extract (including silver), and where there were 'scale economies' in setting up slave-based production. Elsewhere, where there was less obvious low-hanging fruit on offer, and conditions were somewhat more favourable for human inhabitation, poor Europeans migrated and brought their democratic institutions with them,[82] albeit these were not so democratic for the Plains Indians, who, being some of the tallest people in the world, seem to have had a reasonably high standard of living – until Europeans entered the scene.[83] In regard to Africa, it is of course common to argue that 'underdevelopment' is a result of the slave trade and colonization. Recent research suggests that Africa has not always been poor (relatively speaking), only becoming so after the Europeans entered the story. Connections have been made between the slave trade, a lack of state development, ethnic conflict and general distrust amongst the population, all of which resulted in political institutions that were unfavourable to growth. Colonization has similarly been argued to have adversely affected political institutions, both through its authoritarian nature and through the way it encouraged 'self-serving manoeuvering' amongst African elites, with wealth and prestige in the colonial era being earned through political manoeuvering with occupiers, rather than through promoting wider prosperity.[84] In other words, colonialism 'divorced political ambition from public service'.[85] Indeed, before colonial rule, almost one in two African societies had rulers who were kept in check by councils, and almost 90 per cent of centralized states had a judiciary. These figures fell to a quarter and 40 per cent respectively in the twentieth century.[86]

However, in addition to external political forces, often attracted like a bee to a honeypot, internal forces can also stand in the way of continued prosperity.[87] After all, economic stagnation and growth reversals also beset parts of the world in which Europeans were not interfering from the outside. Understanding how a region can seemingly bite off its nose to spite its face hangs on the idea that economic prosperity creates 'losers' as well as 'winners'. Economic advance involves a process of creative destruction: the replacement of older machines with newer versions and archaic products with more innovative ones. Along the way, some sectors of the economy shrink whilst others expand, and some businesses boom whilst others go bust. It is a process that is almost inescapable – unless, that is, we want to stand in the way of progress. However, there are necessarily those who have an incentive to block change: those with a vested interest in older techniques and those who possess obsolete skills. In addition, there are those who fear losing political power when others succeed.[88]

Mancur Olson, author of *The Rise and Decline of Nations*, famously argued that the resultant 'vested interests' build up over time and, by gaining political influence, bring about policy changes that make the economy increasingly sluggish. According to Olson, the problem is that these vested interest groups are much better at representing themselves to government than are those who gain from the economy's dynamism: the millions of consumers, current and future, who benefit from cheaper and more innovative products; and the younger generations equipping themselves with newer and more relevant skills.[89]

According to Joel Mokyr, an economy is best insulated from such pressures where government takes a hands-off approach, making it less liable to 'capture'.[90] The shift towards laissez-faire, as trumpeted by Adam Smith, was, Mokyr argues, one of the reasons why Britain was able to successfully sustain economic growth from the late eighteenth century onwards. That compares with medieval Italy, at the time the home of cloth production, which, in response to rising competition from north-western Europe, chose to enact various regulations which limited the use of new techniques and new dyes. The justification was that it would preserve the quality of Italian cloth; the upshot was that Italy could not compete.

The benefits of the laissez-faire approach are evident to any historian. However, such an approach also had its downsides. As the British economy rapidly industrialized in the nineteenth century, cities became overcrowded insanitary hives of disease, taking a toll on people's health – and, with it, on the economy's ability to keep growing. The market alone was not enough to solve this problem. Markets can and do fail and in a way that can put sand in the wheels of continued economic growth. Economic prosperity therefore demands a state that is neither non-interventionist nor interventionist but that can judge which interventions are reasonable and which are not; a state that can think and question for itself, rather than being captured by outside groups. The state also needs to be able to adapt to the changing needs of the economy. After all, the kinds of policies that work well at one point in time might not work well in another. The education system, welfare system and national health policy need to keep up with the economy to prevent success turning into failure.[91] Democracy is, of course, crucial in terms of providing the right incentives to bring this about, and, as we will see later, democracy and women's freedom are intimately linked.

## Conclusion

In this chapter, I have drawn five lessons from current thinking about how the West grew rich. Along the way, I have touched on some of the key factors that economists and historians typically identify when attempting to explain what ignites economic growth: markets, institutions, science and wages. However, we have seen that many of these factors can also be found in parts of the world that did not experience the type of transformation that began in Britain more than two hundred years ago. Something is missing from this story of prosperity creation, something much more distinctive of the West than markets, institutions, science or wages. It is a missing link that explains not only what turned on the ignition but what has enabled the West to sustain growth – and has allowed a handful of other countries to follow suit. It is the elephant in the room. It is women's freedom.

Whilst women's freedom was by no means perfect in Europe, relative to the rest of the world it gave the West an advantage that was difficult to beat. If the West wants to stay ahead, that's worth remembering today.

# 2

## Uncensored: The Secret Recipe of Economic Success

In 1995, in Beijing, some fifty years after its initial formation, the United Nations made a declaration that was unanimously adopted by 189 countries. It stated that they were 'convinced' that the '[e]radication of poverty based on sustained economic growth, social development, environmental protection and social justice requires the involvement of women in economic and social development, equal opportunities and the full and equal participation of women and men as agents and beneficiaries of people-centred sustainable development'. In 2012, the World Bank dedicated its annual development report to the same topic, noting that gender equality is not only 'a core development objective in its own right' but that 'greater gender equality is also smart economics'.[1] The idea that gender equality is 'good for growth' is now central to the international development agenda.

However, within the ivory towers that house 'expert' economic growth theorists, gender hardly features. And when economic historians debate between themselves how precisely the West grew rich, they have a tendency to focus on people like Isaac Newton, James Watt, Isambard Kingdom Brunel and Richard Arkwright, all of whom are men. It's as if we could have got to where we are today without any women at all. Women's freedom only seems to enter the story as a by-product of economic prosperity.[2]

Where gender *is* taken seriously by economists, there is in fact little in the way of agreement. There are those who argue that gender equality aids growth, but there are also those who argue the very opposite: that economic growth has been built on the exploitation of women.[3] The empirical evidence has not always helped to resolve the debate.[4] Even World Bank researchers have sometimes expressed difficulty with finding evidence of a link between gender equality and growth.[5]

In this chapter, I will consider the whole wealth of evidence from history. After defining freedom, I will then take a short global tour, highlighting the difference between women's freedom in the West and 'the rest' on the eve of the Industrial Revolution. From investment and education to entrepreneurship and democracy, I will then identify the various channels through which women's (relative) freedom in the West supported growth, no more so than in Britain.

Women are too often seen as passive beneficiaries of economic growth, as the people who should be forever thankful to the many male inventors and industrialists of the past for creating the riches that enabled women's rights to flourish. We imagine that, by targeting economic growth, everything else will follow. As we will see, it's time to look at things the other way around. It's time to see women as active creators, not passive beneficiaries. Indeed, as we will see in chapter 3, whilst women's freedom creates growth, growth doesn't always pay women back in return. Freedom comes first, not last.

## Que Sera, Sera

I admit it. I am a control freak. If there is one thing I cannot bear, it is not having control. In her famous song, Doris Day recalls asking her mother 'What will I be?' Seemingly superficial but also profound, the answer has gone down in history: *que sera, sera, whatever will be, will be*. The notion that our future is predetermined, a mere product of fate, is not something that particularly appeals to me. We all know that being happy is not just about having enough money to live a comfortable life; it is also about feeling in control of your life. After all, there were plenty of people living in times gone by who managed to find happiness in conditions which, by today's standards, would seem pretty shabby, without, for example, the convenience of an indoor toilet. Amongst the historic aristocratic elites who were, by contrast, relatively well endowed, there were plenty of women who, admired for their exquisite silk gowns and with tea and cake on tap, felt like little more than caged birds. Historic novels contain a constant theme of the wealthy but caged woman, living an affluent life but one over which she has no control and one in which the slightest social transgression could lead her husband to commit her to a mental asylum. These women wanted for nothing except, that is, for that one vital ingredient: control over their own lives.

However, when economists measure the success of an economy, they look at what the average person can afford to buy; if this is increasing over time, they are judged to be experiencing improvement. That was, at least, until Amartya Sen radically proposed that development was not about money; it was about freedom.[6] According to Sen, economic development is a process in which people gain the ability to take charge of their lives. Control is an often overlooked difference between a modern western economy and many poorer countries in the world today and, of course, a key difference between today's Europe and that of the feudal Dark Ages, when we 'serfs' were under the control of local lords. Sen argues that poverty is often characterized not only by a lack of money but also by coercive relationships, a lack of free choice and political rights, and exclusion from economic opportunities and protections.

Sen's thoughts on freedom cut through a major debate amongst philosophers. Isaiah Berlin famously distinguished between negative and positive freedoms. Negative freedom concerns *freedom from* the interference of others. Positive freedom concerns *freedom to* go out and do things; it requires not only non-interference but also the capabilities needed to do something with one's life.[7] Sen's notion of freedom – and his related 'capability approach' (developed in conjunction with Martha Nussbaum[8]) – relates closely to two other concepts: agency and empowerment. The World Bank defines agency as 'the capacity to make decisions about one's own life and act on them to achieve a desired outcome, free of violence, retribution, or fear'. Empowerment is a broader concept, defined by the World Bank as 'the expansion of assets and capabilities of poor people to participate in, negotiate with, influence, control, and hold accountable institutions that affect their lives'. Empowerment can be thought of as encapsulating agency, plus a little bit more: 'as control over resources, as self-determination, and as the ability to generate change'.[9] In other words, empowerment equals resources, agency and success in bringing about change.[10]

Now when economists more generally discuss freedom, they tend to focus on the market. When academics employ the term, they instead focus on things like free speech and free inquiry. However, freedom for merchants, entrepreneurs and the intellectual elite wasn't the only thing that mattered in the story of how the West grew rich. Neither, as Sen knew, should we confine ourselves to thinking about freedom in the context of the public sphere, in the market, in the political forum or in intellectual debates. Freedom for women was just as important, and that requires us to begin with life in the privacy of the home.

# Women's Freedom Across the Globe: An (All Too Brief) Historic Tour

In their recent book, Jan Luiten van Zanden, Auke Rijpma and Jan Kok[11] argue that female agency is central to understanding how the West grew rich. To see if that's truly the case, we need to consider the degree to which women were free in the West compared with other parts of the globe, especially given that those western freedoms were far from where they are today. Gender inequality indices tend to measure things like labour market participation, wage gaps and the proportion of women in parliament, but economic historians Sarah Carmichael, Alexandra de Pleijt and Jan Luiten van Zanden have designed an index which both goes back much further in time and measures the deeper roots of gender inequality: practices within families.[12] They have christened it the 'female friendliness' index, a measure of how 'female friendly' family practices are. This helps to capture the extent to which the different family norms that exist in different parts of the world help to support (or not) female agency. Using their index, they make a connection between the decline of many of the world's oldest civilizations in the East and the rise of the West. Their findings suggest:

> that the 'reversal of fortune' which happened in EurAsia between 1500 and 2000 was not only related to colonial institutions ..., or to the long-term effects of hierarchical institutions emanating from the process of ancient state formation following the Neolithic Revolution ..., but that there is also a gender-dimension to this story: growth occurred after 1500 in particular in those parts of EurAsia that had relatively female friendly institutions.[13]

The subjugation of women is, they argue, at the heart of why many of the world's first civilizations – in the Middle East and Asia – were unable to sustain economic growth and eventually went into relative decline.

Whilst for millennia Europe had been on the back foot in the global economic race, in the centuries before the Industrial Revolution it developed a secret weapon: women's freedom. The position of women in society was one of the things that most distinguished Europe, especially in the north-west, from other parts of the world. Life for women was, to say the least, far from perfect. However, women had significantly greater freedoms in this part of the world than they did elsewhere and indeed compared with many poor countries today.[14] To see the extent of these greater freedoms, we need to begin with

family life, for as Monica Das Gupta notes '[k]inship systems pro-
foundly influence our values and social constructs in ways of which
we are usually not conscious.'[15] Whilst for Engels, the famous compatriot of Karl Marx, the oppression of women (like the oppression
of the working class) is rooted in private property, historically invested
in men,[16] Claude Lévi-Strauss has long argued that the oppression of
women is rooted in kinship systems – in society, particularly in the
way individuals form families or clans.[17]

Although there was (and still is) significant heterogeneity in family
systems across the world, there were also some regional commonali-
ties that allow us to compare the daily lives of everyday women in
different parts of the world, adding flesh to the bones of the female
friendliness index.[18] As we take our tour, there are certain things to
watch out for: property, marital consent and attitudes to sexual relations. Engels's work would suggest that we keep our eyes open to
rights over property. Lévi-Strauss's work suggests that women may
themselves be treated as property, signs of which would include women
being given as gifts, tribute or as exchanges between families, in the
form of an arranged marriage, rather than having full rights over
themselves. Finally, we should be alert to the ways in which family
life values women. If it's simply for her body and fertility, it's likely
that a woman's sexual honour will be closely guarded and she will
therefore have very little freedom.

Let's begin by comparing Europe with Asia, at the start of the
family life cycle, which is with marriage. Whilst the consent of the
bride became a necessity for marriage in Europe during the Middle
Ages,[19] elsewhere individual consent took a back-seat role: 'In both
India and China, child or infant marriages were common' and 'parental
consent (at least for the woman) was a prerequisite until the 1950s,
if not still.'[20] Once married, northern European women tended to
reside in their own homes, independently of their parents and parents-
in-law, but in Asia they were more commonly found living in the
homes of their parents-in-law, where they had limited agency. Indeed,
'the traditional position of the daughter-in-law in China and India is
uniformly described as pitiful.'[21] As Das Gupta notes:

> Women are at the bottom of two hierarchies: the gender hierarchy as
> well as the age hierarchy. A young bride enters her husband's family
> as a marginal person with little autonomy. Layers of people are above
> her in the decision-making hierarchy: not only the men of the house-
> hold, but also the women who are senior to her. By contrast in the
> North European stem family, women are subservient to their husbands,
> but not to anyone else in the household. The relative absence of an

age hierarchy means that the woman has considerable autonomy in the running of the household.[22]

Polygamy – the practice of multiple wives – was much more common in Asia than in Europe, as was purdah, the seclusion of women. The inheritance practices of European families certainly favoured men, but European widows could inherit their husband's property, and, in the event that a parent died without a son, a daughter was able to inherit. By contrast, '[i]n China, South Korea, and Northwest India, the logic of patrilineality is very rigid.' Rather than allowing a daughter to inherit, a father would adopt a son or 'take another wife or concubine' in order to produce one.[23] According to Bina Agarwal, the historic concentration of property – in the form of land – in male hands is a key driver of the gender gap.[24] A less egalitarian gender distribution of property has been shown to be bad for economic prosperity, restricting women's access to collateral to start new businesses, and lowering wages.[25]

In the Middle East, the position of women was 'relatively strong' compared with India and China. In particular, women were able to own property and were entitled to a (half) share of inheritance, and marriage did not involve a complete transfer into a different kinship group, meaning that 'a woman could always count on the protection of her father and brothers'. However, there was a downside: male members of her family carefully guarded her sexual honour, which was seen as key to overall family honour. Transgressions could be severely punished.[26] Although in property terms, Middle Eastern women were in a stronger position than many women in Asia, and also compared with many married women in Europe (though less so single women and widows), in other aspects of life they 'possessed very little autonomy',[27] not only in terms of more severe sanctions for sexual transgressions but also in terms of arranged marriages (often to older men) and the very strict separation of men and women. The employment rates of women in the Middle East have, as a result, historically been some of the lowest in the world. Women's engagement with the market was almost always discouraged as it risked sexual transgression and was a sign of severe poverty – a sign of desperation. In Europe, by contrast, particularly in the north-west, not only was marriage more consensual, but women were commonly active in the market.[28] Whilst they were often excluded from producing or selling certain types of goods, particularly where guilds were strong, there were still opportunities for employment and engagement with the marketplace, albeit not always the best ones.[29] Laurence Fontaine points to the way in which, where the law was flexible enough, women's legal autonomy was enhanced as market opportunities presented themselves, and especially where local authorities wanted to avoid the alternative: the welfare costs of looking after the poor.[30] Indeed, as Martha Howell argues, the nuclear family – dominant in the northwest of Europe – often necessitated a wife's involvement in the family business compared with more extended family systems.[31]

In Africa, the central entities of society consisted not of a nuclear family but of lineages, comprising around 100–200 people with a common ancestor, and clans, a collection of lineages.[32] Lineages could be patrilineal (common in northern sub-Saharan Africa), matrilineal (common in West Africa and equatorial Africa) or bilateral (in southern Africa). In matrilineal societies, women arguably had a greater degree of agency, including through property, divorce and the ability to hold some positions of leadership.[33] Economic autonomy appears to have been greater than in both Asia and the Middle East. Women farmed the land and were often involved in trade, particularly in West Africa.[34] However, the other side of this coin is that wives were almost entirely responsible for providing for their own children, with relatively little support from husbands. This was an unenviable task, given that women tended to marry young, resulting in big families.[35] Since, unlike in Europe, marriage was always 'an exchange between lineages' rather than requiring individual consent, women were involuntarily condemned to this unenviable hard labour.

Unlike in Europe, women had less control over whether and who they married, and polygamy was common. Since labour was scarce relative to land,[36] African women were commonly seen as a productive resource from which men could extract, to borrow the Marxist phrase, 'surplus value'.[37] To quote Claire Robertson, '[l]abor acquistion and control formed the basis of most wealth in under-populated precolonial Africa. Female-generated agricultural surplus helped men to acquire more wives and children, hence wealth and political power.'[38] As Catherine Coquery-Vidrovitch points out:

> The King of the Ganda, in central Africa, is said to have possessed several hundred and even thousands of wives; Mutesa, in the nineteenth century, had three or four hundred. Any lineage aspiring to political office did well to give several of its daughters to the king. The man who wanted a favour or pardon for an offence would offer one or two daughters.[39]

Women's involvement in production and their intricate knowledge of the land could have been channelled into productivity improvements. Their need to produce in order to support their families – together with the scarcity of labour – certainly would have provided an acute incentive. In some ways, therefore, Africa wasn't far off usurping Europe. The problem, however, was that, unlike the men responsible for production in Europe, African women lacked the requisite capital, power and formal skills needed to bring about productivity-boosting change. To quote Claire Robertson once more, there was 'a tendency for resources to flow toward men and away from women'.[40] Furthermore, witchcraft trials and accusations, which died out in Europe after the seventeenth century, persevered in many parts of Africa,[41] meaning that it was dangerous for a woman to stand out by trying something new (such as an improved seed variety) or by challenging existing (male) authority. Indeed, submission to men was taught and socialized from a young age, which could include painful initiations. Whereas it would be wrong to paint a picture of African women as victims,[42] it would also be wrong to suggest that they had more choices or control over their lives than was in practice the case.

One factor that we haven't so far mentioned is bride price and dowries. Research suggests that around 66 per cent of human societies have family structures that involve the groom paying for a bride, including sub-Saharan Africa, whilst 4 per cent feature dowries, including South Asia.[43] Bride price has been associated with land-based agricultural societies, and dowries with more market-based societies, but where women lack access to markets and, upon marriage, pass into the household of their parents-in-law (taking their dowry with them). Maristella Botticini and Aloysius Siow argue that if dowries are seen as inheritance for daughters, then they may incentivize economic activity amongst men as, once their sisters are married, the sons of a family have more of a reason to work hard as they will receive all remaining family wealth. In Europe, dowries were more common than bride price but declined over time, suggesting that women were gaining opportunities outside of the home and that the family structure was evolving.[44] This contrasts markedly with modern-day India, where dowries have been on the increase, indicative of quite different underlying conditions facing women.[45]

If we were to condense our global comparisons into a single quantitative measure that can help us to see the difference between women's experiences in Europe and those elsewhere, it would have to be the average age of women at first marriage. In general, where women marry later in life, as we will see in the next section, it is indicative of less coercion and greater agency. It is a stand-out feature of northern Europe – the home to the Industrial Revolution – that women did not marry until their mid-twenties.[46] This compares with the Middle East, where '[w]omen married soon after reaching puberty'[47]; China,

**Table 2.1**  Female average age at first marriage before 1790

|  | Average age at first marriage |
|---|---|
| England | 25.2 |
| Belgium | 24.9 |
| Netherlands | 26.5 |
| Scandinavia | 26.1 |
| Germany | 26.6 |
| France | 25.3 |

*Source:* Clark, *Farewell to Alms* (2007), Table 4.2, p. 76

where women generally married between the ages of 14 and 18; and Africa and India, where child marriage is still common today.[48]

None of these regional comparisons should be used to suggest that women's lives were easy in Europe. That could not have been further from the truth. Women had far fewer legal and political rights than men, and marriage law treated women as dependents until the late nineteenth and twentieth centuries. Fewer men than women could read and write,[49] and they rarely received formal training in the form of an apprenticeship or access to top schools.[50] Indeed, women were commonly paid half that of men, even for the same task,[51] and often lost control of property upon marriage, along with the ability to enter into contracts.[52] However, relative to most other parts of the world, and having seen the whole range of experiences elsewhere, it should be clear that there were advantages to being a European woman, particularly so in the north-western region.[53] As Merry E. Wiesner-Hanks notes, '[v]isitors from southern and eastern Europe frequently commented on what they regarded as the "freedom" of women in northern European cities.'[54] In terms of marriage, men and women in northern Europe both tended to marry in their mid-twenties, with grooms typically being no more than two or three years older, whilst in much of southern and eastern Europe it was common for women to marry in their teens and to men who were in their twenties, thirties or even older, a sign of significantly lower autonomy.[55]

It cannot be ignored that, as we mentioned previously, there was a negative turn against women's freedoms throughout Europe in the sixteenth and seventeenth centuries,[56] which may of course be interpreted as a backlash against how far women had come. This negative turn involved the rolling out of rather rigid Roman law, cancelling out many of the legal gains that women had made at the local level, increasing surveillance of unmarried women, along with higher abortion penalties and a significantly higher incidence of witch trials.

Britain did not escape this backlash but fared relatively better. Unlike the rest of Europe, the practice of common law meant that Roman law did not make headway, whilst the shift to Protestantism resulted in more liberal attitudes towards sex and women's bodies. There were also notably fewer witch trials in Britain (along with the Netherlands and Scandinavia). Although far from perfect – and the heavily gendered aspects of Britain's international relations were an abomination that showed how much further there was still to go (in gender and race terms)[57] – the relative degree of gender equality for British women compared with those in other parts of the world at the time, and compared with most other parts of Europe, seems to stand out. Once we open our eyes to the experiences of women, there is an obvious candidate for why the West not only caught up with but overtook the rest of the world in the global economic race. And why Britain was first.

## Being 'Me': The Birth of Individual Freedom for European Women

In the modern world, we value – even celebrate – individuality. We each have our own little quirks and our own likes and dislikes. I personally could not survive without tea and cake, even if it does mean that I live up to a rather British stereotype. This modern sense of 'individuality' is, however, a rather recent phenomenon. In the past, family came first and the individual came second. The family unit provided for us in ways which have become far less common today. With the family therefore came a safety net, a guaranteed minimum standard of living. However, this required that families worked as a team rather than as a set of individuals. Rights came with responsibilities. The inevitable result was restriction – albeit not malicious – on personal freedom. Higher income earners were compelled to help support poorer family members; but the greatest restriction of all came in terms of marriage. The notion of 'family first' was nowhere more apparent than in the practice of arranged marriage.

In the world of arranged marriages, the choice of mate is designed to be 'right' from the point of view of the wider family unit. Marriage is about uniting two families in a way that can be mutually beneficial. The search for a partner falls under the control of the parent and begins well before children reach maturity. The result is that girls tend to get married earlier in the traditional family unit than if they were themselves responsible for finding a partner. Indeed, there is an added incentive to arrange an early marriage – the longer one waits, the greater the chance that the child will be in a sufficiently strong position to object and the greater the question mark over a woman's 'sexual virtue' and so 'value'.

This traditional family system was, as we have seen, present in many parts of the world throughout history. In China, until very recently, marriage involved a contract between two families – not between two individuals. It was very much a family, and not a personal, matter. In India and in the Middle East, arranged marriage is still common, and girls are regularly punished if they object. In pre-Colombian Latin America, '[v]illage headmen held the privilege of distributing the most beautiful virgins among the notables.'[58] However, arranged marriage was also once a common feature in Europe, and in ancient Greece men in their thirties and forties regularly married women half their age.

Whilst arranged marriage served the purpose of the family, it inevitably limited the freedom of young women, something noted in the modern world in the work of Alberto Alesina and Paolo Giuliano.[59] A woman's inability to choose her own partner affected the power balance within marriage. Where marriage takes place through mutual choice, the two individuals are placed on a more level playing field. This can be very different in the case of arranged marriage. Furthermore, with arranged marriage often comes a difference in age between man and wife, which can further add to inequality within the home.

In the West today, marriage is purely a matter of individual choice for the two parties involved. Each party has the personal freedom to enter into a marriage of their own choosing and is protected by law from being forced into a marriage to which they do not consent. But where did this modern idea of marriage come from?

The Catholic Church adopted the principle of 'mutual consent' in the ninth century. By the twelfth century, the Church was clear that the consent of both the man and woman – and not the consummation of the marriage through sexual intercourse – was of central importance in establishing whether a marriage was valid. After all, in the words of one notable contemporary, 'where there is to be union of bodies there ought to be union of spirits'.[60] Marriage was now the personal choice of the bride and groom. Indeed, if a bride was coerced into marriage, she could have the marriage declared null and void and since, from the Church's point of view, such coercion was a sin, her parents could be refused the sacrament.

However, freedom on paper is one thing. Freedom in practice is another. Whereas a European woman's consent was in theory required for marriage, her ability to exercise personal freedom was often limited; that limit was financial. Unless a woman could support herself financially (such as through work), she had limited bargaining power with her parents when it came to a marriage proposal. If her parents wanted her to accept a proposal, it was difficult for her to object. The risk of doing so was starvation (or a life in prostitution). When it comes to women truly gaining enough freedom to decide whether and who to marry, job opportunities and the wages they offer are, therefore, vitally important. The market provides women with opportunities outside of the family. It thereby allows them to stand up to social norms that restrict their freedom. To do so, however, the market must be 'free' – free from the kinds of restrictions that have been adopted throughout history to limit the entry of newcomers through regulations and guilds.[61]

In Britain's case, the early emergence of markets provided women with economic opportunities that, though far from perfect, bought them economic freedom, enabling them to escape from being under the thumbs of their fathers. In medieval Britain, around a half of the population already worked for wages, and it was perfectly normal for women to work.[62] Evidence from the marriage records of the sixteenth through to the eighteenth centuries reveals that the average woman did not marry until she was around 25 years of age, and at least 10 per cent of women never married. That compares rather strikingly with many other parts of Europe at the time, such as Italy, where women regularly married in their late teens (often to older men), and, of course, to modern-day poor countries.[63]

In the late medieval period through to the sixteenth centuries, the Italians, Spanish and Portuguese were busy looking outwards, developing magnificent port cities with endless connections overseas, but with relatively remote and underdeveloped internal territories. Britain was doing the opposite: building a deep and well-integrated internal market, in part supported by natural geographical advantages and in part through the emergence of a reasonably centralized state that limited what would otherwise have been significant barriers between regions.[64] As a result, England was initially little noticed on the international stage, but these deep internal markets provided better foundations for economic advance in the longer term, particularly through the opportunities provided for women.

## Women and the Wealth of Nations: The Four Channels

The relative freedom which markets offered women supported prosperity creation in at least four different ways. As we will see, it affected population dynamics and, with it, wages, but also human capital, investment, entrepreneurship and institutions, including the propensity to democracy and the capabilities versus incompetencies of the state.

## 1 Population dynamics, fertility and wages

In the previous chapter, we saw that sustained economic growth is often best supported by high – not low – wages. Where wages are low, businesses may have little incentive to raise productivity by investing in new technologies and mechanizing production as they can instead exploit cheap labour. The extent to which wages were higher in Britain than elsewhere (and for which groups) is still being debated. It is nevertheless crucial to note the way in which women's freedom can help to support a high-wage economy, particularly in a world before reliable birth control.

According to Malthus, the 'passion between the sexes' risks overwhelming the economy's natural resources, pushing the wage down to subsistence level. He suggested two possible outcomes for the economy: a low-wage or a high-wage equilibrium. The low-wage equilibrium is the result of a system in which fertility is high and unresponsive to the economy. That is typical of family systems in which young women are 'married off' at a young age and have little or no ability to take charge of their own bodies. In the resultant high-pressure population regime, population can easily overwhelm resources, leading to starvation and undernourishment. The result is that high fertility is met with high mortality.

In the alternative high-wage equilibrium, fertility is instead responsive to economic conditions. In a nuclear family system as opposed to a more traditional one, people can only marry and reproduce if they are able to financially support their offspring. That in turn helps to ease the pressure of population growth, meaning that fewer people have to – literally – starve to death in order to keep population in line with the economy's ability to support it. Rather than mortality doing all of the work to ensure equilibrium between the population and resources, fertility adjustment is able to help check population growth. The result is a much less harsh population regime, one in which population is kept under control through fertility, not just through mortality. This lower-pressure regime enables the economy to support a higher wage and so a higher standard of living.

Key to this high-wage equilibrium is the way families operated. John Hajnal famously distinguished between two types of household formation systems, what we tend to refer to as the traditional and the nuclear. Whilst traditional family systems have, he argues, been dominant across the world and throughout history, they were replaced with more consensual nuclear ones in north-western Europe in the two centuries before the Industrial Revolution.[65] Rather than being married off at a young age, women living in this part of the world became free to decide for themselves whether, who and when to marry. And, having the taste of freedom, they had no intention of moving in with either set of parents upon marriage. This meant that, after finding partners of their own choosing, young couples had to save up and make sure they were in a financially stable enough position before they could get married and start a family. The result was that the age of marriage tended to be high and, all importantly, responsive to economic conditions. When the economy was going through a rough period, people had to delay marriage until the situation became more stable. After all, it would be risky to start a family if unemployment was on the cards. When times improved, such as during the Industrial Revolution itself, people could afford to marry sooner. This responsiveness of marriage to the economy helped to keep fertility – the number of babies being born – in line with the ability of the economy to support them.[66] Furthermore, within Europe, we could find a high degree of monogamy, which is a stand-out feature, given that 85% of human societies have featured polygyny.[67] By itself, a shift from polygyny to monogamy has been shown to increase the age of marriage and lower fertility by 40%, increase savings by 70% and raise GDP per person by 170%.[68]

Markets that provided opportunities for women gave them a release valve, a release valve that enabled them to stand up to early marriage and take some control over their own lives,[69] something that changed the way families functioned and, with it, population dynamics and ultimately the mechanization and technological base of the economy.

## 2  Investment and skills

Women's freedom and the associated development of more consensual nuclear families also affected saving and skills, both of which are vital for rising prosperity.

Unlike in traditional families, in nuclear families the children one day have to make their own way in the world.[70] That required preparing them for life outside, particularly by investing in their skills. Marrying later in life – in their mid-twenties as opposed to teens – also meant that young people had the time needed to invest in or acquire their skills, such as through apprenticeships. Furthermore, by marrying later and so having smaller families, parents could now better afford to educate their own children, increasing the skill base of the economy. Evidence certainly suggests that bigger families are more likely to live in poverty, even today, and that children with more siblings – particularly more younger siblings – can suffer a penalty.[71] Jane Humphries finds, for example, that children in larger families during the Industrial Revolution were, out of necessity, sent out to work as child labourers at a younger age, cutting their schooling short.[72] Jacob Weisdorf and Marc Klemp find that one less child per family boosted literacy by 7.3 per cent and those entering skilled jobs by 7.9 per cent.[73] All of this suggests that the smaller families that came along with family systems in which women were relatively freer helped to boost the skill base of the economy.

Smaller families also made it easier for parents to save for the future. And, as nuclear families meant that you could no longer rely on your children looking after you in old age, it became absolutely necessary to do so. This increased incentive to save helped to provide a greater pot of investment for the economy.[74] It encouraged the development of private capital markets, including pensions and life annuities.[75] These in turn provided a ready demand for government bonds as a safe place for financial institutions to invest the contributions they collected, thereby supporting the ability of the state to borrow and invest. As we will see later in the book, Britain's fiscal system led the way in the eighteenth and nineteenth centuries.

## 3 Capitalist spirit

According to Max Weber, a 'Protestant work ethic' is responsible for the rise of the West: the Reformation, in other words, gave birth to capitalism. Protestantism supposedly encouraged a culture of entrepreneurism, hard work and higher savings in a country like Britain.[76] However, this 'capitalist spirit' deserves to instead be seen as a product of women's freedom. And to see why, we need to compare traditional and nuclear families.

In traditional families, where parents are in charge of the marriage decision and where newly married couples are absorbed into the household of the groom's parents, young women (and sometimes also young men) have relatively little control over their private lives. It is the wealth of your family that will determine your ability to marry and whom you marry. In the nuclear family system, by contrast, young couples instead choose their own partner and set up their own independent households after marriage. This was particularly the case in England, where very little support was provided by parents upon marriage.[77] This meant that young couples simply could not afford to get married until they had the independent financial means to do so. Your ability to have an independent home life depended entirely on your own efforts – on whether you yourself were doing well enough at work and how much of your income you had managed to save. Unless you earned enough to support a family, you could not afford one. In a world before reliable birth control, marriage meant children – children that no one other than you and your partner would pay to feed and clothe. In other words, if you wanted to have sex with your partner, you needed to be in a strong enough financial position to support the consequences that would likely result from it. Tough love ruled, creating an acute incentive for individual effort and aspiration. No private life – and no sex – without your own hard labour.[78]

The capitalist spirit – working hard, skilling up, being entrepreneurial and saving for the future – was in part a response to the kind of family system which supported as opposed to suppressed women's freedom.[79]

## 4  Democracy and the state

Economists have noted that stronger kinship ties mean that families tend to look after themselves. With nuclear families, by contrast, people need to interact and work with non-family members. This helps to develop the type of cooperation and generalized trust levels that are needed for the emergence of the state.[80] But nuclear families only tend to emerge in situations in which women are (relatively) free: where they are free to make their own independent decisions about marriage. The state and women's freedom are, therefore, intimately linked.

Furthermore, if our state is to be democratic as opposed to authoritarian, women's freedom is even more important. According to Emmanuel Todd, democratic norms are rooted in the family.[81] It is within the family that we each have our first taste of life – that we are each 'socialized'. Where families are patriarchal – where women have little voice and where an 'elder' dominates – we learn to respect authority and to keep our mouths shut. Status trumps merit. Where families are more consensual – where men and women are equal and where young people are allowed a voice – we become socialized into democratic norms from an early age. We get used to having a say, to forming an opinion through discussion and debate and to holding others to account. We speak up rather than shut up.[82] Authoritarian and undemocratic political institutions are, in other words, rooted in authoritarian family forms. Rather conveniently, patriarchy, by giving everyday men some power within the home, placates those who might otherwise rise up and challenge undemocratic rule.

It is not too surprising, therefore, to find democratic institutions successfully taking root sooner in north-western Europe, where the family system offered women a greater degree of agency and equality. It also suggests that 'bad' institutions – of the kind that limit economic prosperity – cannot be tackled without at the same time questioning inequalities of power within the home. Autocracy and patriarchy stand or fall together – another reason why feminists are right to argue that 'personal is political'.

Not only are democratic states and women's freedom intimately connected, so are women's freedom and the kind of state capabilities commonly taken for granted in the West today. Research has connected votes for women with the expansion of the state into the provision of public goods, health care and education, all of which helped to support increased economic prosperity in the twentieth century.[83] It was also in the parts of Europe where women first began to earn their freedom that a welfare system began to emerge.[84]

In traditional societies, 'welfare' is provided within the family.[85] Higher-income earners help support those on lower incomes whilst women spend their time taking care of the young and elderly – and even being pawns in the marriage market to enable their family to access more resources. Individual freedom and family needs can, as a result, conflict. Where markets enable people to 'escape' such practices – giving them a way out – it leaves a welfare gap that needs to be filled. Through the emergence of a welfare state, the state and the market can therefore work in tandem to both support women's agency and economic prosperity.

Rather than being seen as a burden to market activity, the early English welfare system, known as the Old Poor Law, has been seen in such a light.[86] As Thijs Lambrecht notes when comparing the English welfare system with those in place elsewhere in Europe, in England 'the care of the elderly in particular became a community responsibility'.[87] By doing so, it supported women's ability to work and engage in the marketplace.[88] According to Lambrecht, we can see the state's endorsement of patriarchal family practices in other countries – practices that place greater caring requirements on women – as a strategic means to minimize their expenditure.[89] 'Conservative' states and patriarchy are natural bedfellows, exploiting the 'free labour' of women within the family, which, counterproductively, restricts the ability of the economy to grow. Needless to say that, as Adrienne Roberts[90] argues, the English welfare system was far from perfect and had rather mixed effects, with the laws of settlement having received particular criticism. Clearly, there is still room for improvement today.

## Conclusion

In 1869, John Stuart Mill argued that the subordination of women was 'one of the chief hindrances to human improvement'. He was right. Few economists (other than feminist ones[91]) took note. Evidence from the long span of history is, however, unequivocal: women's freedom is vital for economic prosperity. It boosts wages, skills, saving and entrepreneurial spirit, and it delivers a democratic and capable state.

# Part II

## Inequality

# Introduction

In the last two chapters, I argued that women's freedom was vital to the rise of the West, and that, therefore, increasing women's freedom will similarly be key to building prosperity in today's poorest economies, as well as pushing prosperity further in the West. In this next part of the book, I'd like to begin by asking: can we rely on women's freedom (and with it prosperity) to naturally increase over time? Sadly, as we will see, we cannot. We will take a historical tour from the Stone Age to the modern day to see how women's freedom can retreat as well as improve. Somewhat paradoxically, whilst women help growth, growth doesn't always return the favour, as we will see happened with Britain's Industrial Revolution. The lesson is that women need to be forever on guard.

Having considered the historic path of gender equality, we will then go on to consider why gender inequality is relevant to another much talked-about form of inequality: income inequality. Typically, economists consider income inequality as entirely independent of gender inequality. But, as we will see, income inequality cannot be addressed without keeping our eyes open to gender.

The recent rise in income inequality began not long before I was born, and born into a family that was most definitely situated on a lower rung of the ladder. Where I grew up in northern England, people survived by living on the dregs left behind by the rest of society. Everything had a value; nothing was thrown away. As a treat, my grandparents would take me to the local market to buy a magazine. However, these were not the kinds of magazines that you could purchase from a local newsagent; they were well-thumbed out-of-date magazines, presumably bought second-hand from the local doctors' surgeries. From a nearby stall, you could also buy bags of misshapen and broken biscuits – local people didn't waste money on the neatly packaged versions available in supermarkets. As my grandparents explained, 't'is all same once in t'belly.' However, even these market offerings were sometimes too expensive. Instead, my grandfather and I would walk along the canal to an old red-brick cotton mill, then owned by a local biscuit manufacturer, to queue at the back gate where you could purchase the bags of biscuits at the cheapest possible price.

As a young child, this way of life was perfectly normal. However, as I grew up, I realized that somewhere someone else must have been buying the neatly packaged and pre-sorted biscuits and fresh off-the-press magazines. Otherwise, how would we be able to get our hands on all of the leftovers? It was only once I left the north, aged eighteen, to study at the University of Cambridge that I came into contact for the first time with the 'someone else', the people who actually shopped in places like Marks & Spencer every single week.

Whilst I began my march up the social (or, more accurately, academic) ladder, most other people I knew were, unfortunately, left behind, including many of those closest to me. Mine was an unusual story; it was the exception and not the norm. At the opposite end of the spectrum were friends and family who left school pregnant and never took their GCSEs. I have no delusion about life: it can be very tough, even in our supposedly rich western economy.

However, despite the issue of 'class' attracting growing attention, gender is the missing element. This was something I realized for myself at the age of fourteen, when my parents separated, leaving my mum to care for and financially support myself and my two younger sisters. It was at this point that things became particularly tough, when we missed meals and turned to charity shops. Gender is the elephant in the room; it is difficult, if not impossible, to fully address the issue of income inequality without also facing up to gender inequality.

In the final of these three chapters, we will consider an aspect of inequality that has so far gone under the radar: inequality between women who monetize their bodies and those who monetize their brains. It's an inequality that affects some of the poorest women in our society, and one that is being tackled in precisely the wrong way. As we will see, underlying this inequality are strong social taboos, ones that the Enlightenment together with the nineteenth-century cult of domesticity contributed towards. Society needs to fundamentally transform the way it thinks about both sex and women's bodies if this important but overlooked aspect of inequality is to be addressed. The benefits on offer go well beyond improving the lives of sex workers: the same taboos that serve to sideline sex workers are also those that keep women 'in their place' more generally in society. That includes the notion that women's bodies are the root of sin.

In sum, if we want not only a richer economy but also one that is more equal than at present, enhancing rather than decreasing women's freedom is the place to begin.

# 3

# When Did Sexism Begin?

In the first part of the book, I argued that women's freedom is vital to the creation of economic prosperity. Today, the global gender gap, a catch-all measure of gender inequality, contained in the World Economic Forum's *Gender Gap Report*, stands at 32%, meaning that 32% of the gap between men and women in the dimensions of health, education, the labour market and political representation remains to be closed.[1] However, we tend to think that the course of human history will move us onwards and upwards, that all we have to do is wait. In the United States, for example, and as Claudia Goldin has documented, the wage gap declined from just over 50% in the late nineteenth century to just over 40% by 1930. It then stagnated and began to fall further in the 1980s to not much more than 15% today (Figure 3.1).[2] But, as we will see in this chapter, patriarchy and the associated gender gap has in fact been on the ascendancy as often as it has been on the decline. Rather than being on the side of women, history has often been against them, and economic growth has not always been their friend.[3] Why gender equality has moved backwards as well as forwards over time is the subject of this chapter, and it has an important lesson for the present day: gender equality should never be taken for granted.

## The Origins of Sexism: the Three Ps

We tend to assume that for most of history women have been oppressed and that it is only in the last century that advances have been made. We

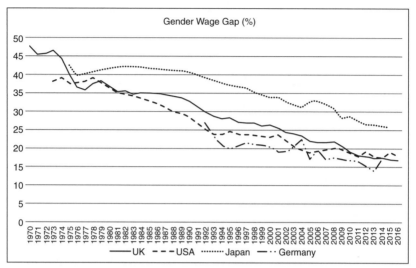

**Figure 3.1** Gender wage gap in the UK, the USA, Japan, and Germany, 1970–2016
*Source:* OECD (https://data.oecd.org/earnwage/gender-wage-gap. htm#indicator-chart)

are more used to asking 'When will sexism come to an end?' than 'When (and why) did it begin?' However, according to the anthropologist Melvin Konner, author of *Women After All*, our hunter-gatherer ancestors experienced much greater gender equality than we might at first imagine.[4] Nature, he argues, grants women, not men, the advantage: women are destined to be dominant in the natural state of the world.

So, you might wonder, when did it all start to go wrong for women? The answer is, perhaps paradoxically, with a great technological and institutional leap. Ten thousand years ago, between 10,000 and 6,500 BC, something big happened: the Neolithic revolution. 'Mankind' began to settle down and farm the land. In the words of Konner, this was the time when 'men killed men and seized women or enslaved both'. However, he wasn't the first to draw attention to the significance of this period of history for its inequalities which still persist to this day. The idea has a long pedigree. Although he might not be instantly recognizable as a feminist, Friedrich Engels, the famous supporter and compatriot of Karl Marx, wrote a whole book on the matter, one which he titled *The Origin of the Family, Private Property, and the State*.[5]

Engels was born into a relatively privileged family in Germany, but when he began to show left-leaning tendencies, his father sent him off to work in Manchester, England, in the hope that it would shake him of such feelings. As it turned out, and much to the dislike of his family, Engels's Manchester excursions achieved the very opposite. Living amongst the working people of the mills and factories made him even more, not less, sympathetic to the cause of working people. Whilst Marx was busily blaming capitalism for the divide that seemed to have opened up between rich and poor, Engels turned instead to the divide between men and women.

Engels argued that the hunter-gatherer state was one of primitive communism, one in which everyone was equal and people worked cooperatively to achieve common goals. Men and women might have carried out different tasks to aid subsistence with, for example, men doing the hunting and women collecting other types of foodstuff, but they made equal contributions to the tribe's survival nevertheless, and were recognized for doing such. However, the egalitarian nature of society started to change as the hunter-gatherer existence gave way to farming.

What was key for Engels was that farming brought ownership.[6] Here, Engels's particular focus was on livestock, such as cattle. In the way that Marx saw private property as being at the root of wealth inequality, Engels saw private property as being at the root of gender inequality. He argued that only men could stray from the home to herd and look after livestock, whereas women needed to be close to the homestead for the purpose of looking after small children – after all, in those days, before modern birth control, many women were regularly pregnant or lactating. Engels reasoned that the rights of ownership came to be vested in men. In his own words, women 'became the slave of his [man's] lust and a mere instrument for the production of children'.

Engels's explanation of the roots of gender inequality still lives on today, albeit in a slightly different form and with a less Marxist twist. Although Engels's own focus was on private property, more recent research suggests that it was the more general transition from a hunter-gatherer system that opened up the possibility of gender inequality. However, sexism did not arrive equally everywhere. The degree of inequality that emerged was highly dependent on local conditions, both geographic and technological, which in turn affected the types of agricultural technologies that were adopted.

If there is one particular technology which appears to have had significantly adverse effects on women, it is the plough, a machine which worked to the advantage of muscle power. The plough – which required significant human strength – was, according to economic historians, the enemy of womankind. Countries with a longer history of using the plough still fare worse today when it comes to gender equality indices. Examining over 1,200 ethnic groups, Alberto Alesina, Paulo Giuliano and Nathan Nunn have found that regions which made greater use of the plough in the past are those where gender differences are greatest today. History casts a long shadow.[7]

Barbara Smuts has an alternative to the technologically driven explanation of the battle between the sexes, but which similarly relates to the Neolithic revolution.[8] Smuts argues that patriarchy was an evolutionary response to the fact that the mother of a child can always be known but the father cannot. This uncertainty created an evolutionary advantage for men who sought to monitor and restrict the freedom of their female partners. In other words, with sex came a desire for control, a desire that enabled men to make sure that their own genes – and not someone else's – were safely passed on. This control only became feasible as society shifted away from hunter-gatherer communities to settled agriculture, at which point subsistence was no longer dependent on women's freedom to move about to collect foodstuff.

Whether it's through the birth of private property, the plough or paternity (what I would sum up as the three 'Ps'), the first big technological revolution for mankind did not exactly work out well for women.

## From Agriculture to Manufacturing

Whilst settled agriculture closed a door, it also opened a window: it enabled the development of manufactured goods. When life was nomadic, people were continually on the move, which meant that belongings needed to be kept to a bare minimum. Once we settled down in one place, this constraint was lifted, ushering in a whole series of technological developments which led to the production of textiles, pottery and metal ware. These included the handloom and the spinning wheel. If muscle power was what first gave men an advantage in the field, technological developments in the realm of manufacturing began to erode this advantage. However, where a patriarchal culture had already become deeply rooted, it would take centuries until this change in technology was capable of bringing women on board.[9] And one of the key ways in which patriarchal culture was consolidated for so long was through the development of the state.

As agriculture advanced, and as towns developed, so too did the state. The fact that settled agriculture meant that people stayed in one place enabled the development of fixed states.[10] Towns and cities also needed governance and, naturally, it was not always of a modern-day democratic nature. Patriarchal family structures provided a model of governance for the first political institutions; a state that was similarly autocratic and domineering. These political institutions in turn affected the way family members saw one another, the extent to which it was the 'norm' to see others as equal or to bow to those in power. Political structures and the family fed back on one another. It was therefore in the parts of the world that first 'advanced' technologically speaking – undergoing the Neolithic revolution early on – that patriarchal family structures began to take hold.[11] Outside of the three main centres of civilization – the Middle East, the Indus Valley and China – a more equal family structure, one which embedded a reasonable degree of equality for male and female members and had its roots in simpler times, prevailed. This included Western Europe.

## Equality Consolidated

The early backwardness of Europe was, it turns out, to the advantage of women. The Black Death in the middle of the fourteenth century consolidated these early – more gender equal – foundations. The population of Europe declined dramatically, by between one third and one quarter, making it one of the most significant shocks in history. The result was a shortage of workers, in response to which male wages rose and employers were left on the lookout for alternative sources of labour. The power balance between landowners and labourers moved in favour of the latter, reducing inequality within the economy. This period of labour shortage meant new opportunities for young people, changing the bargaining power between parents and the younger generation. This had a particularly large effect on young women: teenage girls now had the ability to financially support themselves. This economic freedom dramatically changed women's lives and with it the structure of families. The nuclear family was born.[12]

With their new-found economic freedom, young women could choose whether, who and when to marry (free from parental interference). As we saw earlier, they entered into the workforce and waited to marry until they found someone of their own choosing. Since neither party could be forced into marriage and, instead, chose their partners of their own accord, it was a marriage of equals. However, people now had to wait to marry. The other side of the coin to

choosing one's own partner in life was setting up your own independent marital home upon marriage. Couples therefore had to save up
and wait before getting married, meaning that the average young
couple did not marry until their mid-twenties. Smaller families were
the inevitable result, which, as we saw earlier, helped to boost the
economy in a number of different ways.

The Black Death also consolidated women's empowerment in another
surprising way: by turning us into meat eaters.[13] The labour shortages
resulted in higher wages, which enabled us to purchase more meat. In
response, farmers began to shift away from crops and towards animal
husbandry. The plough lost its dominance. In the United Kingdom,
the share of economic value in farming created by raising animals as
opposed to growing crops rose from 47 per cent in 1270 to 70 per
cent by 1450. New job opportunities opened up in the agricultural
sector for female labourers.

Of course, the changes to women's power did not come without
resistance. Men responded by trying to restrict women's freedom,
such as limiting where they could work, what professions they could
join, their rights to borrow and spend – and even what they could
or could not wear.[14] Changes in the structure of the family had the
potential to empower women but the extent to which they were
capable of doing so also depended on institutional structures that
existed outside the home.[15] Where, for example, women's entry into
formal and skilled employment was restricted by the existence of
guilds and the power of the law, as was the case in Germany and
France though less so in Britain and the Netherlands, women's progress from the home into the public sphere was limited – until, that
is, institutions outside of the home began to take their lead from the
increasingly equitable family structures.


## From Farm to Factory

Women already accounted for a surprising third of the labour force
in Britain in the first half of the nineteenth century.[16] However, as
with the first giant technological leap of mankind, this period of
revolutionary technological advance began to hurt rather than help
women. Whilst the cotton mills of Manchester provided new income-
earning opportunities for women, 58 per cent of cotton industry
workers being female,[17] the 'factory girl' was certainly not representative of women more generally in the economy. Rapidly expanding
heavy industries like coal mining and iron and steel relied largely

(though not solely) on male labour. This was a marriage of muscle and capital, one that is perhaps best summed up by the murals of Thomas Hart Benton that graced the walls of the New School of Social Research in New York. Farming became increasingly mechanized, and women and children up and down Britain were made unemployed. Cottage industry – manufacturing conducted within the homes of villagers – was out-competed by dark satanic mills, reducing the opportunities for women in the countryside to supplement their income from farming.

Women's work became concentrated in areas such as domestic service and clothing.[18] Not only were the opportunities for women to earn declining, unpaid work demands within the home were on the rise. Perhaps in part due to changes in the labour market, women began to marry sooner. The average age of first marriage for women fell from 25 to 23. With it, fertility rose.[19] This was a baby boom, old style: more pregnancies, more breastfeeding and more drudgery.

Before the Industrial Revolution, it was normal for women to work.[20] However, over the course of the Industrial Revolution, female employment fell and labour market disparities between men and women increased.[21] By the end of the Industrial Revolution, only one in five women was officially recorded as being part of the workforce.[22]

As the labour movement gathered strength, working-class men pushed for regulations which restricted the employment of women and children. Areas of labour which were predominantly female, notably domestic service, the largest single category of employment in Victorian Britain and late nineteenth-century United States, failed to attract the interest of trade unionists in the fight for better pay and working conditions.

It was against this backdrop that the 'male breadwinner model' was born. Men were now cast in the role of providers and women of caregivers.[23] Often considered a historical relic, this model of family life only really came into existence in the nineteenth century, soon becoming the 'ideal' template for society. It certainly remained common for young unmarried women to work but it was increasingly uncommon for married women to do so. This 'cult of domesticity' not only brought inequalities along gender lines but also along racial–ethnic lines. As Teresa Amott and Julie Matthaei have noted, white middle-class women relied on lowly paid female servants, a high proportion of whom were women of colour or recent immigrants, to take on the drudgery, reserving themselves for the 'higher level' aspects of domestic life.[24] In 1900, more women worked in domestic service than any other sector, and that included more than 40 per cent of African-American women and European immigrant (such as Irish) labour.[25]

Whilst women's freedom was central to laying the foundation of the Industrial Revolution, it didn't pay women back for the favour. For men, the Enlightenment and industrialization involved a struggle between man and nature, one in which men came out on top. However, for less privileged groups it was clear that other struggles were taking place, ones created not by nature but by human society.[26] Feminists did not take their struggle lying down. Wollstonecraft had made the argument for equal rights in the eighteenth century. A new group of feminists began to push even further, pointing to the drudgery of the domestic sphere. In their 1825 *Appeal of One Half of the Human Race, Women, Against the Pretensions of the Other Half, Men*, Anna Wheeler and William Thompson wrote that '[a]s women's bondage has chained down man to the ignorance and vices of despotism, so will their liberation reward him with knowledge, with freedom and with happiness.'[27] By the late nineteenth century, the US feminist movement was gathering force and, in a neat parallel with the Black Death, was helped by the scarcity of male labour during the civil war.[28] It was, however, a divided movement, blind to the way in which gender and race intersected in the struggles of the day,[29] and with major disagreements between those calling for equal rights and those calling for a 'maternal' welfare system – disagreements that persist to this day.[30]

## The Twentieth Century

After retreating in the nineteenth century, women's involvement in the labour market began to expand again in the twentieth century. Claudia Goldin suggests that women's labour force participation has followed a U-shaped trend, initially falling as the economy develops and then recovering thereafter.[31] Looking over the longer span of history, as we have done, suggests that this U-shaped process has been repeated, with long cycles of successive Us, as opposed to a single U.

Since it remained common in the nineteenth century for unmarried women to work, the change that came in the twentieth century was significantly less dramatic for this part of the labour force, with the associated labour-force participation rates in the United States rising from around 40–45% in the early decades of the twentieth century to an average of about 60–65% for more recent decades. The greatest change was visible for married women, whose labour force participation expanded in an 'extraordinarily rapid and all-embracing' way, from 6% in the United States in 1900 to 73% by 2000.[32]

The increasing prevalence of women in the workforce is often attributed to the feminist movement. However, feminism did not come from nowhere. It developed fastest where economic opportunities for women held firm in the nineteenth century, including my home city of Manchester, famous for the cotton industry and also for the Pankhurst family.[33] Feminism subsequently spread at the very same time that a new economic wave began to create opportunities for women. Labour shortages during the two world wars, and the 'Golden Age' that followed the second of those, created another period of labour scarcity, giving women and people of colour more bargaining power to push for change.[34] And, as the economy advanced and as manufacturing shifted overseas, the West began to move into a new area of activity: services.[35] From office work to retail and hospitality, a whole host of new employment opportunities opened up, ones which, unlike heavy industry, did not work to the advantage of men. Economic opportunity, in other words, provided a reason for women to push for change in the political and social sphere. It also, however, created reasons for men to put up barriers, including, for example, marriage bars, especially when there was fierce competition for jobs.[36] Whilst men monopolized the better-paid service-sector jobs, women dominated in dead-end clerical jobs and in the types of jobs that had been created in response to a decline in domestic service, such as child and elderly care and food and retail. A similar split could also be found along racial/ethnic lines. The service sector is a story of two halves – and one that continues to the present day.

## The Future

Technological development in history has been at the root of rising prosperity, but it has also sometimes brought rising inequality, and not only in terms of income (as at present) but also in terms of gender. However, technology is not necessarily destined to increase inequality between men and women. Having once worked to the advantage of men, we have been passing through a phase in which new technology has been more gender neutral. In the words of Claudia Goldin, technology has led to the 'replacement of brawn by brain power'.[37]

In the way that technology eventually replaced muscle power, it is now beginning to replace brain power, something which threatens the livelihoods of both sexes. It is emotional and human skills – skills that are more difficult for a computer to replace – that are set to become the most valuable feature of human beings. The sectors of the economy that are now expanding the fastest are those in which female labour is dominant.[38] These sectors have also tended to be those offering the least financial reward, but these very same skills may, due to their increased value, at last receive some of the highest rewards. Furthermore, cyberfeminists argue that the digital age of technology is shaking the boundary between machines and humans, and, with it, the very idea of gender.[39] The tables are turning as they did once before, and now, rather than men having the advantage, it is women who will likely be the beneficiaries.

But, if modern technology creates the potential for change, that potential has to be won for it to be achieved. Society does not instantly adapt to changes in technology; where a patriarchal culture holds firm, technologies that are gender neutral can still be dominated by male workers. In fact, not only is feminism needed to push for legal and other changes that allow women to take advantage of opportunities opened up by new technologies, but the way technology develops may in turn reflect the position of women in society. Economists used to assume technology is 'exogenous', a force that follows its own path and its own direction, meaning that the resultant effects on gender equality (and income equality) are difficult to resist. However, history has revealed that technology is open to influence – that the direction in which it travels depends on the different resources available.[40] We now need to recognize that this direction can similarly be influenced by gender gaps. Whilst technology shapes gender equality and even gender identity itself, gender equality can in return also shape the direction of technology and how that technology is used.[41] In the words of Judy Wajcman, 'technology as such is neither inherently patriarchal nor unambiguously liberating ... the politics of technology is integral to the renegotiation of gender power relations.'[42]

## Conclusion

Women's struggle in the twentieth century, from the time of the suffragettes onwards, was not just about breaking new ground; it involved regaining lost ground. Industrialization had pushed many women out of the workplace: the male breadwinner model was born. The sidelining of women was crystallized by two accompanying forces: the development of a powerful trade union movement, which represented male interests; and state interventions which, as we will see in chapter 7, rendered women dependent upon spouses. It was also, as we will see in the final part of the book, something which economists encouraged.[43]

When women are told that they've never had it so good, they are presented with a vision of history in which they are expected to be forever grateful, a vision of history which is supposed to pacify us, leave us unconcerned by what the future holds and, more importantly, off guard. What history really tells us is that we need to be on guard: we can move backwards as well as forwards.

# 4

# Income Inequality: What Does Sex Have to Do with It?

Over the last decade, not only have we faced the biggest global economic crisis since the Great Depression of 1929 – something which, just years before, economists had predicted would never happen again – we have also seen increasing inequality, the stagnation of wages and a slowdown in economic growth. And, as so frequently happens in cases of economic turmoil, political turmoil has followed. The politics of the West are being rewritten.

In this chapter, and after outlining the longer-term trends, we will consider the common explanations for the increase in income inequality. We will go on to note the exclusion of gender from the popular discourse, including in the work of Piketty. I will draw on existing research to identify some of the links between income inequality and gender inequality.[1] I will then propose a new diagnosis for the situation we currently find ourselves in: one that places sex front and centre.

## Poverty and Income Inequality: The Long Term Trends

Over the course of human history, and as two recent bestselling books have shown, income inequality has not followed a simple trend, whether upwards or downwards.[2] Instead, it has followed a wave-like pattern, sometimes rising and at other times falling. Economic history, however, once taught economists to be optimistic. Economic development was assumed to be associated with an initial increase in inequality, but Simon Kuznets argued that this would be temporary; that, with time, inequality would disperse, leading the benefits of economic growth to be spread more widely and more equitably throughout the population.[3] It was, in other words, supposed that inequality would follow the path of an upturned U: initially rising and then falling in the course of economic advance. For a while at least, this seemed to ring true. From the 1930s onwards, inequality in the West followed a declining trend. That was until the latter part of the century, when the optimism turned to pessimism. In the 1970s, inequality in many western countries reversed course, reaching levels not seen for decades by the early twenty-first century.[4]

However, when looking at *global* income inequality – instead of that within the West – the recent trend is precisely the opposite. Global inequality rocketed in the nineteenth and twentieth centuries as western countries grew and diverged from the rest of the world, peaking in the 1980s. However, in more recent years it has begun to fall.[5] This is, of course, a natural result of other parts of the world starting to 'catch up' with the relatively richer West, including the giants that are China and India. Calculating global earnings inequality from 1970 to the present day, Olle Hammar and Daniel Waldenström find that the global Gini coefficient has fallen from a value of around 0.7 in 1970 to less than 0.6 today, and that it was driven not by declining inequality *within* countries but by falling inequality *between* countries.[6] As Max Roser notes, in the 1970s the global income distribution was bimodal: it had two rather than one peaks. Countries were in two completely different camps, converging either to a high- or a low-income equilibrium. More recently, these twin peaks have disappeared, and the global income distribution has shifted rightwards, meaning that the bulk of the world's population is now positioned at a higher level of income than before.[7]

Global poverty data also shows reason for optimism. For most of human history – for thousands of years in fact – life was pretty miserable. It was nasty, brutish and short, and you'd have been lucky to live to the ripe old age of forty. The economy was incapable of supporting a rising population. Death rates were high, meaning, as a parent, you would have witnessed the death of multiple children. That would have been the norm. And then, about two hundred years ago, something big happened. The world population began to increase without bound and, despite this rising population, people began to get richer and richer. Global poverty rates have fallen spectacularly alongside (Figure 4.1). Not only is poverty falling in percentage terms, the number of people actually living in extreme poverty is falling. According to the World Bank's estimates, it has more than halved, from around 2.2 billion in 1970 to 705 million by 2015.[8]

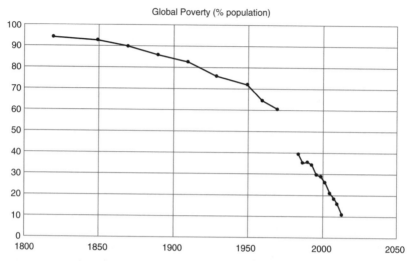

**Figure 4.1**  Global poverty as percentage of population, 1820–2013
*Source*: Bourguignon and Morrisson (2002), pp. 731–2 to 1970; World Bank
from 1981 (https://data.worldbank.org/indicator/SI.POV.DDAY)

However, after the good news comes the bad news. Whilst the aggregate picture looks reasonably positive, not everyone has been a beneficiary of this global trend. First, a large part of the decline in global poverty over the last thirty years is due to one region alone: East Asia, including, of course, China. Sub-Saharan Africa and South Asia remain regions of high poverty. In fact, in these regions the number of people living in extreme poverty has barely budged. That compares strikingly with East Asia and the Pacific, where the number of people living in extreme poverty has fallen from around 900 million in 1987 to 71 million in 2013.[9]

Second, although across the world income inequality has declined, in the West it has been on the rise. The top 1% of earners in the United States now takes a fifth of the nation's total earnings. The top 10% of earners takes half the pie. In Europe, the situation is a little better, although not much. In Britain, the top 10% receives 40% of the cake, whilst in France and Germany it is a third. Such figures are also reflected in another measure of inequality: the multiple of earnings of directors compared with the average worker. In the 1990s, the executive pay packet was around sixty times that of the average worker. Now it is closer to two hundred. Alongside, the real incomes of working-class men have stagnated or even fallen. Whereas in 1969, three-quarters of men aged 25 could expect to earn a wage that would independently support a family of four, by 2004 it took until men reached the age of 30 for them to earn enough to do so.[10]

Branko Milanovic's famous 'elephant chart' helps to show what has been going on. It presents the real income gains of different income groups, from the poorest in the world to the richest in the world since 1988, and looks (unsurprisingly) like the cross section of an elephant.[11] It shows positive gains for the bottom 75% of the population, along with the top 10%, but for the people in between it's a different story. These are the people feeling the pressure, commonly referred to as the western working class (in global terms, the upper-middle class). Whilst the world is becoming a better place, it is clear that pockets of severe poverty and inequalities still remain.

## Rising Inequality in the West: The Standard Diagnosis

Economists have offered two key explanations for the rise in income inequality in the western world, both of which can in theory also explain why, simultaneously, inequality and poverty have been falling elsewhere in the world. They are the two 'Ts': trade and technology.[12] In regard to trade, globalization is seen as the all-powerful force at work, reshaping our economies and integrating the far corners of the world into a single marketplace. The world becoming smaller and flatter has allowed each nation to specialize in exporting the goods and services that it can produce relatively more cheaply than others. In particular, each economy has tended to specialize in producing the types of things most suited to its resources, whether that's skilled or unskilled labour. In the richer countries, we find an abundance of skilled labour and so, with trade, the West has specialized in skilled labour-intensive types of goods and services, importing unskilled labour-intensive goods from poorer countries where unskilled labour is abundant and so cheap. Rather than producing such goods for themselves, richer countries now import such goods from countries such as China and Bangladesh. This has increased the demand for unskilled workers in the export sectors of those poorer countries, increasing the wages of unskilled workers there. In the West, by contrast, imports have replaced home production of labour-intensive goods and services, having the very opposite effect.[13] Unlike elsewhere, it is skilled workers who have gained, as they are now able to sell their skills to buyers in poorer countries, where there is relatively little supply. Unskilled workers in the West have, by contrast, lost out. They are now competing with unskilled workers overseas, and this has arguably affected both wage growth and jobs.[14] One estimate suggests that increased imports from China have cost America 1.4 million manufacturing jobs.[15] With unskilled wages in poorer countries having risen from rock-bottom levels at the same time as those in richer countries have fallen from relatively higher levels, the two have begun to converge. That means that global inequality has fallen, whilst in the West it has risen. In other words, poorer groups in the West have lost out not only to skilled workers in their own home countries but also to unskilled workers elsewhere.[16]

However, despite the recent backlash against globalization, most economists argue that the second 'T' – technology – is much more responsible for the uptick in inequality.[17] Whilst computerization has helped professional and skilled workers at the top, making them more productive and so increasing their wages, lower-paid workers, such as those in retail, hospitality, cleaning and care, have been largely unchanged by the advent of computers. Low productivity growth in such sectors has, as a result, meant that wages have also been held down, leading to a rising gap between the wages of skilled and 'unskilled' workers. There was a time when technological change once benefited unskilled workers, as was the case in the Industrial Revolution, when machines out-competed skilled weavers and spinners.[18] But, as Claudia Goldin and Lawrence Katz note, from the late nineteenth century technology began to complement as opposed to replace skilled labour. They argue that expanding educational opportunities were, therefore, key to the way in which the American economy was able to achieve both rapid growth and declining inequality in the course of the twentieth century. However, from the 1980s onwards, the supply of skills has not kept pace with demand for them, leading to a growing gap between the wages of skilled and unskilled workers. This slowdown in educational expansion is, they argue, in part a result of the increasing cost of university education together with the obstacles presented by poverty amongst single-parent families and racial minorities.[19] To quote, '[t]he slowdown in the growth of educational attainment ... is the single most important factor increasing educational wage differentials since 1980 and is a major contributor to increases in family income inequality.'[20] The latest technological developments mean that computers are now fast replacing semi-skilled and middle-management jobs – those in the middle of the income distribution. From driverless cars to online sales and legal advice, computing technology is encroaching into more and more lines of work – and not in a way that helps to raise the productivity of workers but that physically makes them redundant. According to Carl Frey and Michael Osborne, one in two of our jobs will be under threat by computers in the next twenty years.[21]

It seems that the future could be hourglass in shape. Whilst the jobs of skilled workers at the top will be relatively safe, opportunities in the middle are fast disappearing. The implication is that those in the middle must move in one of two directions: upwards, if they can acquire the requisite skills or, failing that, downwards. Unfortunately, evidence gathered so far suggests that it is more likely to be the latter: researchers at the University of Oxford have found that more people in Britain are moving down as opposed to up the social ladder.[22] And low-wage sectors, where productivity growth is minimal, are on the increase. This has implications not only for inequality but also for the growth of the economy.

Although most economists have been busy debating the relative contributions of technology and trade to rising inequality, the economist Tony Atkinson took a rather different stance, placing the blame on social and political factors, including the shift towards laissez-faire government in the 1980s.[23] Following in his footsteps, Joseph Stiglitz has argued that rising inequality is not inevitable; it is a political choice.[24] Others have pointed to the interactions between politics and economics, arguing that globalization has made people and capital much more mobile, reducing the ability of governments to tax and regulate the economy, thereby pushing policy in a more free-market direction. Nevertheless, the economist Peter Lindert has crunched the numbers and argues that 'the rise in income inequality since the 1970s owes nothing to any retreat from progressive social spending.'[25] Although his conclusion is the subject of debate, there is one takeaway point. Rather than politics taking all of the blame for rising inequality, underlying market forces – whether they be technology or trade – cannot be ignored.

So where does Piketty enter our story? So far, we have said quite a lot about income inequality but much less about wealth inequality. In his *Capital in the Twenty-First Century*, Piketty argues that increasing income inequality feeds through to wealth inequality, not only because people on higher incomes can afford to save and invest but also through the act of inheritance, creating an increasingly uneven playing field for the next generation.[26] He notes that if the return on wealth (r) is greater than the economic growth rate of the economy (g), meaning that the value of wealth increases at a faster rate than average wages, the wealthy will move further and further apart from everyone else in money terms. It's for this reason that he recommends a global tax on wealth. However, the problem is not simply that r is rising; it is also that g – the growth rate of the economy – is falling. If economic growth was keeping up with the returns on investments made by the wealthy, as was the case in the twentieth century, then average wages would increase at a faster rate. We would all be sharing in the growing pie. To reduce inequality, we need to grow the economy. As we will see later in this chapter, both rising income inequality and a fall in the growth rate of the economy – one that has helped to pushed g below r – have a common cause. And it is one that has so far gone under the radar, and one that any standard redistributionist package alone cannot solve. It is a global sex problem, one rooted in women's lack of bodily autonomy.

## Gender Inequality Meets Income Inequality

Whilst gender and race feature in sociological debates about inequality, they are all too often missing from the economics of inequality. As Kathleen Geier writes of Piketty's book, '[t]hough *Capital* has many virtues, attention to gender, alas, is not one of them.'[27] Zillah Eisenstein notes the hypocrisy of many male economists, politicians and religious leaders who take a stand on wealth and income inequality: '[e]ach of these men denounces excessive inequality, but without recognising the way that structural racism and patriarchy intimately define economic injustice.'[28] Even the way that inequality and social mobility are measured circumvents a proper consideration of gender. Social mobility is commonly tracked by comparing the occupations of fathers and sons, which sidelines differences between men and women. For example, 35 per cent of men born into the poorest quintile of the population will remain there in adulthood. The equivalent figure for women, by comparison, is 47 per cent.[29] And, when it comes to measuring income inequality, the standard approach compares *household* income. However, given evidence that the division of the household pie between men and women is not always equal, inequality measures can underplay the true picture of inequality.[30]

When we turn to the bare-bone facts, we find that women are both under-represented amongst the rich and overrepresented amongst the poor. Starting at the top, the female share of global billionaires in 2014 was 10.5%. Amongst the self-made, it was a mere 2.6%.[31] As Forbes 400 data reveal, the wealth of females is based much more on inheritance than is that of men (Figure 4.2), suggesting fewer women 'make the grade'. Moving to the bottom of the distribution, and given that poverty calculations are difficult to break down by gender, the United Nations has famously albeit controversially claimed that 70% of the world's poor are female.[32] Single mothers are also significantly more likely to live in poverty than single fathers.[33] As a recent media campaign noted, 'poverty is sexist'.[34]

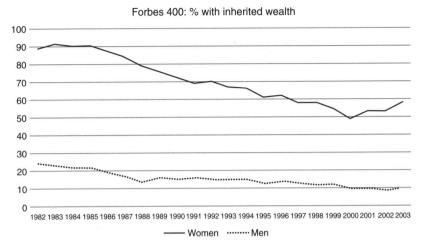

**Figure 4.2** Percentage of individuals with inherited wealth on the Forbes 400, 1982–2003
*Source*: Edlund and Kopczuk (2009), Table 4, p. 164

Globally, women earn only 57 per cent of what men earn each year, a figure which is higher than the gender wage gap as it also takes into account women who do not earn.[35] Research suggests that occupations dominated by women tend to pay relatively less, even for the same skill level.[36] Alice Kessler-Harris and others have argued that women's low pay is not just a result of market forces, but of our 'gendered imagination' which assumes that 'female' jobs are undeserving of the same pay as jobs associated with men. That particularly includes jobs associated with care which, as the population ages and as more women have entered the labour force, have been on the increase.[37]

Tackling inequality will require greater efforts to close the gender gap. That, however, will not happen until we deal with unpaid – as well as paid – care.[38] According to the International Labour Organization, unpaid caring responsibilities are the key barrier to women 'getting into, remaining and progressing in the labour force'. Where women have an unfair burden of responsibilities within the home, it feeds through to create inequalities in the marketplace, both directly, by affecting women's ability to engage in paid work, and indirectly, through the way in which society undervalues the types of jobs associated with being female. Globally, women perform more than three-quarters of unpaid care, equivalent to two billion people working full-time without pay.[39] And it is not sufficient to excuse it by saying it's women's free choice to prioritize family caring activities over paid work. Not only do women feel the weight of their family's expectations, but evidence suggests that globally, 44 per cent of pregnancies are unintended.[40] That means that a lot of care work is taking place that women have not voluntarily signed up to.

Before we leave our all too brief summary of existing research on gender and income inequality,[41] we also need to confront a paradox highlighted by Stephanie Coontz: that gender inequality and income inequality have in fact been moving in opposite directions over the last fifty years. As the gender gap has fallen, income inequality has increased. On the one hand, women's greater participation in the labour market has helped to boost family incomes. Research suggests that '[w]ithout changes in women's earnings during that fifty-year span, inequality would have grown 52.6 percent faster'.[42] On the other hand, there is an increasing propensity for higher-earning men to 'marry their like', magnifying the income differences between the top and bottom of the ladder. Calculations suggest that, if couples in the United States formed randomly (such as by picking partners out of a hat), the Gini coefficient (a measure of inequality ranging from 0 to 1) would have a value of 0.34 instead of 0.43.[43] Sociologists also point to a growing gap in terms of other aspects of family life. At the top, couples increasingly wait to marry and have children once their careers are well established. However, at the bottom, women tend to have children relatively early in life and increasingly have to take full responsibility for raising them as single parents.[44] Unfortunately, many of these children are unplanned, leaving women in a far more precarious financial situation than need be the case, and one that interrupts their educational and working life. In the United States, for example, 60 per cent of births to young unmarried women are unplanned, which is not good when the before-tax poverty rate for single mothers is close to 50 per cent – hardly surprising, given not only the gender pay gap but also the burden of unpaid care.[45] Despite it, women's access to birth control and abortion is increasingly under threat.[46] Whilst double (high) income households are the norm at the top, an increasing number of single-parent households can be found at the bottom, most of which are female headed, struggling to juggle work and care, and fare far worse than their male-headed equivalents.[47] The resultant poverty can have implications for generations to come.[48]

Addressing inequality will require something more than a standard left-leaning redistributionist package, based on an understanding of class alone; it requires a greater focus on gender equality, one of not only equal pay for equal work but basic female bodily autonomy, along with training and educational opportunities throughout the life cycle, something which neither policy nor the current labour market, based on a male breadwinner model, are set up to provide. The 'predistribution' agenda, one that we will come across in chapter 6, can help more generally to ensure that market outcomes are not biased against women, thereby helping equalize outcomes for female- and male-headed households. However, we also need a much greater focus on the distribution of caring responsibilities in the economy,[49] the inequality of which has its roots, as we have seen, in the nine- teenth century 'cult of domesticity'.[50] At the end of the day, equality in the market cannot be achieved until there is equality within the home; but equality within the home will not be achieved until there is equality in the market. The two types of inequalities are mutually reinforcing. However, making sure that women have more (rather than less) bodily autonomy would, at the very least, be a good place to start.

## The Global Sex Problem

Rising income inequality in the West is not only linked to women's (lack of) bodily autonomy there but also to the lack of bodily autonomy of women across the globe.[51]

Mention sex, and any good economist should instantly think of Malthus. As a bunch, economists have historically been famous for their 'dismal science', and Malthus was one of the original doom- sters. He was an eternal pessimist. Despite being a religious man, he thought that helping the poor (such as through redistribution and benefits) would be futile. His reasoning was that the 'passion between the sexes' meant that population would overpower resources in the economy, keeping the standard of living trapped at a low level for the general population. So, looking back to Malthus, sex and inequality are intertwined.

Malthus's 'model' of the economy has been largely discredited by modern-day economists but his thinking about population is still highly relevant. One of the key developments in the last 35 years has been a major expansion in effective labour supply driven by the greater integration of the world economy.[52] The result has been decreased bargaining power for workers in the West (contributing to rising inequality) and businesses substituting capital with the now cheaper labour (resulting in lower investment rates, a fall in interest rates and slower productivity growth).

If today's world might look troubling on this count, history shows just how bad things can become. As population recovered from the Black Death and throughout the sixteenth, seventeenth and eighteenth centuries, wages were on a persistent downward trend in most of Europe.[53] At the same time, many European economies began to stagnate. However, all was not bleak. As Bob Allen shows, there was one exception to the rule: north-western Europe. In Britain and the Netherlands, wages resisted the downward trend and economic expansion took hold. It was this high-wage part of Europe – not the parts with lower wages – that went on to industrialize and lead the globe. Wages and productivity entered a virtuous circle: high wages encouraged the kinds of technological changes that made workers more productive, which pushed wages up further, encouraging more such productivity-improving investment.

As we saw earlier in the book, the position of women in the economy is central to understanding why the north-western part of Europe was able to sustain a higher wage economy. From early on in history, women in this part of Europe began to gain economic independence; they went out to work and delayed marriage – and so reproductive activity – until they were in their mid-twenties. This lower-population pressure regime helped to prevent wages from being pushed down to subsistence levels. The economy entered its virtuous circle in which high wages and productivity growth positively fed back on each other. That was until the 1970s, when the wages of the working classes in rich countries began to stagnate, and economic growth started to slow down.

As we have gone global, the West has lost its insulation from developments elsewhere in the world. The virtuous equilibrium established since the Industrial Revolution has collided with an altogether different kind of equilibrium. Outside of the West, large parts of the world are in the opposite of a virtuous circle. They are in a vicious one, one in which wages are low and there is little incentive to invest and invent because labour is cheap. Behind this equilibrium is a situation in which women have little control over their own fertility. With little in the way of financial independence, girls have no power to stand up to their parents and delay marriage. Once married, they then have little power to take charge of their baby-making capacity. The result is a life of poverty. As mortality rates fell in the course of the twentieth century, in part the result of concerted efforts to eradicate global diseases, these high-fertility rates meant that the global population ballooned. In 1920, global population growth was no more than 0.6% a year, no higher than it had been in 1760. By 1962, it had reached 2.1%. Global population growth has since slowed to around 1.2%, but all of those babies born in the peak have contributed to global labour supply right up to the present day, and the population is still growing more than twice as fast as it has done historically. Whilst in 1962 the global population was not much more than 3 billion, today it is more than 7 billion and is projected to rise to more than 11 billion by 2100.

Through globalization, whether directly, such as via immigration, or indirectly through trade, the rapidly expanding global labour supply has become increasingly accessible to western businesses. With it, western wage growth has suffered,[54] putting an end – at least for now – to the high-wage growth and high-productivity growth equilibrium in the West. Productivity growth, economic growth, investment rates and wage growth have all suffered as a result, and inequality has widened. Individual western governments have turned to minimum or 'living' wages as a means to support the standard of living, but they do not have the power to tackle what is really a global problem: a world awash with people.

Rather than restricting immigration or raising trade barriers, we need to resolve the problem at source. If women have agency – if they have control over their bodies – they will, at the ground level, make fertility choices that will help keep their own families away from poverty and so will prevent population growth from undermining wages throughout the wider economy. For a woman to have control over her body, economic empowerment is vital: providing women with opportunities to become educated, to join the workforce and to be represented in political decisions, including about, for example, birth control. Rather than being a pawn to be 'married off' at a young age, destined to produce child after child, women who have an ability to support themselves financially are able to take control of their lives. They have the financial freedom that allows them to stand up to early marriage and can go out into the world and build an independent life, determining for themselves whether, whom and when to marry. Women's wombs then become their own. By acting in their own self-interest, women will, without knowing it, aid the wider (global) economy.

The room for improvement is significant. In comparison with the Britain of old, and according to UNICEF, the proportion of women aged 20–24 who were married by the age of eighteen stands at 41% in West and Central Africa, 38% in sub-Saharan Africa and 30% in South Asia.[55] Asia is home to a half of all child brides; one-third of all child brides live in India.[56] Globally, one in five girls marry before they are eighteen.[57] Once married (and indeed before), many of the world's poorest women lack access to reliable birth control, as the United Nations Family Planning Agency has documented, something that is becoming more of a problem in light of the global gag rule.[58] It's hardly surprising, therefore, that 44% of global pregnancies are unintended.[59]

An important exception in the modern developing world, and one that helps to prove the point, is China. In 1980, China was home to more poor people than anywhere else in the world. However, since 1981, 680 million people have been lifted out of poverty, and the proportion of those living in extreme poverty has fallen from 84% to under 10%.[60] This has been the single most important development in lowering global poverty and global income inequality over this period. According to standard accounts, globalization and market liberalization are responsible. However, women's fertility must surely play a role. By taking steps to restrain population through its 'one-child policy', the Chinese state managed to overcome a population problem that has blighted the standard of living throughout history. Along the way, it freed women to work outside the home, increasing their economic independence and challenging traditional gender roles. Such a policy has, however, come at a high price in terms of restricting choice and 'missing women'. Government attempts to directly control population have a murky history, including forced sterilizations of some of the world's most marginalized and poorest women. Such policies are abhorrent and could never be recommended by any freedom-loving economist. European history provides a much better path, one in which rising opportunities for women – starting in the labour market – transform the family system and allow women themselves to take control of their bodies.

Economists have expressed deep concern about the way in which a slowdown in population growth may harm the economy,[61] and the newspaper headlines like to deliver messages like 'the choice to be childless is bad for America'.[62] This ignores the fact that population growth has too often reflected women's lack of freedom, pregnancies that they would have rather avoided. It also fails to acknowledge the fact that population growth has been built on women's hard labour, both reproductively and in terms of unpaid care. Although a slowdown in population growth clearly creates a challenge in terms of an ageing population, in the much longer term equitable and environmentally sustainable growth can only be delivered if we give women freedom to take charge of their own fertility. Whilst fertility rates have been falling in recent years, we still have a long way to go until women's bodily autonomy becomes a reality for all women, and, given recent policy moves, we need to be very careful that we don't move in the wrong (as opposed to right) direction.[63]

## Conclusion

The words of the Nobel prizewinning economist Robert Lucas neatly sum up what economists once thought of inequality: that 'of the tendencies that are harmful to sound economics, the most seductive and ... poisonous is to focus on questions of distribution.'[64] They argued that lowering inequality would mean taxing the very people who produce the economy's growth, blunting their incentives to work hard and produce. Rather than worrying about inequality, economists argued that governments should instead place much more focus on economic growth – that a rising tide would lift all boats, and that if the pie was getting bigger, we wouldn't need to worry as much about how it was distributed. However, in the West, we have now witnessed *both* rising inequality and a slowdown in economic growth. In the United States, economic growth was 2.23% per year between 1950 and 1980, falling to 1.67% per year from 1980 to 2010, and across the world growth averaged 3% during the 1960s and 1970s, compared with half this rate, only 1.4% per year, between 1980 and 2009.

Economists are now starting to highlight the ways in which rising inequality might be costing the economy.[65] Economic history also suggests a link between the two, with periods of simultaneous economic expansion and declining inequality gaining scholarly attention. The Black Death of 1348–51, which wiped out around a third of the European population, has been a particular focus. By making peasants scarce, it also made them more valuable (at least in the case of male workers[66]), reducing inequality. The resultant higher wages for men and greater labour market opportunities for women have been argued to have fed through to affect the economy in numerous ways, culminating in the Industrial Revolution. They brought about a radical change in society, resulting in greater freedom for women, smaller and better educated families, higher savings and better political institutions. All of these changes added up to a sizeable stimulus to the economy. Greater equality and high – not low – wages helped ignite the fires of economic growth in history. This is not to deny that cheap labour existed, as was the case with female relative to male labour, but to suggest that labour scarcity created the possibility for both economic growth and falling inequality. In the twentieth century, we also find falling inequality and rising growth occurring alongside one another. By this point, the state had begun intervening to ensure higher levels of education (as documented by Claudia Goldin for the United States[67]), along with better funding for science, and health care for all. However, as Teresa Amott and Julie Matthaei also argue, the buoyant times and tight labour markets of the post-Second World War era created a scarcity of labour that gave underprivileged groups the bargaining power to push for an end to discriminatory practices. This is, of course, the period which is well known for both the civil rights and the feminist movements.[68] By contrast, periods in which the economy was doing less well, such as during the 1920s and 1930s, and since 2008, when labour was in excess supply, led groups of privileged workers to put up barriers against others on the basis of gender and race in the former and against immigrant workers in the latter and through to the present. Throughout the twentieth century, the welfare state was only a part of this much wider story and, as we will see later in the book, increased gender and racial disparities in clear, if often under-discussed, ways, trading class inequality for gender and racial inequalities.[69]

Based on history, it is certainly possible to see how events or policies that lower inequality could have beneficial consequences for the economy. However, as we have seen in this chapter, rising inequality and the slowdown in economic growth in the West also reflect a common underlying cause: the lack of freedom of women not only in the West but also in many poorer parts of the world. Until that lack of freedom is addressed, there is a natural limit to what more standard left-leaning inequality-reducing policies can achieve. As Zillah Eisenstein has astutely pointed out:

> Pope Francis has gained enormous popularity by focusing on the excesses of capitalism, the horrors of poverty etc. while fully endorsing patriarchal choices for girls and women in terms of their reproductive lives and health. The very person promising to limit inequality cocoons them into misogyny. It is a well-known and documented fact that the world the pope condones, one without contraception or abortion, is a world with more poverty.[70]

Inequality can only be tackled if we stop focusing on class alone[71] and if we also think beyond a single economy, widening our outlook to the globe. Resolving inequality requires more than 'workers of the world unite': it requires women of the world being entitled to their own bodily autonomy, along with a fairer distribution of the caring labour that results. Nancy Fraser has suggested that we need to move beyond the post-male breadwinner phase of 'universal breadwinners' to a new phase of 'universal caregivers', one that expects everyone to be involved in both work and care.[72] Without them, there would be no economic future. Importantly, not only will getting this right deliver more equitable growth, it will also help us to achieve more sustainable growth, growth that is not undermined by the continual environmental damage that occurs from the population expanding at a rate with which the planet cannot cope.

# 5

# Sex Sells: The Body Versus the Brain

Nothing divides feminists more than capitalism. Except, that is, for the monetization of women's bodies, whether for modelling, for milk (as wet nurses), for surrogacy – or for sex. And the two are not entirely unrelated: if there is one thing that can help explain why so many women have an underlying discomfort with the market, it is the marketization of women's bodies. With sex work labelled the oldest trade, markets and sex seem inseparable. In this chapter, I therefore want to highlight a neglected form of inequality: inequality between women who monetize their brains and those who monetize their bodies. It is an inequality that has so far gone under the radar, one that isn't even measured. And, whilst we're more used to focusing on inequalities between men and women, this inequality, in what we might call the body versus the brain, drives inequalities between women themselves. As I will argue, present policy in many western countries – one of attempting to end demand for sex work – is tackling it in precisely the wrong way.[1]

## The Sinful Eve

For centuries, in fact ever since Eve supposedly tempted Adam, women's bodies have represented sin. In the middle of the fourteenth century, in the Italian town of Siena, an antique statue of Venus was torn down and destroyed by order of the authorities, the town's misfortune having been attributed to its supposed sinful nature. Before long, fragments of the statue were being secretly buried in enemy towns in the hope of bringing similar bad luck to Siena's rivals. Even today, when women uncover too much of their bodies – or attempt to make money from them – it is often seen as inappropriate and shameful. They are commonly labelled 'trashy'. Despite its ubiquitous presence in western art from the time of Botticelli's *Birth of Venus*, the female body remains a taboo, both its naked presence – in revealing clothes or for protest – and its monetization.

Society's discomfort with women's bodies is something I have experienced personally. When giving a public lecture at the launch of a new research forum in London in 2017 on the topic of society in the 1960s, I chose to address the audience in a cutting-edge piece of feminist fashion by designer Jenna Young. It was a sheer black bodysuit that was designed to raise questions about women's bodies. I thought it would be an interesting test of how far society had come in terms of women having the freedom to do whatever they want with their own bodies, thereby fitting neatly with the theme of my lecture. Soon afterwards, I noticed that the accompanying lecture given at the same event by a well-respected male colleague, who wore his usual suit, had been made available online. Mine had not. I was subsequently told that two female attendees had complained that what I did was inappropriate: that I was objectifying myself. They claimed to be feminists. Unlike his, my message never escaped the room.

It is a disapproval I've also faced on other occasions when using my naked body as a vehicle to deliver a feminist message. That includes the nude portrait of myself that went on display at the Mall Galleries in London in 2014, which I'd commissioned from the artist Anthony Connolly. In this and other such art work I aim to question the traditional division in the art world between a male artist and a female nude, one where the male artist is in command, and one which has resulted in the portrayal of women's bodies from the point of view of men. I wanted to 'take charge' in order to challenge the standard depictions of women's bodies, showing the body not of a goddess but of an everyday woman, sending out the message that behind every image of a naked woman is a real thinking being – and one who can talk back. In my view, there is nothing shameful about the female body; shame is a societal construction used to keep women 'in line', so much so that I was happy to put my name to the painting, which is what then resulted in a media storm.

Although paintings of anonymous nudes (whether historic or new) do not attract much in the way of criticism, those with names do. We are happy for women to be painted in the nude so long as we know nothing of them except for their body. I tested the idea by exhibiting another of my nudes – a nude sculpture – anonymously. Unlike the one with a label, it didn't raise eyebrows.

Despite the blatant inconsistency in the way we think about anonymous versus 'real' nudes, some argued that my painting was objectifying, to which I responded with a public defence.[2] A few months later, in the Oxford University annual Encaenia address, summarizing the achievements of the University of Oxford and its various alumni, my 'apparently' empowering portrait got a mention. The choice of the word 'apparently' says it all, seeming to cast doubt on whether this artistic endeavour really was, as I had termed it, empowering. As if I – the woman in question – am not capable of judging for myself. As if what I think and feel comes second to what other people – primarily heterosexual men – might think and feel in response to my nude portrait. It reflects a society in which the 'male' way of seeing women's bodies takes precedence, a society in which, if men see women's bodies as sexual, then a woman who reveals her body cannot possibly be thought of as 'empowered'.

In many countries, the daily life of women is entirely dictated by the way heterosexual men see women's bodies. It is this male way of viewing that overrides what a woman herself would like to do and how she herself witnesses the world. If she wants to cool down, that comes second to concerns about how a man might view her uncovered legs and arms. If she wants to show off her personality by dressing in an 'outrageous' way, that is, once again, overridden by how a man might interpret it. The woman has to be constrained 'for her own good'. It is only the male way of looking, thinking and feeling that matters.

Worryingly, as I've seen in the response of female officials to my own naked protests, women can themselves be complicit in enforcing such outcomes. Women themselves may internalize the dominance of the 'male gaze': they can come to see other women purely through (heterosexual) male eyes; they imagine what heterosexual men might think or feel before determining their response to cases in which women dress too revealingly (or don't dress at all). In fact, at least to date, I have only ever been forced to cover up by female organizers and officials, never by male ones. As we know when it comes to practices surrounding women's bodies (such as foot binding and female genital mutilation [FGM]), women are all too often complicit in restricting the freedom of other women.

Freedom from the 'male gaze' does not, of course, mean that people cannot think or feel whatever they want. I am certainly not naive. Instead, it means that those thoughts and feelings should not have to dictate what a woman chooses to do. For women to have true freedom over their bodies, they should be allowed to use their bodies for their own purposes (whether that's monetary or non-monetary), irrespective of what others think about it. The feminist mantra must always be 'my body, my choice' in the broadest sense of the term.

When it comes to my art and protest, I often have to pose the question: why should I have to cover my body because of what certain men think? Surely I shouldn't be prevented from being free just because of what some heterosexual men may think – or because of what other women think those men may think? As we will see, it is the very same arguments that I face in resistance to my ongoing artistic nudes and naked protests that are also employed by feminists against sex workers.

If women should be free to dress as they wish, model for artists and engage in naked protest, why shouldn't they also be free to sell sex, should they choose to do so? It would, of course, be hypocritical of me to think otherwise. At its roots, society's dislike of sex work (as with its dislike of revealing clothes and naked protest) stems from the sinfulness with which we see women's bodies – and sex itself.

## Feminism Meets Puritanism

Sex trafficking. Sweatshops. Surrogacy. It's not difficult to find stories of markets 'exploiting' poor and vulnerable women. Or of profit-seeking pimps, pornographers and even charity workers doing the same, along with couples from rich countries looking to rent the wombs of women in poorer parts of the world. Capitalism seems to see women's bodies in cash terms. It puts women's breasts, their vaginas and their wombs up for rent. For those who see capitalism as inherently exploitative, nothing would appear to be more indicative of it. Natasha Walter suggests that young women are being turned into 'living dolls', and, according to Kat Banyard, the modern-day state is conspiring with market forces. What we have is not a liberal and democratic state but, she argues, a pimp state.[3] For many feminists, the monetization of women's bodies seems to provide the ultimate example of capitalist exploitation.

Not only are feminists in the West enraged by the marketization of women's bodies, so are extreme conservative social forces. Extremist groups see western capitalism as a threat to female modesty. Their rejection of western values – and their desire to wage war with western civilization – is, in my view, rooted in a belief that western capitalism 'ruins' women. Acutely incentivizing their behaviour is the desire to protect 'their' rights over 'their' women, women who will, in their view, become worthless if they are brought up in a world in which scantily clad women grace advertising billboards and magazines. Women's bodies are the ideological battleground we face today. The association of women's bodies with sin has a lot to answer for.

Feminists who embrace the market – libertarian feminists – believe that individual women should have the choice to use their bodies as they wish; that what they do with their bodies is nobody else's business. This fundamental difference of opinion in regard to women and their bodies is not going away any time soon.

Alison Phipps distinguishes between 'sex radical' and 'sex negative' feminists.[4] 'Sex negative' feminists argue that the sale of sex is inherently violent, that it amounts to rape. They see sex as central to gender inequality and, to quote Phipps, 'porn and prostitution as the pinnacle of women's objectification and the power of men over women's bodies'. Julie Bindel, author of *The Pimping of Prostitution*, writes that 'prostitution is inherently abusive, and a cause and a consequence of women's inequality' and that we should regard 'prostitution as a form of violence in a neoliberal world in which human flesh has come to be viewed as a commodity, like a burger.'[5] By contrast, 'sex radical' feminists see sexual freedom as an essential part of women's liberation and society as inherently repressive of women's sexuality. They emphasize the free choice of women, including of sex workers. They see sexuality as a means of empowerment and sexual freedom as a form of freedom of expression. Within this context, Annie Sprinkle defines sex workers as people who 'challenge sexual mores, help people, are creative, "hot and hip", free spirits, healers and not afraid of sex'.[6] For 'sex radical' feminists, a sex worker certainly should not be assumed to be exploited and vulnerable.

'Sex radical' feminists have a point. For centuries, men have restricted and regulated what women can (or cannot) do with either their bodies or their brains. Over the last century, women have made great strides in terms of their ability to use their brains. However, the same cannot be said of their bodies, which remain taboo. Whilst making money from your brain is to be celebrated, making money from your body is, apparently, not. Perhaps in part because historically women were seen purely in bodily terms – as being without a brain – the monetization of their bodies in the modern day is perceived as anti-feminist. But in a world in which women have the opportunity to make use of their brains or their bodies (or some combination), why should the monetization of the body be seen as inferior to the monetization of the brain? Isn't it inconsistent to allow women to make money from their brains but not from their bodies? In my view, 'sex negative' feminists risk looking like a group of 'clever' women ganging up to pull the rug from under the feet of women who have physical assets that they would like to monetize; women who monetize their brains are, in other words, denying other women the ability to earn an equal living from their bodies.

The justification we are given is twofold: that women who monetize their bodies don't always know their own minds, and that what an individual woman chooses to do has significant (and negative) consequences for the rest of womankind.

In regard to the first justification, 'sex negative' feminists outright deny the possibility that any woman could freely choose to engage in sex work. They argue that free choice cannot be assumed, that women can be 'socialized' into wanting to objectify themselves. The reasoning goes that in a different – more equal – world, they would not 'choose' to reveal their bodies, parade around in high heels or sell sex, and so, for their own good, should be denied the opportunity to do so in *this* world. They should become accountants, politicians or lawyers instead. The Nordic Model Now! submission to the Liberal Democrat's consultation on sex work – from a campaign group that is pushing to criminalize the buying of sex – thereby argued that: '[S]ince prostitution itself causes harm, positioning "voluntary" or "consensual" prostitution as fundamentally different from forced prostitution is misguided … [it is] damaging for society to consider prostitution consensual sex.'

For libertarian feminists, such as Nadine Strossen, Wendy McElroy and Joan Kennedy Taylor, such thinking represents a complete denial of individual agency; it is a denial that *any* woman could possibly choose to monetize her body.[7] It locks out the voices of consensual sex workers by devaluing their voices; devaluing by assuming that their voices are not truly their own.

Now, of course, not all women want to reveal or to monetize their bodies. But just because you might not want to engage in sex work does not mean that we should assume that no other women want to. No group should be assumed to speak for every woman. If I'm honest, I don't understand why anyone would want to experience the risks and pain of boxing or extreme sports. But to outlaw those things because I can't understand why other people might want to do them – or because I think they *shouldn't* want to do them – would be to behave in an authoritarian fashion. Once, I did not understand why anyone would want to pose or protest naked; now I do it myself. How can I, therefore, assume to know the mind of every other woman?

In the words of the sex worker and activist Laura Lee:

I don't ask you to like what I do … what I do ask for is to be allowed to do my job in safety and to be treated with dignity and respect …

there is no greater feeling than meeting a disabled person who has never been with a woman and affording them their first orgasm. To bring such happiness and fulfillment into someone's life is something I treasure. Sex work is work, just like any other. And those of us in the industry deserve support and respect – not to be reviled and stigmatized.[8]

And, in the words of Kirio Birks, a defender of Grid Girls:

[S]urely a woman has a right to be the object of somebody else's desire if she wants and surely it doesn't matter if she is being paid for it? ... Rather than sending Grid Girls off into the wilds of unemployment, or providing one less place for would-be models, a far better solution would have been to make sure that they're unionised, properly paid, and protected. If they are, then they have empowered other women to take up work they might otherwise have avoided, in a safer way.[9]

By denying the agency of women who choose to monetize or reveal their bodies, we conflate two groups: those who really are involuntarily involved in sex work, who should of course be the focus of our concerns, and those who are not. Rather than recognizing the difference, and pointing to the possibility of different degrees of agency,[10] those who claim to be working voluntarily are instead argued to be misguided, socially conditioned and suffering from false consciousness. But for other people to assume they know better than you – to assume that they can judge how free you are better than you yourself can judge – is a dangerous road to go down. It risks replacing patriarchy with a female-led plutocracy. It leads us to a world in which the very concept of individual freedom becomes lost behind what a particular group or community thinks you should or shouldn't want.

None of this means ignoring the fact that many women have been forced into monetizing their bodies, either directly, by people trafficking and modern-day slavery, or indirectly, where a particular individual is left with no other option. Austerity, benefit cuts and benefit sanctions – which have had particularly adverse effects on women – have been linked to sex work. If any woman feels she has no choice, then it is of course tragic. However, the solution is not to ban sex work, which merely makes her options even more restricted, it is to tackle the underlying poverty. Similarly, if women are directly forced into sex work, then the element of force needs to be tackled, such as through criminal law and human slavery legislation. To attempt to stop all sex workers, including those who choose to freely engage in such work, because other women are being forced into the business simply does not make sense. Would we seek to stop all women from being cleaners on the basis that there are, sadly, numerous cases of domestic slavery, or to stop people from working in agriculture on the same basis? As with any other area of activity, sex work by choice and sex work by force cannot be treated in the same light. Unless we separate the two, our moralistic thinking about what women should (and shouldn't) be doing with their bodies biases our policy response. Tackling those who traffic women, and ensuring that all women have choices other than sex work, improving education and welfare policy, can be achieved *alongside* improving the lives of voluntary sex workers by recognizing and supporting their work. Or, at the very least, by not making their lives more vulnerable. If we continue down the route of trying to eliminate sex work, by criminalizing the purchase of sex, by preventing sex workers from having bank accounts or from being able to advertise online, then all we do is make the lives of sex workers more (not less) difficult.[11] Why would anyone want to do that – unless, that is, they really do think that sex is evil.

## The Effect of Sex Workers on Society

The denial that sex work could ever be voluntary – the idea that women do not know their own minds – isn't the only problem that stands in the way of equal rights for women who monetize their bodies with those who monetize their brains. The second supposed justification for denying individual women the freedom to do what they want with their own bodies is the idea that their choice can have a serious adverse effect on other women: that it encourages heterosexual men to look at *all* women in a way that is objectifying. Individual freedoms – of women – must, apparently, be restricted in order to put the wider good – of all other women – first.

Josephine Butler is commonly seen as Britain's first anti-prostitution campaigner. She was born in 1828 and dedicated her life to helping sex workers. She argued that '[t]he degradation of these poor unhappy women is not degradation for them alone; it is a blow to the dignity of every virtuous woman too, it is dishonour done to me, it is the shaming of every woman in every country of the world.'[12] Catherine MacKinnon has followed in her footsteps, arguing that pornography is used 'to train women to sexual submission'.[13] Andrea Dworkin similarly argues that '[p]rostitution in and of itself is an abuse of a woman's body' and that prostitution reflects male supremacy:

> Male dominance means that the society creates a pool of prostitutes by any means necessary so that men have what men need to stay on

top, to feel big, literally, metaphorically, in every way ... Every man in this society benefits from the fact that women are prostituted whether or not every man uses a woman in prostitution ... prostitution comes from male dominance.[14]

The 2014 British All Party Parliamentary Group on Prostitution argued that '[p]rostitution is incompatible with attempts to tackle gender inequality.' The submission received from the European Women's Lobby argued that '[t]he prostitution of women and girls constitutes a fundamental violation of women's human rights and a serious form of male violence against women'. The Nordic Model Now! group's submission to the Liberal Democrat Party's own consultation on prostitution argued that 'the system of prostitution perpetuates the archaic practice of female sexual submission for male entertainment'; that it involves an exchange in which 'he has all the power and she has to do what he says', one that 'feeds the punter's sense of entitlement and the sense that she has no rights'.[15] Their submission was made jointly with eighteen other women's rights and feminist groups.

However, there are big holes in this increasingly popular argument. First, it runs dangerously close to suggesting that gender inequality is a result of women themselves selling their bodies; that, in other words, it is women's own fault, an accusation which 'sex negative' feminists only get around by arguing that all sex workers are involuntary. Sex workers are either treated as the enemy – or as victims. Second, it is of course realistic to suggest that if a society is unequal in gender terms, more women will feel forced into selling their bodies because they have few other options. At present, too many women who are struggling to feed their children find themselves with little option but to enter sex work. But preventing women from selling their bodies does not tackle those underlying gender inequalities. All it does is make the lives of sex workers more difficult. For example, policies that restrict sex workers' ability to screen clients and advertise on line push women onto the street; policies that criminalize the buying of sex push sex work into dangerous avenues, where buyers are less likely to be caught; policies that restrict women's ability to work together mean that they have no one keeping check; and the whole set of policies aimed at 'ending demand' for sex work reduces the price of sex, leaving sex workers poorer than before. A much better approach would be to tackle the barriers affecting women's entry into education, training and the professions, along with addressing the unequal distribution of caring responsibilities in the economy and making sure that those that do unpaid care are not treated by the state as a welfare burden when they are in fact providing the public good on which we will all in the future depend: the next generation. In all of these respects, feminist thinkers have a great deal to offer policy makers, and without interfering with women's freedom to do what they want with their own bodies.[16] Seeing women who sell their bodies as the underlying cause of women's objectification or of gender inequality is to confuse cause and consequence.

By placing the supposed 'social good' (the interests of womankind taken as a group) ahead of the freedom of the individual to do what she likes with her own body, 'sex negative' feminism also creates a slippery slope. If the way women use their bodies affects all other women, then we could easily end up in a society where women are not permitted to wear 'revealing' clothes; where they are expected to wear floor-length skirts and to cover their hair so as to discourage men from looking at them in a certain way. That may seem far-fetched, but it wasn't that long ago that a woman showing her knees, or even her ankles, was seen as objectifying herself, including by other women. If we see people who choose to deviate from the 'norm' as the cause of the problem, we end up, as Friedman and Hayek knew too well, in an authoritarian state, a state that demands that women cover up 'for their own good'.

Once we start placing the supposed 'social good' ahead of the freedom of an individual woman, we end up in a world in which not only would we be insisting women cover up, but where we deny women proper access to birth control on the basis that it would resolve the current demographic crisis (one that economists Coen Teulings and Jason Lu have argued is costing the economy[17]) or of restricting people's ability to move abroad so as to avoid the adverse consequences of a brain-drain at home. Such policies would also be doing nothing more than placing the interests of wider society ahead of individual freedoms – and yet, unlike with sex work, we would reject them. That presents a blatant inconsistency. Either you believe that individuals should be free to choose or that their right to choose comes second to the 'social good'. You cannot have it both ways.

## The Effect of Society on Sex Workers

It is common to think about the effect of sex work on society, but it is much less common to think about the reverse: how society affects the lives of sex workers. As Francesca Bettio, Marina della Giusta and Maria Laura di Tommaso point out, whilst economists have studied stigma in sex work, they have neglected the way in which such stigma is socially constructed.[18]

For centuries, sex work has been demonized and stigmatized. As Kate Lister writes, '[i]n the nineteenth century, sex work was known as "the great social evil" and was a source of acute concern to Victorian moralists.'[19] Alexandre Parent du Châtelet (1836), author of *Prostitution in Paris*, wrote that '[t]he profession of prostitution is an evil of all times and all countries, and appears to be innate in the social structure of mankind.'[20] F. Arnold Clarkson described sex workers as follows:

> In the first place, a great many of them would be classified as pathological liars who garnish the sad tale of their downfall with a romance which would do credit to Munchausen. Poverty has comparatively little to do with their initiation, for prostitution increases regularly with wealth, and no raising of wages can abolish it. Domestic servants, who have a fairly sheltered life, furnish the most recruits. The mental characteristics which are most common are indolence and the love of luxury, including fine clothes. Passion does not seem to play as large a part as is usually supposed ... Once firmly established in this life, few of them seem anxious to change their occupation, and there has always been difficulty, in America at least, in finding girls for the philanthropic 'Rescue Homes'.[21]

Society has created a myth that they are bad people so as to create a 'them' and 'us' – a world in which women are divided into 'good girls' and 'whores'. Lena Edlund and Evelyn Korn explicitly model women choosing between the two.[22] Evidence suggests that even when it comes to our choice of clothing, never mind the monetization of the body, we tend to be more empathetic towards modest women.[23] It is this artificial division of womankind into two groups that allows individuals to get away with subjecting sex workers to the worst kind of horrors. By calling for the criminalization of the buying of sex, sex negative feminists are adding to the stigma, implicitly imposing a view that there is something wrong, shameful or sinful about monetizing the body.[24] After all, if sex work was not thought to be 'wrong', why would they want to end the demand for sex workers? As any economist knows, suppressing demand pushes down the wage, hurting the livelihoods of sex workers. As Marina della Giusta, Maria Laura di Tommaso, and Sarah Jewell show, increased stigma actively achieves that result.[25]

Sex work is, of course, known for high levels of physical and mental abuse, something which campaigners often use to make the case for the buying of sex to be criminalized. In the words of Rahila Gupta, '[e]very prostitute who has left the industry describes the horrendous violence she has faced from pimps and punters, an occupational hazard that characterizes this kind of work.'[26] However, such harm cannot and should not be separated from society's stance towards women who use their bodies in a particular way. In the words of sex worker and blogger Marleen Laverte, '[f]irst and foremost, it is social prejudices about prostitution that render it difficult for us to protect ourselves. That is because they lower the threshold to use violence against us – among clients, among the police, among everyone.'[27]

The disapproval of society can, understandably, result in common feelings of shame and, with it, mental harm and social isolation for women who monetize their bodies, unlike those who monetize their brains. It encourages clients to treat sex workers as subhuman and can lead them to take out their own feelings of shame for purchasing sex work on the sex worker. Society's disrespect also influences the law, which in turn affects violence towards sex workers. Criminalizing the buying (or selling) of sex places women in a more vulnerable position: unable to practise in safe conditions, unable to call on the support of the authorities and police and unable to benefit from the same rights as other occupations.[28] It leaves women at the behest of those in a position of power. According to Laura Lee, '[t]he result is we're forced to work alone, sitting targets for would-be attackers who know that we are vulnerable, on our own, and carrying money.'[29] And in the words of Margaret Corvid:

> Criminalisation doesn't end demand – it just makes clients more afraid, and destroys any trust between worker and client. It makes it difficult to screen our clients or to practise safer sex. In street-based sex work, clients and workers now avoid well-lit areas, and meet in isolated places or in the client's home. In indoor sex work, it's harder to screen clients by phone, or with deposits, and our clients can't really trust us. How can this possibly help us?[30]

## Society's Three Hang-Ups

Full equality for women means not only making sure that no woman feels backed into a corner but treating women who voluntarily monetize their bodies in the same way as we treat those who monetize their brains. Rather than criminalizing market exchange, it is instead society-wide disapproval and disrespect for sex work that needs to be tackled. This requires tackling three deeper hang-ups that we have as a society.

First, setting brain over body: to assume that it's perfectly all right for people to effectively pimp their brains but not their bodies. If you're born with or work hard to hone numerical or literary skills, it's entirely acceptable to make money from them, to sell your talents to others and for those other people to buy them. But if you're born with a great body, exercise hard and are able to hone your erotic skills, that's somehow considered different. Economic thinking, which grew out of the Enlightenment, hasn't helped here. Economics developed in a period in which science moved centre stage. Arts and emotion were out. Logic and reason were in. The brain came to be seen as superior to the body, capable of bringing about never-before-imagined riches. Anyone at the time identified primarily by their bodies – women and people of colour – was rendered second-class.[31]

Ever since the Enlightenment, there has been a tendency to view 'clever' people as somehow superior to everyone else. Consistent with this, and within sex work itself, stigma is lower for parts of the industry that involve more brain than brawn.[32] Implicit in this way of thinking – that it's OK to sell access to your brain but not to your body – is a gender element: the association of the brain with men and the body with women (as well as with people of colour).[33] Since the brain has traditionally been considered masculine and therefore seen as man's great asset, our patriarchal society past and present has been perfectly happy with the idea of pimping the brain. But, since the body has been traditionally more associated with women and since women have traditionally been seen as inferior to men, then by default it has been assumed that making money from the body is somehow less respectable. And, of course, it has been in the distinct interest of men to leave sex workers in a vulnerable position, unprotected by the law, thereby reducing the sexual power that women can have over men. 'Sex negative' feminists fall into this same trap, one which devalues women who earn income from their bodies – in fact, not only devaluing it but aiming to eradicate it. 'Sex positive' feminist Catherine Hakim, by contrast, suggests that we adopt a concept she calls 'erotic capital' alongside the more common concept of 'human capital', one that recognizes the value created by bodily assets.[34]

The second hang-up is that, historically speaking, we have tended to locate a woman's value in her sexual virtue and to see sex as 'dirty'. Throughout the world, women are tortured and killed by their families if their sexual virtue is brought into question. Here in England, we revere Elizabeth I as 'the Virgin Queen'. We slut-shame. Christianity has not helped, historically seeing the naked female body as evil, sinful and shameful. The problem is not sex work; it is the way we value women on the basis of their sexual virtue. In the words of Andrea Dworkin:

> to the extent that people believe sex is dirty, people believe that pros-
> tituted women are dirt ... The prostituted women is, however, not
> static in this dirtiness. She's contagious ... In general, the prostituted
> woman is seen as the generative source of everything that is bad and
> wrong and rotten with sex, with the man, with women.[35]

Third, there is a tendency to see a woman's body as the property of men, that her (assumed to be) male partner should be the only one with access to it and that, until a woman meets her partner, she should remain 'pure'. A woman using her own body is, as a result, seen as a threat to male sexual control. Throughout history, sex workers have been depicted as a threat to men and as a threat to the sexual virtue of women. It's for that reason that in medieval times they had to mark themselves out by the way they dressed (such as by wearing striped hoods), so that no other woman could be mistaken for one, and why female nudes in art were most commonly depicted as unaware of the male viewer and in an unthreatening pose, such as looking away from the onlooker.

As a society, we need to face up to and tackle these three prob-lematic ways of thinking about women and sex, rather than regulating what women can and cannot do with their bodies. As suggested by the anthropologist Joke Schrijvers, a particularly good way to evalu-ate the place of women in a culture is to ask to what extent women have control over their own sexuality and fertility.[36]

## Conclusion

Trading sex has a long history – and is not unique to humans.[37] It's also big business. However, women who monetize their bodies remain a taboo. Although the feminist mantra 'my body, my choice' seems to be perfectly acceptable in some situations – such as in regard to birth control – it doesn't seem to apply to sex workers. As a society, we surely have further to travel in gender equality terms but, once we achieve that utopia, the question is this: will sex workers, glamour models and revealing clothes be welcome? I personally think that a utopia that restricts the way that women use – or reveal – their bodies is no utopia at all. My utopia is, instead, one in which not only is no woman forced into a career that is not of her own choosing but that making money from the brain and body are placed on an equal footing. The inequality that exists between the two is not natural and is not the fault of the market; it results from deep-rooted social taboos about women, sex and their bodies. Confronting these taboos, as I myself aim to do by using my own body in art and protest, could have a transformative effect on the lives of some of society's most vulnerable women – women who are vulnerable because they are unprotected by the law of the land and by the basic market supports available to those working in virtually any other profession.[38]

# Part III

## State

# Introduction

In this part of the book, I want to get to grips with the debate that has hung over economics since the time of Adam Smith: state versus market. It is a debate that raged throughout the last century, not only in lecture halls but in the form of the Cold War. As we will see, when it comes to capitalism, feminist thinkers are deeply divided.[1] This does, however, have one big advantage: wherever one stands on the political spectrum, feminist thinking has a lot to offer.

Whilst we tend to assume that by the end of the twentieth century, with the fall of the Iron Curtain and the liberalization of China, capitalism had won, it's clear that the state has remained a powerful force in all western economies. The numbers speak for themselves. Little more than a century ago, governments administered no more than 10% of the typical economy's annual income. The typical government is now in charge of some 30–55%[2] of their economy's annual income (Figure III.1); it taxes the public to fund a whole host of activities, such as education, health, transport, utilities, energy, pensions, scientific research and welfare; and it employs around 15–30% of the total workforce within Europe, or around one in seven workers in the United States.[3]

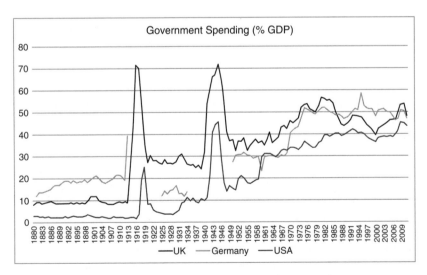

**Figure III.1**  Government spending as percentage of GDP in the UK, Germany, and the USA, 1880–2011
*Source*: Ortiz-Ospina and Roser (2018); Mauro et al. (2015)

However, that does not mean that the ideological battles of the past are dead and buried. The events of the last decade – a global financial crisis that rivals that of 1929, together with increasing concern about inequality – have caused popular dissatisfaction with the status quo. Something has happened that has never been seen before: people have lost faith in both capitalism and the state. Politics is in the process of being remade.

We might like to think that the state versus market question is rather old hat – that we have a much less polarized and more pragmatic view today than we did during the Cold War – but economists on both the left and the right are digging in their heels. On the left, they increasingly point to the failures of markets, highlighting new points of focus for the state, whether in the form of 'nudges', regulation or tax and spend.[4] On the right, by contrast, contemporary economic problems, including the global financial crisis and rising inequality, have been re-spun, not as a result of too much capitalism but of too little.[5] On one side, the focus is on criticizing the market and trumpeting the virtues of the state. On the other, we find the exact opposite.[6] Blinkers are back in fashion, to the distaste of anyone in the centre.

It's time to remove our blinkers, and, in the process of doing so, it's vital that we listen to what feminist thinking can offer. Feminist economists and thinkers have been pivotal in offering critiques of capitalism.[7] Being on the edge of the economy, all too often in the vulnerable position of needing to feed their families with few financial resources and the burden of unpaid care, women have also often borne the brunt of its most exploitative elements. In the same way that Marxists argue that capitalism leads to the exploitation of the poor, Marxist feminists have argued that capitalism leads to the exploitation of women. According to this line of thinking, capitalism keeps women in their place; it is not in the interest of the system to promote equality when it can instead be taking advantage of women. For these thinkers, feminism is about more than the pursuit of equality of opportunity within the current system; it involves overthrowing the system. Capitalism and feminism are, we are told, inherently incompatible.

For libertarian feminists, by contrast, the idea of replacing capitalism with an opposite kind of system could not be more terrifying.[8] On the face of it, alternative systems might look appealing. The bright red revolutionary posters of the Soviet Union depicting healthy and strong factory women certainly give that impression. They promise equality and freedom, putting what's good for society ahead of any single individual. In practice, however, alternatives to capitalism place greater power in the hands of the two bodies that history has shown to provide no guarantee of women's freedom: the state and society.

Given its rather diverse thoughts on capitalism, feminist thinking provides the perfect backdrop against which to reflect critically on both the state and the market. In what follows, we will begin with Marxist feminism, which provides a critique of the market, before moving on to highlight the often overlooked social benefits of the market. Along the way, we will, however, acknowledge that not every market is the same, meaning that the market can be made to work better, the two limiting factors being the degree of progressiveness of society and the capabilities of the state. In the second chapter, I will consider the role of the state in greater detail and, as with markets, will note that not every state is the same; some are much better than others. I will look at the formation of the modern-day state, explaining how countries such as Britain managed to build their relatively capable states, pointing to the essential role played by women's freedom. Along the way, two questions should be in the back of our minds: how have women affected the development of the state, and what has the state done for women in return? And, more generally, can the market and state work together to deliver more equitable and sustainable prosperity?

# 6

## Marx Versus Markets

---

Marxism has had a strong influence on feminist thinking, leading many feminists to be highly sceptical of markets. In this chapter, I therefore want to take a fresh look at the market, considering not only its downside, as told with the help of Marxist feminism, but also its upside, an upside that differs substantially from those more commonly emphasized by economists and which, according to Stiglitz, looks increasingly slippery.[1] We will see that rather than being the enemy of radicals, bohemians and non-conformists, the market can help to undermine the social norms and state-imposed restrictions that keep people – including women – where society would like to see them: 'in their place'. But, as we will also see, not all markets perform this task in an equally effective way. That's because markets do not exist independently of the state or society. Wherever an economy lies on the political continuum, society – not the state or the market – is always the key obstacle where women's freedom is concerned.

### Marx: The Secret Sexist

Karl Marx isn't known for his feminism. In fact, if you read *Das Kapital*, you get the distinct impression that he was a secret (or not so secret) sexist. In a section titled 'Labour of Women and Children', he notes that women's entry into the labour force hurt male wages and meant that wives were unable to undertake their 'free labour' duties within the home. Marx's friend, Friedrich Engels, did, however, take gender inequality seriously. His explanation for it was, however, simple: the birth of private property. Like other forms of inequality, gender inequality was reduced to class. Overthrowing capitalism was the panacea.

As feminism spread across the social sciences in the course of the 1970s, Marxists began to take it more seriously, with Heidi Hartmann pushing for a 'progressive union' between the two.[2] In 1986, Maria Mies penned what was to become a classic work in the Marxist feminist literature. Entitled *Patriarchy and Accumulation on a World Scale*, she argued that capitalist production depends upon the exploitation of women, as both cheap labour within factories and the home. As she writes of the latter: 'It is my thesis that this general production of life, or subsistence production – mainly performed through the non-wage labour of women and other non-wage labourers as slaves, contract workers and peasants in the colonies – constitutes the perennial basis upon which "capitalist productive labour" can be built up and exploited.'

In her *Caliban and the Witch*, Silvia Federici went further, suggesting that capitalism relied on violence – against women, the poor and ethnic minorities – in order to create a class of landless labourers who were entirely dependent on capitalists.[3]

This Marxist vein of feminist thinking continues to the present, though with more of an ecological and intersectional focus. Emma Dowling recently argued that:

> Capitalism as a system organises production and reproduction in such a way as to enable the private appropriation of the social wealth that is produced, relying on sources of unpaid labour and, as is becoming acutely obvious in the face of climate change, extensive ecological resources to do so ... What is at stake then is the question of how the material relations of power and wealth that underpin the control over the reproduction of livelihood are organised, maintained and reinforced.[4]

As the world has gone global, Marxist feminism has highlighted the way in which professional western women rely on the labour of poorer women elsewhere in the world, whether indirectly in the form of cheaply produced clothing and household goods or directly in the form of cleaners and nannies – and even surrogate mothers.[5]

According to Nancy Fraser, liberal-leaning feminists have engaged in a 'dangerous liaison' with capitalism.[6] They have been fooled into believing that they could pursue equality of opportunity *within* the current system, rather than seeking to challenge the system. Marxist feminism suggests that the strategy of 'lean in' will never be enough, that women need to 'lean out'. 'Leaning in', a term coined by Sheryl Sandberg, involves 'fixing women' – making them more in tune with the workings of the market. Rather than fixing women, Marxists argue that we need to fix the world.

The implication of Marxist feminism is that gender *inequality* is good for capitalist growth, and that capitalism is, therefore, bad for women. Feminists have, of course, regularly pointed out that globalization relies on cheap female 'sweatshop' labour, and the economist Stephanie Seguino has found evidence that a greater gender wage gap can boost economic growth by allowing the export-oriented manufacturing sector to take advantage of lower-paid women.[7] Turning to history, Oxford economic historian Jane Humphries has argued that it was cheap female and child labour that fuelled the British Industrial Revolution.[8]

But, just because cheap female (and child) labour existed, it does not mean that it was ultimately helpful to the process of industrialization or economic growth; it could have instead reduced the pressure on businesses to automate, thereby limiting the pace of productivity advance and economic growth. Low wages also make it more difficult for families to invest in their children's skills or to save for the future, thereby hurting growth.

Evidence that cheap female and child labour was hurting as opposed to helping the Industrial Revolution can be found in the Factory Commission Report of 1833. At the time, there was a popular outcry about the working conditions facing women and children, and so one of the purposes of the report was to ascertain whether regulating female and child labour would hurt the expanding industrial sector. The Commissioners therefore sent inspectors to talk to factory owners, supervisors, workers, doctors and midwives in industrial towns. One of the questions asked of factory owners and managers was how they would respond to restrictions on the use of cheap labour, including of child labour. The answers were clear: they would have to adopt more automated machinery.[9] In other words, the pockets of cheap labour that no doubt existed during the Industrial Revolution were not always helping the Industrial Revolution, they were limiting it. They were allowing businesses to get away with using cheap labour when they would have otherwise had to increase the rate at which they were developing and adopting new technology. Even though it makes life temporarily easier for businesses, cheap labour is not good for growth in the longer run. As Naila Kabeer writes: 'Women's lower costs and lesser bargaining power in the market place have been the basis of export-oriented growth based on labour-intensive manufacturing ... [but] there is ... no trade-off between gender equality and economic growth once the focus moves from short-run gains to long-term, sustainable and pro-poor growth.'[10]

In sum, Marxist feminism, is correct to alert us to the way in which power imbalances can distort women's wages, and how their unpaid reproductive and caring labour is made invisible, leaving women in a much more vulnerable position than would otherwise be the case – such as with lower wages. However, this does not mean that markets and gender equality cannot coexist. Gender equality is, as we saw in part I, good for growth – and it's also better for the planet, leading to growth that is more sustainable.[11] And, importantly, that gender equality, as we will see more below, is often supported by the market. Furthermore, and as we will see in the next chapter, we cannot always rely on the state to do the same. Markets are a necessary ingredient. The question this will leave us with is how can we make sure that markets produce more equitable and sustainable outcomes?

## Why we Need Markets

Staring history in the face, it's easy to portray Karl Marx as the radical of his age. At a time when capitalism was in its early stages, he offered a seemingly devastating critique, suggesting not only that it oppressed the masses but that it would eat itself alive. According to Vladimir Lenin, only imperialism – what he called the highest stage of capitalism – could postpone its ultimate demise, a last ditch attempt to find additional buyers and, of course, additional labour to exploit. Although it might appear radical, such thinking was not, however, without precedent. For centuries, the Church had taught us that the pursuit of riches – including profit – was evil. It was immoral and corrupting. What was really radical in the eighteenth and nineteenth centuries was instead the work of free-market economists.

When economists like Adam Smith and David Ricardo were making their pro-market arguments, free markets were far from the 'norm'. As the historian Laurence Fontaine has shown, whereas this pre-capitalist period is often presented in a romanticized way, whether in the work of authors such as E. P. Thompson and Karl Polanyi or in the numerous paintings which depict a happy peasant life in rural idylls, it was in fact no utopia.[12] It was instead a time when politicians and the aristocracy (and there was, naturally, a lot of overlap between the two) had a stranglehold over all of our lives. According to Rubinstein, of all the British millionaires who died between 1809 and 1859, 179 were landed and only 10 were not.[13] As he writes, 'an observer entering a room full of Britain's 200 wealthiest men in 1825 might be forgiven for thinking that the Industrial Revolution had not occurred.'[14] Where government intervened it was often in the interests of privileged groups, including the landowning elite. When it came to business activity, the state wielded its power to grant licences to companies that were themselves, like the East India Company, the size of a small economy. The access of smaller traders and producers was regularly blocked by guilds or by government regulation. In the eighteenth century, even the production of beer was heavily regulated, requiring permission from a single local judge.[15] Free markets were not supported by the wealthy or by 'big business'; they were resisted by them. It was the working classes and the 'new money' – the industrialists producing cotton and steel – who could see the benefit in reduced government interference, a way out from under the thumbs of those in power. It placed power in the hands of individuals, allowing them to work for whoever they liked and to set up businesses producing whatever they liked. Markets had to be fought for. Concentrations of power in politics and society had to be confronted.

Although economists have focused on the efficiency properties of the market, the social consequences are just as important. Markets can give the individual the power to escape societally imposed constraints. It is, here, notable just how many pro-market economists have themselves faced the wrath of society. Adam Smith is known for being something of a social 'outsider'. He certainly was not a natural 'social animal'. David Ricardo became estranged from his Jewish family after marrying a Quaker, and, as a non-conformist Christian, John Stuart Mill would have been unable to join the esteemed scholarly ranks of Oxford and Cambridge. Milton Friedman was from a Jewish immigrant family, meaning he was well aware of the way in which society in Europe had demonized the Jewish minority population, with disastrous consequences. To such thinkers, it could not have been more apparent that society does not always support our individual freedom. The state was not, therefore, the only target of free market supporters. In the words of J. S. Mill:

> Society can and does execute its own mandates: and if it issues wrong mandates instead of right, or any mandates at all in things with which it ought not to meddle, it practices a social tyranny more formidable than many kinds of political oppression, since, though not usually upheld by such extreme penalties, it leaves fewer means of escape, penetrating much more deeply into the details of life, and enslaving the soul itself. Protection, therefore, against the tyranny of the magistrate is not enough: there needs protection also against the tyranny of the prevailing opinion and feeling; against the tendency of society to impose, by other means than civil penalties, its own ideas and practices as rules of conduct on those who dissent from them; to fetter the development, and, if possible, prevent the formation, of any individuality not in harmony

with its ways, and compel all characters to fashion themselves upon the model of its own.[16]

For those who see society as something other than a happy and harmonious place – as something that can potentially constrain us and restrict our freedom – the market provides an escape mechanism. That includes for women. It was a relatively small leap from Mill's idea that society could constrain our liberties to the idea that society was in fact constraining women's freedom. Mill became the first politician to demand votes for women and is often considered to be one of the first male supporters of feminism, publishing *The Subjection of Women* in 1869.

Looking to history offers some support for the notion that markets can help to set women free. Economic historians Jan Luiten van Zanden and Tine de Moor point to the way in which women's involvement in the labour market in medieval Europe led to substantial changes in family life that empowered women, including providing them with the ability to escape early marriage, ultimately laying the foundations for economic growth.[17] Amy Froide, in her recent book *Silent Partners*, points to the way in which early financial markets in Britain before and during the Industrial Revolution provided opportunities for women that had been denied by incumbent societal practices and institutions.[18] Those included the guilds that locked women out of skilled work and the professions. Using the sex ratio at birth as a measure of preference for sons, Melanie Xue finds greater gender equality today in parts of China more historically associated with cotton production, which offered jobs to women.[19] As Swedberg notes, '[m]any improvements in the household have incidentally come about when some of its actors – young people and women – were given access to the alternative of the market.'[20] As anonymous markets developed, though they were by no means perfect, they often opened doors for women, as well as for other people who had been sidelined by 'mainstream' society. Indeed, one of the most noticeable aspects of the period in the twentieth century which was associated with a return to free-market thinking was a social revolution. Rapid social change culminated in dramatic changes in the laws affecting homosexuals, ethnic minorities and women. Individuals were fighting for their freedom against a backdrop of a heavy-handed state – one that represented a majority of citizens who were conservative with a small 'c'. In the words of Jason Hickel and Arsalan Khan:

The hallmark of the [social] revolution of the 1960s was the defence of individual liberty against the constraints of mass conformist society.

Resistance to the draft; the defence of free speech; the right to divorce, abortion, contraceptives, and other sexual freedoms all references the desire to make choices for oneself, through one's own reason and according to one's own conscience.[21]

Following in the footsteps of Friedrich Hayek, Milton Friedman's *Capitalism and Freedom* captured the wave.[22] Friedman argued that political and economic freedom are inextricably linked; that 'a society which is socialist cannot also be democratic, in the sense of guaranteeing individual freedom.' He was well aware of the fact that society was not always harmonious and that there was therefore the risk of an inherent conflict between society and the individual. Friedman argued that the market could ease the resultant tension, allowing us to engage in an anonymous fashion without having to agree with one another. The result was that we could all live side by side and meet our daily needs in a way that avoided enforced conformity. To quote Voltaire: 'Go into the London Stock Exchange ... and you will see representatives from all nations gathered ... Here Jew, Mohammedan and Christian deal with each other as though they were all of the same faith.'[23]

Not only do markets allow us to try to escape the norms of society, enabling us to be ourselves, market competition adds a further release valve: it means that individuals have at least some chance of escaping individual cases of abuse. The market might be brutal but so can the state be too. And whilst in human nature 'bad apples' are inevitable, they are, in general, more likely to face the consequences of their actions in the marketplace than they are in any state-run economy. Without competition to expose them, the state can cover up wrongdoing, meaning that abuses continue. Indeed, it has an incentive to do so in order to hold on to its reputation for 'social good'. In the marketplace, even though cover-ups can and do happen, competition pushes in the direction of rooting out wrongdoers. Either consumers get wind of it and stop buying a particular producer's goods, or workers move on to another producer. Although the mechanism for this to happen is not perfect – consumers do not always find out the full facts and workers facing abuse are not always mobile – at least it provides a possibility of punishment and escape that is missing when the state has a monopoly of power – and, all importantly, a monopoly of force, which enables it to imprison or even kill those who speak out.[24]

Exploitation and violence levelled at women is regularly blamed on capitalism but society is, more often than not, the underlying cause. That includes Federici's classic example: the tens of thousands of women burnt at the stake in Europe during a 200-year period of witch trials in the course of the sixteenth and seventeenth centuries. Witch burnings reflected the way in which society felt threatened by increasingly independent single women. And, as new research shows, they were also a response to increased competition between different Christian religious sects as a means to demonstrate their purity value to the masses.[25] In the modern world, witch burnings and other forms of violence towards women – including FGM – are similarly the result of bad social practices. Although it's far from perfect, and needs to be backed up by a legal system that takes violence against women seriously, the market can help to provide a way out.

## The Big 'But': Markets can (and Should) be Made to Work Better

Until recently, we tended to think that markets were modern. In 1944, for example, Karl Polanyi argued that a 'great transformation' to a modern market economy took place around the time of the Industrial Revolution. Over the last twenty years, economic historians have, however, identified a more prominent role for markets than that envisaged by Polanyi throughout many different periods of human history and in many different parts of the world. But, of course, this does not mean that one market is equivalent to another. As Ha-Joon Chang and Alex Marshall have noted, there is, in a sense, no such thing as a free market.[26] Markets can take many different forms, depending on the foundations upon which they are built: laws, institutions (both formal and informal) and the regulations we choose to put in place, including what can or cannot be bought or sold. Although markets may appear entirely 'natural', well-functioning markets – those that deliver equitable and sustainable prosperity – are the product of careful design and periodic updating of laws, regulations and institutions. Markets do not, in other words, exist independently of the state or society.

As Steven Pearlstein noted in response to the controversial question 'Is capitalism moral?':

> [T]he way markets distribute rewards is neither divinely determined nor purely the result of the 'invisible hand'... In our current debate over capitalism, too much attention is focused on whether, how or how much to redistribute the incomes that markets have produced, with too little focus on the institutional arrangements that determine how that income is divided up in the first place.

History provides plenty of examples. In his study of labour markets in the British Industrial Revolution, Mark Steinberg notes that the laws which provided the 'rules of the game' within which labour markets operated were not neutral but were 'embedded in a legal system structured to serve capitalists' interests', which included the Master and Servant Act of 1823.[27] In the late nineteenth century, we find a further example, one in which the state regulated the working hours of women, in part due to pressure from the rising (and very male) labour movement. In regard to gender equality, past and present, we know that family law, property law, the regulation of abortion and birth control, and laws aimed at sex workers all have significant effects on the extent to which market outcomes are equitable in a gender sense.[28]

Many economists who initially began to embrace the market – those of the eighteenth and nineteenth centuries – recognized that markets would only work well if they operated against the 'right' backdrop, where what was 'right' needed to be debated and was ultimately determined by normative considerations. According to Avner Offer, this means that neoliberalism is a 'radical departures from the ethical legacy of Enlightenment and utilitarian economics' and certainly is 'not consistent with Adam Smith's own position'.[29] When determining the appropriate backdrop for markets, early economists confronted numerous ethical questions, including about what is or is not 'fair'. This included debating the laws on bankruptcy, the notion of lender of last resort and guarantees for savers, whether people who owned shares should be personally liable for a company's debts and whether inventors should be able to patent their ideas.[30] In the late nineteenth and early twentieth centuries, they also debated equal pay legislation, though they came out against rather than in favour of it, which goes to show just how much social norms creep into the laws that underpin markets.[31] However, before long, Milton Friedman began to argue that economics could divorce itself from moral and ethical questions, meaning that the contributions of both earlier liberal thinkers and of early institutionalism were lost.

These early insights have, however, been reborn in modern debates about the market versus the state in at least two ways. First, we've seen a revival of interest in the work of Karl Polanyi, who argued that markets became increasingly disembodied from society in the course of the Industrial Revolution. His modern followers suggest that in order to work better, markets need to be 're-embedded' in society and subjected to non-economic (not just economic) norms.[32] A reassertion of social democracy, involving greater social protections, along with encouraging small local efforts to design, trial and demonstrate alternatives to the capitalist firm (along the lines of J. K. Gibson-Graham's Community Economy), is on offer in place of a full-scale anti-capitalist revolution.[33] Second is the idea of 'predistribution', or, when applied to gender alone, what Elisabeth Prügl has sceptically termed 'neoliberalism with a feminist face'.[34] The idea here is that we do not have to simply accept market outcomes as given, redistributing *ex post*, but that we can instead work on the very foundations of markets to ensure that those initial outcomes are 'fairer' and more successful. Here, rather than society taming capitalism, it is about changing the rules of the game so that they do not rig the game on one side or another. Redesign can include: tackling property and inheritance laws that are different for men and women; laws that ban married women from working, girls from attending certain educational institutions or accessing particular careers; laws that restrict women's ability to control their fertility or their access to financial services and credit; and laws that criminalize sex work. Market outcomes that are not inequitable can also be a result of a lack of female (or other such) representation in the development of those laws, regulations and institutions, which means voices that need to be heard are sidelined.[35]

Whether we move in the direction of Polanyi or predistribution, or develop some combination, it necessarily requires starting big debates within society about what we think is – or is not – 'fair'. Most pressing are, I would suggest, debates about whether rights should be equally invested in immigrant and domestic labour, in citizenship as opposed to paid work (the latter being the case with health care, etc. in the United States), how we think care should be distributed, whether we think individuals should be financially responsible for their own children (or whether there should be some collective responsibility due to their 'public good' nature and, if so, whether or not there is a 'right' number of children where such responsibilities are concerned), and whether women should be free to monetize their bodies.

But, change is never easy. Social norms that penalize women – norms that are in turn embedded in laws, regulations and institutions – must be confronted.[36] This requires being aware of the potentially divergent interests of different groups; whilst empowering women might be good for everyone in the longer term, it can also create conflicts of interest in the short term which, unless they are factored in, can lead to worse rather than better results for women. That includes greater violence against women within the home, including, as has been found in India, female relatives being killed in response to changes in inheritance rights.[37] Furthermore, as Nancy Fraser notes, the geographical political boundaries within which laws and institutions are constructed – the nation-state – can prove to be a severely limiting factor where justice is concerned. Once again, that's relevant not just to class but also to gender. National boundaries force us to ask who are the relevant subjects that we must consider when determining the laws and institutions that so affect market outcomes? That can lead us to ignore the interests of foreign workers and the world's poorest women. We need to question whether the 'appropriate unit of justice' really is the territorial state, and what more can be done to effect more equitable and sustainable outcomes where that is not the case.[38]

## Conclusion

The value of the market cannot be reduced down to economic concepts of efficiency and productivity. What gives markets their power is the very way in which they enable bottom-up as opposed to top-down action, supporting individual freedom: markets allow us all to try different things and to be whoever we want to be, unconstrained by what other people think. Marxism makes the mistake of assuming that we can all happily associate with one another once class has been eliminated; Karl Polanyi assumed social norms and social protections (such as a welfare state) could be entirely innocent. Perhaps the two greatest thinkers of the left, they both completely ignored the way in which society can be vicious, particularly to those it disapproves of, whether that's working women, single mums, people of colour, the LGBT community or immigrants. The reality of life is that, starting from an early age, we frequently come into conflict with one another *outside* of the marketplace, no more so than in the playground. Every human being is different, and we gain utility from being free to be ourselves. Non-conformity does not, however, always please others, which means that, in a social setting, people often have to hide their individuality or risk open conflict. That includes women who want to escape from heavily gendered social norms – and women who disagree with other women about appropriate behaviour (such as how much of their body it is appropriate to cover or uncover). The market offers a solution by catering to all lifestyles and allowing us to exchange with one another in an anonymous fashion, meaning we don't have to get on with one another.

Whilst markets thrive on diversity, society and the state can punish it with the heavy hand of force. They can respond to the diversity and freedoms that the market has enabled by putting a lid on it: to restrict, as we see today, our freedom to move across borders and our freedom to buy or sell whatever interests or best suits us, which can include monetizing our bodies as well as our brains. Some commentators, such as Nancy Fraser, believe that it's possible to 'forge a principled new alliance' between social democracy and emancipatory movements: that we can have more state interventions and social protections at the same time as allowing every individual to be themselves.[39] I am altogether less optimistic, as was Friedrich Hayek.[40] Not only, as we will see in the next chapter, have many state interventions historically sidelined women, but sex work provides a perfect example of where well-intentioned state interventions designed to be emancipatory are trampling on (rather than supporting) the individual freedom of a heavily marginalized social group. There is a limit to how much we can trust anyone who is given free rein to intervene in the market, even if they are a self-declared social progressive.

Although it must surely be embraced, the second agenda – that of predistribution – also has its limits. As it suggests, the foundations on which market exchange is built – laws, regulations and institutions – can vary quite significantly across place and time and come to embody society's views on what is or is not acceptable and what is or is not 'right'. Where markets fail to deliver equitable outcomes to women, it is often a result of laws, regulations and institutions that embody unprogressive views. Redesigning markets is essential, but it can also be very tricky when society is unprogressive in its views. Society is always the limiting factor.

The market is far from perfect, but it must be understood in the context of both an imperfect state and a society that can be something other than progressive. When we blame the market, sometimes that blame would be better directed at society.

# 7

# Why Women Make Better States

In the previous chapter, we saw that markets are a necessary ingredient of any successful and progressive economy – and indeed society. In this chapter, we will explore the relationship between the state and economic prosperity in greater detail. As we will see, it is not simply the size of the state that matters but how capable it is. Where states are capable, they can work with (rather than against) the market, leading to a whole that is more than the sum of its parts. However, as we will also see, what economists define as a 'capable' state is not always enough for ensuring that the state works in the best interests of women and, in turn, for delivering equitable and sustainable growth. When judging states, gender needs to be brought into view. We will go on to explore how today's most successful states developed, pointing to the largely neglected role of women's freedom. The history of the state is intimately tied to the history of women.

## Why do Richer Countries have Bigger States?

It's fast becoming a well-known fact amongst economists, but one which isn't often aired in public: there is a surprising correlation between the state and prosperity. And it's not a negative correlation. It's strikingly positive. Alongside the astronomical rise in living standards in western countries over the last two centuries, one thing stands out: the expansion of the state. Whilst the twentieth century is often associated with expanding markets and globalization, it also witnessed ever growing states.[1] And, perhaps ironically, it wasn't a low-tax, low-debt part of the world that spurred the process of modern economic growth. It was high-tax, high-debt Britain that gave rise to the first industrial revolution in the late eighteenth and nineteenth centuries (see Figure 7.1) – high both compared with Europe and Asia.[2]

Not only does the time-path of history suggest that states and prosperity sometimes can go hand in hand, so too do comparisons across countries in the modern world. Indeed, some of the poorest parts of the globe lack well established and capable states. They tend to be fragmented and experience significant internal conflict, including civil war. As economists Noel Johnson and Mark Koyama point out, '[t]oday's richest countries possess both sophisticated market economies and powerful, centralized, states. In contrast, the poorest people in the world tend to live in regions with dysfunctional markets and weak or failed states.'[3] As Acemoglu et al. note, '[i]t is now widely recognized that the weakness or lack of "capacity" of states in poor countries is a fundamental barrier to their development prospects. Most poor countries have states which are incapable of or unwilling to provide basic public goods such as the enforcement of law, order, education and infrastructure.'[4] Even in the United States, where there is a tradition of arguing that the state is inimical to growth, there is increasing evidence of a link between the state and prosperity. That includes the work of Daren Acemoglu, Jacob Moscona and James

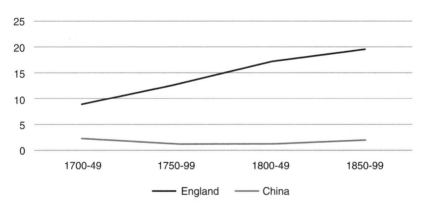

**Figure 7.1** Taxes in history: high-tax England vs low-tax China. Central government tax revenue per head (measured in the number of days an unskilled worker would have to work to pay the tax).
*Source*: Ma and Rubin (2017)

Robinson, who, using postal stations as a proxy for state infrastructure in history, find a strong link with innovative activity, as measured by patents.[5]

So how do we explain the fact that many of today's richest economies also have big states? There are, in fact, three possibilities: that states can be good for prosperity; that prosperity leads to expanding states; or that there is a common factor that produces both.

The first of these possibilities is that states have learnt how to support prosperity. Markets are a necessary but not sufficient driver of economic prosperity, and, if the state uses its capacity to work with them (rather than against them), it can make an important contribution to prosperity. First, you don't have to dig too deep into any economics textbook to find all kinds of situations in which markets 'fail', along with a series of policy implications. Whether that's dealing with externalities such as pollution, funding public goods, including, as Marianna Mazzucato emphasizes, the science base, or making sure that everyone has access to education and training, allowing us to make the most of the most scarce resource our economy has: human talent. Furthermore, since care is central to economic activity, and yet is so often provided outside of the market and on a rather longer timescale to production, allowing the economy to free-ride on what has largely been women's reproductive and caring efforts, feminist economists would also suggest that the state has a role to play here too, both in terms of limiting the adverse implications for gender equality and in terms of making sure that care is not depleted in a way that harms us all in the longer term.[6] Second, the same forces that create prosperity (such as technology and trade) also cause disruption for human life, the most obvious of which is the loss of jobs in declining sectors of the economy. A good state is one that can help make people resilient to this continued change and empowers them not only to make the most of new opportunities but to actively create them. If it does not, the process of economic advance can in fact exacerbate inequality and lead to a waste of human talent. Third, and as we saw in chapter 6, the state also has a more fundamental role to play when it comes to markets. Markets only work well, both to achieve prosperity and an equitable and sustainable outcome, if they are built on the right foundations: both formal ones (legal and political) and informal ones (family and society). Markets do not have an independent life of their own and can be redesigned to make them better deliver. Fourth, markets help to deliver prosperity in the long term but economic instability is to some extent inevitable along the upward path (see chapter 9). The state may have a role to play in helping alleviate such instability. Finally, prosperity is not, as we saw in chapter 3, guaranteed to lessen gender inequalities, which can feed back to hurt the economy going ahead. Economic growth in the short term cannot be assumed to deliver equitable or sustainable outcomes.[7]

However, although we can in theory see the need for state interventions, we also know that in practice a bad state can do more harm than good. States can themselves do great damage to the environment, take advantage of women's reproductive efforts (and limit their reproductive choices) and add to, rather than alleviate, instability.[8] Ask any New Yorker about William M. Tweed, one of the most corrupt politicians the city has ever known, and you'd soon understand why Americans are in general much more sceptical of big government than are Europeans. It's difficult to deny the fact that big government can be bad for the economy, either directly by harming efficiency and productivity, as seen in the former communist bloc, or indirectly, as discussed in chapter 6, through the social conformity and lack of diversity that arises when markets are not available to support exchanges between people who have different social beliefs.

Size, in other words, isn't all that matters. The same-sized states can have very different effects: size can harm or it can help, depending on how 'capable' a state is. Where, for example, tax revenues are used to fund infrastructure that connects people or that supports their ability to engage in the market, it can have a beneficial effect. Where the same funds are instead used to build fancy palaces, suppress opponents or wage unnecessary wars, the outcome is likely to be altogether different. In a recent study of China, Yi Lu et al. found that the number of communist party officials in a region had a negative effect on economic activity before the introduction of market reforms in 1978, but it had a positive correlation with numerous measures of economic performance thereafter, including growth in agricultural output, mortality rates, educational outcomes and local infrastructure development. In their own words, 'state capacity could indeed accelerate development, but the effect is substantial and unambiguous only when the state seeks to complement the market instead of substituting it.'[9]

So whether a state is good or bad depends not simply on its size but also on its capabilities. Recently, economists have introduced the concept of state capability. They define state capability as the capacity to collect taxes to fund public goods like defence and infrastructure and to enforce law and order across the nation's territory, in other words, in fiscal and legal terms. In addition to capability, they also point to the importance of constraints on the state. They argue that if it is to support the market, the state needs to support property rights, and that is more likely when the state is constrained to act in the will of the people through a system of political representation like democracy. Throughout history, we have seen time and time again the way that unelected monarchs have trampled on people's property, extracting wealth from minority groups – or from those unable to vote. Political representation that acts as a constraint on the ability of a state to act in its own self-interest is, therefore, thought to be important.[10]

The way I think about state capability is, however, quite different to the way other economists tend to define it. It is instead about judgement: the ability of the state to judge which interventions are best for the economy, including the types of laws, regulations and institutions that are required to ensure that the market delivers. Rather than being substitutes, the market and the state can, in the right circumstances, be complementary. However, the state can also over-reach itself, suffocating prosperity. A capable state is one that can work out the difference. That is, unfortunately, not easy to get right – which, of course, likely explains why capable states are quite rare. Having fiscal and legal capability is one thing, but the state also needs to be able to judge when and how best to use that fiscal and legal capability. Unfortunately, there is no straightforward recipe for when the state should or should not intervene. Ideology – capitalist or communist – isn't the best guide. Laissez-faire provides a simple hands-off approach but, in the words of John Ramsay McCulloch: 'The principle of laissez-faire may be safely trusted to in some things but in many more it is wholly inapplicable; and to appeal to it on all occasions savors more of the policy of a parrot than of a statesman or a philosopher.'[11]

On the other hand, if a state is too keen to intervene without question – if it is too ready to assume that markets fail and that intervention is always the answer – it is likely to be captured by vested interest groups. Any intervention is, on the face of it, easy to market to a politician. Being a capable state therefore involves great judgement. In each and every case, the state needs to be able to judge whether it can improve upon market outcomes or whether by intervening it will make things worse. The relevant question should not be whether markets are failing but whether the state has the ability and knowledge required to improve upon the market outcome.[12] Here there are no hard and fast rules. No wonder there are so few relatively capable states.

State capability should not, of course, be divorced from gender equality, something which, as we've already seen, is vital for building equitable and sustainable growth. Whilst the situation facing women in the West was historically somewhat more favourable than elsewhere, the state hasn't always helped.[13] As Alice Kessler-Harris has argued, the 'gendered imagination' – the association of women with domesticity and men with paid work – led to a welfare system, tax code and the sanctioning of workplace practices (such as marriage bars and discrimination) that penalized those in the United States who did not fill their prescribed socially dictated roles.[14] The twentieth-century welfare state operated on the assumption that women were dependents, supported by their husbands, giving them less favourable tax and pension treatment and presuming that they were available to pick children up from school halfway through the afternoon, acting as a constraint on labour market involvement. The trade union movement with its fight for 'family wages' also, like the state, served to crystallize the male breadwinner model.[15] Population and immigration policies have also had consequences for women. No wonder, as Pedersen argues:

> Welfare policies meet social needs but they also construct social norms and inflict social punishment: they can foster as well as ameliorate distinctions or inequalities. Welfare states provide entitlements: but to whom, and in what form, and under what conditions? When it comes to welfare states, the devil is always in the detail ... Welfare states reflect social patterns but they also reify them, nowhere more than in the assumptions they make about gender relations and family life.[16]

More recently, feminist economists have pointed to the way in which structural reform packages in developing countries and the austerity policies that followed 2008 excluded any consideration of the very gendered effects, which took a particular toll on women.[17]

A state cannot be deemed 'capable' if it is blind to and perpetuates gender inequalities, which explains why feminist economists now push for 'gender budgeting': a consideration of the gendered consequences of each new state intervention. Now we might suppose that once a state opens its eyes to gender equality, it is relatively straightforward for it to judge what it needs to do. But, as Mala Htun and S. Laurel Weldon have shown by looking across a whole range of different countries, state interventions on the gender equality front are often highly inconsistent. Countries that are ahead in addressing violence against women (VAW) can also be quite backward in terms of labour market policies (like paid parental leave), family law (such as divorce and inheritance) and reproductive freedom (such as birth control and abortion). And vice versa. That is even the case for Scandinavian countries, the supposed pinnacle of success. To quote, 'states can be both progressive and regressive ... They can extend greater rights and freedoms to women and men with one hand while taking them away with the other.'[18] Understanding why this is the case can help us to see why some states are more capable than others in gender terms.

Htun and Weldon argue that gender equality interventions can be categorized on two grounds: on whether they are doctrinal or not (i.e. whether they touch on religious doctrine, as family law and abortion do), and on whether they are 'inflected by class differences' (i.e. where they fit on the right–left political scale).[19] This categorization, which allows us to divide gender equality interventions into four groups, explains why states often make progress in some ways but not in others.[20] The attachment (or dependence) of the state to religious institutions and its political inclinations (right versus left) will affect what states are willing and able to do in gender equality terms.

In sum, states can be either bad or good for prosperity: it all depends on how capable they are, where that capability should be defined to include gender. In the marketplace, competition helps to root out businesses that are incapable, thereby creating pressure for capabilities to be built; democracy and interstate competition could be seen as providing a similar device when it comes to states. Unfortunately, however, and as Stiglitz argues, democracy is not enough to ensure that the state is capable – it also needs to be accompanied by, for example, an active civic society and a free press.[21] When it comes to gender equality, evidence similarly suggests that democracy is not enough.[22] Given that capability is difficult to build, and that democracy is not necessarily enough to push us in the right direction, we can start to understand why economies in which the state and the market work successfully together are in fact a rarity.

There is a second reason why we might find a relationship between the state and prosperity in today's rich countries: one of reverse causation. Increasing prosperity may lead to an expansion in the size and capability of the state. That's certainly how Avner Offer explains the escalating size of the state throughout the course of the twentieth century. As Offer argues, once we are rich enough to meet our everyday needs – food, shelter and clothing – we start thinking about investing in our long-term welfare, such as through health care, education and pensions.[23] The only stumbling block is myopia. Because we are inherently short-termist, we do not always save enough for the future. In addition, we can be overly optimistic about what that future holds, meaning that we put too little aside. In Offer's own words, the state and the tax system provide 'a commitment device which helps individuals overcome myopic preferences'. We actively vote to have our choices restricted in the sense of committing ourselves to the taxes that are required to cover the costs of our longer-term selves in an effort to overcome our short-termism. In other words, as the economy becomes more prosperous, we place more demands on the state – and are of course better able to fund those demands. Unfortunately, however, when it comes to state capability as opposed to the size of the state, there is no guarantee that increasing prosperity will make the state more capable in gender terms. As we saw in chapter 3, there are times when increasing prosperity has come hand in hand with government regulations that have hurt as opposed to helped, particularly in regard to gender equality.

There is a third and final possible explanation for the correlation between the state and prosperity: that there is a common underlying factor that has produced both prosperity *and* relatively capable states in today's richer economies, one that may be missing in parts of the world that remain both poor and lacking in state capability. In other words, rather than thinking solely about how prosperity and the state affect one another, we should also think about outside factors that may have led today's rich countries to build economies in which we find states and markets working in a way that delivers a whole that is more than the sum of its parts.

In what follows, we therefore delve into the history of today's most capable states, looking at how they developed in a way that supported as opposed to hindered economic expansion. As we will see, it is a story that – like so many others – has left women out in the cold. By bringing women into the story, we will identify an often overlooked factor: women's freedom. We have already noted the need to bring gender to bear on how economists define and judge state capabilities; we still need to think more about how gender equality affects the chances of building a capable state in the first place.

## The Invention of the Modern State

A (relatively) capable state is something we all too often take for granted in modern-day western countries. However, as Noel Johnson and Mark Koyama astutely note:

> [f]or many premodern polities, even the term state is an anachronism: there was no state in much of Europe prior to the late middle ages ... the word 'state' only came to acquire its modern meaning in English at the end of the sixteenth century. ... This was not merely a semantic change; when 'the word "state", l'état, stato' or Der Staat came into usage in the early modern period it was 'a word for a new political experience'.[24]

Recently, economists have begun to consider how the West managed to successfully develop both capable states in fiscal and legal terms, and states in which the ruler was kept in check, such as by a constitution and democratic vote. As Tim Besley and Torsten Persson have pointed out, '[e]conomists generally assume that the state has sufficient institutional capacity to support markets and levy taxes, assumptions which cannot be taken for granted in many states, neither historically nor in today's developing world.'[25] The black box that is the state is finally being opened up, and we are at last moving beyond thinking about the state merely in terms of its size.

According to some, states are an inevitability. In *The Social Order of the Underworld*, David Skarbek uses prisons as a natural experiment to observe how states arise.[26] He explores how prisoners develop their own institutions, including their own hierarchies and rules, as a means to resolve common problems – in their particular case, the supply of drugs. Gangs provide both governance and protection, acting like their own mini-states. In prisons, the population is immobile; no one can (in theory) escape. That provides a parallel with the work of James C. Scott, who argues that the state first came into existence when human beings made the shift from hunter-gatherers to farming the land.[27] Once we settled down in fixed locations, we became sitting ducks. As Walter Scheidel explains:

> Confined to territories of arable land, early farmers submitted to a new political order that protected them in much the same way as the mob protects its unwilling clients. The early state was born, erecting ambitious structures of command and control in support of steep hierarchies, vast inequality and endless war. Scott rightly stresses the critical role of domesticated grains – wheat, barley, millet, maize and rice – in sustaining political power: grown above ground, ripening on a predictable schedule and eminently storable, grain invited assessment and appropriation by the taxman. Alongside compulsory labour services, grain taxes formed the sinews of the early state ... Any visitor to Giza, Angkor or Machu Picchu who is left with a sense of admiration rather than dread and compassion fundamentally misunderstands the nature of early states and the steely cages they erected for humanity.[28]

The history of modern as opposed to ancient states begins with the fall of the Roman Empire, a time at which Europe fragmented. Power rested in the hands of local lords, who built castles to defend themselves from incursions from neighbouring lords. The population was enserfed. According to some accounts, freedoms – such as the freedom to move – were given up willingly in return for the safety and security offered by the local lord and his castle. More cynically, it was the natural result of the rich exercising their power over the local population, which was particularly beneficial at a time when population was shrinking due to the instability and insecurities which followed the collapse of Roman rule. By limiting the freedoms of (increasingly scarce) peasants, lords were able to hold down the price they effectively paid for them to work their lands, enabling the extraction of a surplus to fund their lavish lifestyles.

In this post-Roman feudal world, local power was strong. This meant that an overarching state that operated over a larger geographical area could only develop and hold onto power if it negotiated with local lords, leading to the development of some of Europe's earliest parliaments.[29] Although not everyone had a vote, local areas were at least given representation within the umbrella of an emergent state.

As population grew, the balance began to tip in favour of free as opposed to enslaved labour. With a greater supply of people, the market wage fell, making it cheaper for lords to employ free labour through the market. Serfdom went into decline. However, when the Black Death hit in 1348, it devastated the population, wiping out between a quarter and a half of Europeans. The result was a fundamental change in the balance of power between lords and peasants. The power of landowners was diminished as land fell in value, having become relatively more plentiful compared with the number of people whose mouths needed to be fed. In some parts of Europe, serfdom witnessed a revival as a result, and in other areas peasants successfully took advantage of their increased scarcity to push for greater freedoms.[30] Where that happened, such as in England, the diminished power of local lords paved the way for the centralization of the state. The local forces that had in the past resisted centralization were now too weak to prevent it.[31]

Regions were more likely to join together to form states where not only local resistance fell, but also where there were clear benefits to working as one. Economists argue that it can be in our mutual interest to contribute to a common pot of resources – what we may think of as a nascent state – as a result of the need for human societies to provide public goods to support their existence.[32] According to historians, war was, in this sense, the great driver of today's states.[33] War required adjoining regions to cooperate in an effort to defend themselves, which in turn required the creation of a common pot to which different localities would contribute. The threat of Viking invasions is often seen as one of the key reasons for the early formation of a centralized English state. In the case of the Netherlands, the hostile geographical environment, which required cooperation to instigate systems of irrigation and land reclamation, also pushed in the direction of state creation.[34] By contrast, local regions in present-day Italy and Germany were both too strong and too antagonistic to enable the early development of a broader state.

For states to operate, they needed to tax. The expansion in the state's fiscal powers began in England in the seventeenth century.[35] At that point, states mostly taxed to wage war with one another. How the state funded defence and other such activities was a big question. Since historically society had consisted of rich landowners and serfs, the key things that the state could tax were land and imported luxuries. As markets developed – as more people moved beyond self-sufficiency and barter and as serfs gained their freedom – more things were bought and sold. As markets expanded and the economy grew, not only were there more goods in circulation, all of which could be taxed, but a new class emerged: one of merchants. This new commercially oriented class managed to get a seat at the top table, something which economic historians have argued is central to understanding how the West went on to become the richest part of the world. According to Jared Rubin, and in contrast with Europe, 'Middle Eastern leaders were strong enough, due to the legitimizing capacity of Islam, to exclude them.'[36]

As the economy advanced, not only did the new commercial interests push in the direction of representative government but a new political philosophy began to emerge. The seventeenth century is commonly seen as the period in which the 'divine rights of kings' came to be challenged. From Locke onwards, philosophers began to question the idea of fixed social positions, seeing us all as free agents with rights that should be supported by the law of the land.[37] Having grown in strength in the previous centuries, and in some cases stamping on the parliaments that had emerged in medieval times, states seemed to be overstepping the mark. The notion of individual freedom was born.

Not only were merchants and intellectuals beginning to question the 'natural' authority of kings but the Reformation began to wreak havoc both with their religious claims and with their fiscal ones. Rubin notes that in countries that emerged from the Reformation as Protestant, religion proved to be even less of a legitimizing tool than in those that remained Catholic. Hence, in Protestant England and in the Dutch Republic, the state turned to ever more commercial (as opposed to religious) interests in order to legitimize its rule.[38] This also had implications for gender, which further aided the emergence of state capabilities. As we saw earlier, the extent to which religion feeds into the state affects the state's longer-term ability to pursue, for example, changes in family law and the extent to which it gives women freedom over their bodies (such as by legalizing abortion and supporting women's access to birth control). These in turn affect the extent to which growth will be equitable and sustainable.

Whether Catholic or Protestant, religious wars in seventeenth-century Europe meant not only the deaths of millions of Europeans but also greater pressure on taxes. And no one likes tax, particularly when it hasn't been voted for. Rebellion was in the air: not only in England in the seventeenth century but also in France in the eighteenth century. Influential in the associated French Revolution were a group of economists known as the physiocrats. They argued that order did not require the imposition of authority from above but could instead be achieved by leaving free individuals to engage with one another through the market. Where commercial interests had a seat at the top table, such as in Britain, the result was Adam Smith's laissez-faire approach, one of small government where individuals were no longer under the thumb of a heavy-handed state or its partner in crime: religious authorities.

For a while, laissez-faire seemed to pay off. The country of Smith's birth was the first to industrialize. People were free to start new businesses and develop new technologies, leading to another new class: one of industrialists, many of whom came from relatively humble roots. This new class, along with merchants, rivalled the aristocracy, lords whose power dated back to feudal times. However, whereas industrialization brought significant benefits, it also brought squalor, overcrowding and unsanitary conditions. People suffered and, as a result of the associated health problems and pollution, so too did the economy. By the latter half of the nineteenth century, the state therefore began to do more than fund law and defence; it stepped in to help provide sanitation, clean water and public health programmes. The state was building its capabilities – fast.

Revolution, both economic and political, was followed by further democratization. Unlike in the past, this democratization allowed the state to hold on to its authority at a time when it was expanding. As the vote spread to the working classes, the state began to spend even more on utilities, education, health and the welfare state, so much so that across the course of the twentieth century, the size of the state expanded rapidly. So too did tax. The share of taxation in national income rose from well below 10% of GDP in 1910 to, in the present day, 28% of national income in the United States, 35% in the United Kingdom and more than 45% in France and Sweden. We find the coincidence of bigger states and more prosperous economies.

Although this might seem like a natural end point, a cursory look across all today's rich countries suggests that if we include gender in our definition of state capability, then there is room for further progress. States that may appear capable in economists' standard definition of the term are not necessarily capable once we bring gender to bear, as we have seen in this chapter. By rethinking how we judge states, we can start to see how opportunities to keep on building a more successful relationship between the market and the state still remain for the taking. That involves acknowledging a third sphere: alongside the market and the state, there is a whole other realm in which the vital work of care takes place. Making the most of this third sphere may require more to be done than at present by the state, but in a way that supports markets and creates more equitable and sustainable growth. It is a win–win.

## Three Ways Women Helped to Build Today's Most Capable States

In our story of how today's modern states emerged, women have only received a passing mention. In fact, they are entirely absent from economists' accounts of how state capability emerged in today's rich countries. The importance of society is, however, something that has come to be acknowledged, although a big debate rages. Some see the state and society as interchangeable,[39] whilst others argue that they are complementary, pointing to the way in which a well-functioning and cohesive society makes for a more capable state. Johnson and Koyama pinpoint culture and civil society as two deep determinants of effective states.[40] They point to a long line of thinkers who argue that 'social capital' is critical to the successful establishment of liberal democracy. Needless to say, the relationship goes two ways: political institutions that are corrupt foster a wider culture of mistrust and undermine social cooperation.[41] The degree of internal cohesion amongst the population also affects how long lasting the state will be.[42] It is, therefore, of little surprise that states have gone to great lengths to engineer a national identity. Knitting people together – creating a common sense of belonging, whether through national songs and festivals or by demonizing 'the other' in foreign countries – helps the state to hold onto its tax-raising powers and its authority. The fact that society matters helps to explain why attempts to transplant political institutions – such as democracy – have not always generated successful outcomes.

However, there is another underlying factor that can lead to both capable states and economic prosperity: women's freedom. Gender equality (or a lack of it) has had a powerful effect on the way that modern states have developed and helps explain why western states have tended to be less deleterious – more capable – than those elsewhere. Here we will focus on three particular channels: the way in which more gender-equal family systems help to foster democracy; the way in which women's freedom has led to a historical shift in the provision of care from the home to the state; and the way in which votes for women changed the priorities of the state.

## 1  Women and democracy

One of the great ironies of history is that the first states to develop were not those in the now rich economies but those in the parts of the world that are today relatively poor. That includes the part of the world often seen as the cradle of civilization, the Middle East. Being an early developer in state terms was, however, no guarantee of positive outcomes for women. It is precisely where states first developed in human history that we also find some of the highest levels of gender inequality today.[43] By contrast, in regions in which hunter-gatherer ways of life persisted for longer, meaning that there was a longer history of gender equality, modern states formed somewhat later and in a way that proved to be less inimical to gender equality and better for long-run growth. That includes in Europe.

The relationship between the state and gender equality has been examined by Emmanuel Todd, following in the footsteps of J. S. Mill, the nineteenth-century political economist, and Susan Okin, the feminist political theorist.[44] Todd notes that the state and the family – the public and the private spheres – are fundamentally linked. Political institutions are influenced by family institutions in a way that has long been ignored by economists. Power and voice within the household act as a model for wider institutions. Democratic government requires democratic family structures, structures that nurture democratic citizens from a young age. As Jan Kok notes, '[p]eople are socialized within families; it is here they learn the basic rules of interaction, negotiation, dominance and submission.'[45]

Not only does women's freedom push in the direction of democracy, but democracy also fed back to women. As political scientist Valerie Bryson writes of the seventeenth century, when the divine rights of kings was being questioned:

> Conservative defenders of absolute monarchical power argued that the authority of the king over his people was sanctioned by God and nature in exactly the same way as that of a father over his family; this meant that 'patriarchy' (the rule of the father) in the home was used as justification for a parallel power in the state. Opponents of such state

power, who argued that authority was not divinely ordained but must rest on reason and consent, were therefore forced to re-examine arbitrary power within the family as well: logically, it seemed, patriarchy in state and home must stand or fall together.[46]

As we saw in chapter 2, the way families operate differs dramatically across the world, with implications for female agency and, as a result, political institutions and markets. The more egalitarian – nuclear – family forms in Europe helped to not only underpin democratic states but also market activity and the types of institutions needed to support market exchange. Avner Greif argues that the weaker kinship ties in Europe – a result of more nuclear as opposed to traditional family structures – led people to engage with those outside the family.[47] That meant building trust outside the 'kinship' group, which aided the development of markets and trade – and the types of formal institutions needed to support them – in the longer run. By contrast, in the Middle East, kinship ties were stronger, including as a result of practices such as consanguineous marriage. Greif argues that this produced a more collectivist culture, where families had strong ties with each other and didn't need to build as many with the outside world as a result. These strong family ties helped the economy in the early days of trade but, as market opportunities expanded, they became more of a hindrance.[48] In this sense, we see how women's freedom – itself aided by market opportunities – helped to support the commercialization of the economy, at the same time fostering a democratic state and associated institutions that supported as opposed to hindered market activity. Women's freedom is key to enabling both prosperity and a supportive state.

## 2 The emergence of the welfare state

Women's freedom is also relevant to the emergence of a now common role for government in the form of the welfare state. However, women's freedom helped to ensure that the welfare state developed in a way that worked with rather than against markets. Recent research has enabled us to compare welfare spending in different parts of Europe over the last six hundred years. The results suggest that 'from a European perspective the degree to which the English state succeeded in enforcing a nation-wide tax-based system of poor relief was exceptional.'[49] In the words of Johnson and Koyama: 'The revenues generated by the increased fiscal capacity of European states after 1500 was predominantly spent on warfare rather than on other public goods ... One of the few exceptions to the absence of government provided insurance or public goods was the English Poor Law.'[50] The question is: why? Why did England manage to develop a welfare state so early on – and why didn't it cost the economy?

The British welfare state dates back to Tudor times. At this time, local parishes used land taxes to help support the elderly and 'infirm', as well as chasing fathers who had abandoned their children. Although it was far from perfect, this Old Poor Law system helped to fill the hole left by a retreating family-based welfare system as economic opportunities for women outside of the home began to spread, thereby supporting the market.[51] Internationally, England was something of a backwater at this time, compared with the more famous Italian city states, but internally it was becoming highly commercial.[52] England was ahead of its time in developing internal markets centuries before many other European countries, in part a result of geography that was favourable to trade and of the emergence of a relatively centralized state which meant that there were limited internal barriers to trade. The welfare state emerged to pick up the slack as society began to change, moving away from traditional to more nuclear family structures, and from feudal structures to the market. It was by no means a perfect relationship (or a perfect system of welfare), as Adrienne Roberts makes clear,[53] but the state and the market were already starting to dance with one another very early on, at least more so than in other parts of the world. It is, of course, by building on this history – on the way in which state interventions that take on board caring activity can support as opposed to 'crowd out' the market – that we can make further progress in the modern day.

## 3  Votes for women and state priorities

The expansion of the state in the twentieth century has come hand in hand with the expansion of women's political rights. That includes the right to vote. Some have argued that the correlation is far from causal, that women (at least historically) tended to favour conservative values as opposed to big government.[54] Others suggest that the correlation was no mere coincidence: that the state was women's tool for ensuring their interests were met.[55]

As the vote spread to women in the late nineteenth and early twentieth centuries, the story goes that politicians began to appeal to their interests and that these interests were, on average at least, very much 'left' of their fellow men. Whilst state expansion is more commonly attributed to the rising power of the working classes, the rising power of women was, it is argued, just as important. Through the state, women could find insurance against the risk of divorce – a welfare system that would not leave them destitute – and employment in an expanding public sector. John Lott and Lawrence Kenny estimated that women's suffrage led to a 10 per cent rise in tax collection.[56]

Women were also often the very people living a life on the periphery of 'the market', in precisely the conditions where negative as opposed to positive effects could be felt. They were more likely to be in a vulnerable position, one which allowed the market to prey on their weakness, leading to exploitation and abuse. Not only were women acutely aware of the dark side of the market, they also saw the way in which markets failed to fully address problems such as insanitary conditions and a lack of clean water. As those historically responsible for the domestic chores, the everyday tribulations this presented would have been excruciating. Dealing with the day-to-day consequences of environmental degradation, together with time spent fetching clean water, remain big issues for the world's poorest women. For all of these reasons, one could easily equate votes for women with the vote for a more sizeable state.

However, as we saw in the previous chapter, markets can also provide advantages to women, offering a way out of repressive families and heavily gendered social expectations. A bigger state is not always better for women, which may explain why a debate still rages about whether the political emancipation of women really did lead to a bigger state. This does not, however, mean that the women's vote didn't affect the composition of state expenditure: what states chose to do with their tax revenues.[57] Evidence from developing countries shows that, where women have greater influence over household spending, a higher proportion of family income is spent on necessities, education and health care.[58] Furthermore, since they suffer relatively more from the effects of environmental damage, and of bigger families, their political representation has been shown to lead governments to take family and the environment more seriously.[59] Super-sizing this to the level of state spending, it seems likely that the spread of the vote to women would, at the very least, have caused the state to rethink its priorities.

## Conclusion

Markets and the state have long been seen as adversaries. However, the most successful economies are those in which the state and the market work in unison, allowing us to deal with the downsides of markets without throwing away the baby with the bathwater. How a country like Britain was able to develop a (relatively albeit not perfectly) capable state, one that generally worked in favour of prosperity creation, is one of the great questions which face economists today. Historians traditionally pinpoint Britain's peculiar geography and its history of having to defend itself, including against those pesky Vikings, but that is far from enough. As we have seen, just as important was the way individuals engaged on the ground, and that includes within the family. Agency and voice within the family fed through to politics and to wider commercialization.

To understand how a little island off the edge of Europe managed to build a sizeable and capable state, democratic institutions and a whirl of commercial activity, we have to begin in the home. It is also, therefore, by looking within the home that we will find the source of poverty and dysfunctional states within many poorer countries today, together with what more can be done in the West to ensure markets and the state continue to bring out the best in each other. Personal is indeed political.

# Part IV

## Humanity

# Introduction

Throughout this book, I have tried to emphasize not only how crucial women's freedom is for delivering prosperity but equitable and sustainable prosperity. However, as we will see in the remaining chapters, economics is blind to women's freedom and to the associated policy implications. Gender bias is built into economics through its very choice of assumptions and approach. To see why, we need to delve into the history of economic thought; to see how economics first came to conceive of the individual, and what that meant for the direction of economic thinking from the late nineteenth century through to the present.

Despite being so commonly associated with money, economics is first and foremost about people. What's going on in the economy is the outcome of our most personal decisions: whether to go to university; whether to start a business; whether to have children; whether to take time out to look after our children; whether to rent or buy; and whether to stick to that new year's resolution to eat healthily, exercise and save more. Summed up across the population, these and numerous other decisions affect how much our economy is capable of producing, what kinds of products it produces and its ability to invest and grow. When modelling the economy, economists therefore begin by thinking about how individuals make decisions.

Now, of course, the way people behave is something that falls into the realm of neuroscientists. However, you don't have to be a scientist (or – one of my favourite television characters – *Frasier*) to ponder why we do what we do. From the moment we are born, we interact with those around us and, in an effort to prevent ourselves from being exploited, have to try to second-guess other people: if we are too friendly and trusting, we might be taken advantage of, but, if we are too cold and cruel, our reputation risks being sullied in the wider social group. Hence, in some sense, we all have to become amateur psychologists from a young age simply to successfully socially engage with others.

As a teenager, I had far too much time to ponder human behaviour. I was never part of the 'in-crowd' – one of the Pink Ladies or T-Birds of the kind I saw in the film *Grease*. You know the kind I'm referring to – the kind who rebelled by smoking behind the bike sheds, by talking back to teachers, by breaking the school uniform code, and who had a string of older boyfriends with cars and earnings to take them out (albeit, when it came to the cars, not very new ones, and when it came to the cash, sums that only really seemed impressive relative to pocket money).

The result of being an outsider, of not being involved in the everyday action, is that you're able to stand on the periphery, pondering why people do what they do. I wondered why some of my peers paid so little attention to their school work when it was clearly going to affect the rest of their lives. We were, after all, growing up in Oldham, where deindustrialization meant that job opportunities in the traditional industry were shrinking and education seemed to be more important than ever. I also wondered why people became bullies – why they would sometimes snatch the book I was reading out of my hands and tease me before losing interest and turning on someone else. Did they actually enjoy tormenting people or was it a desperate attempt to build a reputation for being tough and cool (in which case it might have left them with sleepless nights of regret)?

One particular event is fixed in my mind. It was a Whit Friday evening back in the 1990s on the edge of the moors to the east of Manchester in a bleak and hilly group of villages known as Saddleworth, where the Moors murders still cast a shadow. I was heading back home with friends after listening to the last of the brass bands playing in the local band contest. As my friends and I started to leave the crowds, we were followed by a rather tough-looking group of girls not from 'our parts'. They threatened to beat us up unless we emptied our pockets. We knew they were serious, and so we reluctantly did as they said. I tipped out my pockets and handed over what was not much more than a few measly coins. 'Is that it?' the ringleader said. What she did next was a real surprise. She handed back the coins. Relieved but puzzled, I wondered if she had had a sudden burst of solidarity, or if she instead reasoned that the pickings were too small to risk being the centre of a police report. And, of course, whether she managed to maintain her tough reputation within the gang.

I might have given the impression that, in my youth, I was an island of good sense. However, looking back on some of my own decisions I am left puzzled. I was eleven when, in the course of a deep economic recession, my father's business failed and, by the time I was fourteen, my parents had separated (perhaps the only advantage of which was, rather strangely, it seemed to buy me 'street cred'.). My teenage years were filled not only with emotional turmoil but with poverty. Most of what my mother earned paid the rent but little else. My grandparents – only on a state pension themselves – would help to top things up. The minimum wage and tax credits were introduced some time later, so there was relatively little help from the state then. However, some assistance did come in the form of free school meals. The problem was that the queue at the school to collect your free dinner tickets was so public that it might as well have had a sign over it reading 'the needy poor'. And, to join the queue, sometimes you had to be excused from class. Of course, the rest of the class knew precisely where you were going. I preferred to go hungry rather than have to join that queue and so begged my mum not to claim. If friends commented on why I wasn't buying lunch, I would just make up an excuse: I was often, it seems, dieting. I soon worked out ways of economizing, for example, buying a pack of cheap scones from the local co-op supermarket and making it last all week for lunches. When you're hungry, you find solutions.

But why was I so ashamed of being poor that I let it stand in the way of doing what would have obviously been best for my health? It's likely cost me in the longer term, including my height of just under 5 ft. The answer is straightforward: I put some value on what other people thought of me. I didn't want to look poor. Life's not just about money, it's also about dignity. Poverty is tied up with all kinds of emotions. That's easy to ignore.

What all of these experiences taught me was that human beings are pretty complex and, more than anything else, their decisions are often filled with tensions: tensions between wanting to be friendly but at the same time having to maintain a reputation for being tough so that they're not taken advantage of; tensions between doing what's best here and now and doing what's best for the longer term; tensions between doing what they themselves want but also feeling that they need to live up to what other people expect of them; and tensions between meeting their physical and their emotional needs – where the latter includes the very respect and human dignity for which we all aim.

However, as we will see in what follows, the way economists think about individuals is much simpler. We are assumed to act as little more than robots; as rational, self-interested calculators. In the next chapter, we will consider how and why these economic assumptions emerged. In chapter 9, we will see how they have been challenged by behavioural economics. In the final chapter, I will suggest that if economics is to open its eyes to gender, it needs to go further: it needs to adopt a behavioral-cum-feminist approach to human life. As we will see in the process, whilst it has become common to criticize economic thinking, these criticisms have both gone too far – and not far enough. New ground now needs to be broken if economics is to take us in the direction of equitable and sustainable prosperity. Feminist economics can point us in the right direction.

# 8

# Me, Myself and I: A History of the Individual

To understand the economy, we need to understand people. In this chapter, I want to look at the way economists have thought about the individual throughout the ages, culminating in the individualistic 'rational self-interested economic agent' paradigm that still exists today. We will see that it has now become popular to critique this model of human behaviour, but there was an underlying logic to economics moving in this direction, adopting what might appear to be a very simplistic and unwholesome model. However, whilst the direction was understandable in the context of the time, it also created a problem, one that will become abundantly clear in the remaining chapters: it helped to crystallize the increasingly gendered division of the economy that emerged in the nineteenth century, one that cast men as economic actors and women as unproductive dependents.

## At the Beginning

As a recent history of economic thought has noted, '[e]conomics is a relatively young academic discipline ... Economic thinking, on the other hand, has a much longer tradition ... As long as humans have lived on earth, they have resolved economic questions.'[1] Markets and money can be found throughout the writings of Greek philosophers, the Bible and in the work of medieval scholars. They were, however, explored in relation to questions of ethics and justice; acquiring riches was certainly not seen as a suitable end goal for individual existence. It was, we were told, by keeping selfish monetary desires in check that a society would be able to lift itself in spiritual and moral terms. That would, at least according to the Bible, ensure that the fruits of God's earth would be sufficient to provide for the fruits of the loins. Poverty was not attributed to a lack of hard work or talent, or even to the class system, but to a lack of faith and of basic morality. Making money, such as through business and merchant activity, was frowned upon, and charity was the means by which merchants and bankers would pay for their sins.

Rather than being seen as the sum of free individuals who had their own rights, society was compared with the human body. Each social group was thought to have its own function to perform, with the aim of keeping the whole being living and breathing.[2] The function of peasants was to labour to make sure that everyone was fed. The function of the elite was to provide justice and to ensure that the nation was protected from foreign incursions. The function of the clergy was to take care of spiritual and moral well-being. Mobility between groups was frowned upon; only by individuals performing their allotted functions could the whole body of society be kept alive. Responsibility to wider society was key, not the rights of the individual. Selfish desires were kept in check by the Church – under threat of eternal damnation. The assumption was that individuals are inherently sinful, driven by passions such as greed, envy and lust which had to be contained by religious and moral teaching.

The Church had provided a structure within which societies functioned from the fall of the Roman Empire. However, by the sixteenth century, the modern-day nation-states began to form. In this new age of state building, a nation's ultimate survival depended not only on its moral fibre but on its ability to defend itself. That required financial means. If a nation was to acquire the riches it needed to achieve its defensive goal, the presumption was that it had to operate like a merchant. The state took control of trade in an effort to maximize the 'balance of trade': to sell more on international markets than the country needed to import. It was by maximizing this surplus that the state believed it could strengthen its position on the world stage. Rather than pinning their own nation's survival on the products of other countries, policy makers aimed to build independent domestic economic capacity.

Trade policy and industrial policy became all the rage as, unfortunately, did imperialism. In an effort to maximize their 'specie', governments used a mix of import taxes to punish and discourage imports (except those that were vital to production), and subsidies to encourage exports. They sought access to foreign lands, trying to monopolize their markets and access their produce. Colonies were acquired and vast trading companies were created alongside; the East India Company in the case of England and VOC in the case of Holland. The desires of individual consumers and of individual entrepreneurs came second to the merchant state. Merchant activity was now acceptable, so long as it was aligned with the mercantile interests of the state. Conspicuous consumption of luxuries was discouraged, portrayed as an economic evil that used up scarce foreign exchange. In other words, the moral case against greed was now also supported by economic logic. This was a time when the state could be self-interested but not the individual.

This hypocrisy could not continue. Either the state had to become 'moral' or a case had to be made for the self-interest which the state enjoyed being rolled out to everyone else. Before long, a radically new way of thinking about society and individuals began to emerge, one that led a number of European states along the latter path.

The Enlightenment, which gathered steam in the eighteenth century, demonstrated the power of human thought to generate an ever-improving understanding of the world around us. Reason came to trump 'passions'. With the capacity for reason came the idea that individuals are born equal and should be free to pursue their own individual goals. Rather than expecting citizens to blindly obey, reason enabled individuals to engage in a social contract with one another, with the state acting as intermediary. Whilst Hobbes argued that this could lead us to voluntarily accept a Leviathan as a means to avoid a violent state of nature, Locke disagreed. The first duty of the state, he argued, should be to uphold the rights of individuals. Rather than limiting their freedoms, the state should be protecting them. Medieval writers had emphasized individual responsibilities towards wider society; Locke pointed to individual rights.

This notion of individual rights and freedoms could not have been more radical. The fear had always been that leaving people to their own devices would wreak havoc. How could the needs of society – our need to be fed, clothed and sheltered – be met simply by leaving everyone to 'do their own thing'? Chaos would surely be the outcome of a society in which neither the Church nor the state imposed order, through either physical or spiritual threats. When Mandeville's *Fable of the Bees* attacked puritan values in 1714, questioning the commonly held notion that it was Christian morality that 'held society together' and suggesting that private vices can in fact be to public benefit, it resulted in an outcry.[3]

Undeterred, David Hume and Adam Smith took up the mantle. Hume argued that without the desire to acquire ever greater riches, we would be idle.[4] Smith pondered how economies developed from a simple state of nature in which we spent our days hunting and gathering to one in which we were surrounded by factories, offices, new technologies and an ever expanding stream of goods and services to tickle our fancy. Drawing inspiration not only from Mandeville but also from the school of French economists known as the physiocrats, Smith argued that order, not chaos, would be the result of leaving everyone to do as they pleased – so long, that is, that we were free to engage with one another through the market and the state took on the role of providing justice. Though it might not seem the most 'moral' of drivers, Smith suggested that the market harnesses selfishness and channels it in a direction that works in the best interests of society. The natural harmony of the market would translate individual desires into a wider social good. In his own words, '[i]t is not from the benevolence of the butcher, the brewer, or the baker, that we expect our dinner, but from their regard to their own interest.'[5] Or, in the words of the French economist Quesnay, '[t]he whole magic of a well-ordered society is that each man works for others, while believing that he is working for himself.'[6] Somehow, with everyone simply doing what is best for themselves – behaving as 'rational', self-interested and calculating creatures – we end up living in a complex and sophisticated economy with access to everything we need to live our lives. Rather than being by design or the result of some big state plan, it is as if by magic.

Smith aimed to show that individual selfish behaviour in the context of the market would not result in chaos and would in general be in everyone's best interests. However, this did not mean that such selfish behaviour had to dominate our every waking hour. His *Theory of Moral Sentiments* showed a different side to human behaviour, one which placed individuals in the context of a wider society and brought morality to bear on self-interest. And, rather than seeing our key goal in life as being the maximization of riches, he instead believed that we should be left to pursue whatever goals we wanted – as separate individuals. By using the market, as opposed to being part of some system of state or societal control, we can more easily and cheaply meet our material needs, but that would leave more time and resources for us to fulfil whatever non-material goals we might have. Unlike in the mercantilist system, the state is not bearing down on us to produce whatever it thinks we should be producing and in the quantities that it demands. And, rather than the Church imposing its own view of what our goal should be in life, Smith believed we should answer to our inner selves – to an 'impartial spectator' that sits inside each of us.

## The Big Picture: Classical Economics

Regularly bundled into the same school of economic thought as Adam Smith is, seemingly paradoxically, Karl Marx. As with Smith, Marx took the view that, when it came to our lives in the market (if not outside), selfish behaviour rules. However, unlike Smith, he did not believe that the overall result would be beneficial for the 'proletariat' or even, in the long run, for the capitalist. Selfishness results in an order but one that oppresses the worker for the benefit of the capitalist and that would, he argued, end in chaos. Capitalists might feast off the exploitation of their workers in the short to medium term, but they can only do so by undermining their own future sustainability. The pursuit of profit to fund capital accumulation would eat into consumption, leading to an economy with an ever-increasing capacity to produce but without the demand needed to mop it up. An over-investment–under-consumption equilibrium would result, and a revolution would ultimately be required, shifting the means of production into communal ownership and spreading the fruits. This new – communist – system would rest on individuals who were motivated by the common good. For Marx, it was capitalism which corrupted our humanity. The death of capitalism would mean the death of selfishness. Marx and the Church, it seems, have a lot in common. Whilst the Church had a moral case against selfishness, Marx had now provided them with an economic case. But, rather than seeing self-interest as inherent in human behaviour, he saw it as a product of capitalism itself. Without capitalism, the Church becomes defunct. Without capitalism, we internalize the needs of our fellow citizens.

Although they may not have agreed on the implications of individual selfish behaviour, Smith and Marx did, however, have one thing in common. They focused on the big picture, on aggregate outcomes. This was an age of revolution – of the British Industrial Revolution, in fact. Evidence from the world around them seemed to suggest that the fate of any economy was not signed and sealed; it was changeable. The rise and decline of economies – and political systems – was centre stage. The big picture with its focus on 'the wealth of nations' was, therefore, ever present. Marx simply added another dimension: distribution, or how that wealth was divided up between the classes.

## The Marginal Revolution

In the latter part of the nineteenth century, economic thought underwent something of a revolution, one known as the marginal revolution.

Led by William Stanley Jevons (1835–82) in England, Carl Menger (1840–1921) in Austria and Leon Walras (1834–1910) in France, and drawing influence from Jeremy Bentham's utilitarianism, economics shifted away from the big picture – from questions of growth and distribution – towards the study of the individual. It began to analyse individual choices, attempting to quantify the notions of pleasure and pain. The assumption that we are all rational, self-interested and calculating beings formally took hold. Mathematical proofs of Smith's invisible hand – of the magical properties of the market – would soon follow.

According to Partha Dasgupta, this marginal revolution was economics' natural defence mechanism against Karl Marx. By placing the individual at the centre of their analysis, economists sidestepped the need to face up to class inequalities.[7] And, as the economy moved from the transformative phase of the Industrial Revolution, Dasgupta argues that the focus began to switch away from the growth of the economic pie to scarcity: to how we could best use the resources that we had (rather than assuming a world of ever-expanding fruits). In a situation of scarcity, the marginal economists argued that we had to make sure every single resource was used as efficiently as possible so as to achieve maximum 'happiness', where for firms such 'happiness' was defined in terms of profits and for consumers in terms of 'utility'. That involved modelling individual decisions on both the production and consumption side of the economy: how businesses could make best use of the 'factors of production' (capital and labour), and how consumers could make best use of their resultant earnings – choosing between all of the different types of products available to them – so as to achieve maximum enjoyment. Self-interest again was key.

Jevons noted that the enjoyment we receive from consuming a particular product is not constant: it depends on how much of that good we have already consumed.[8] Our enjoyment tails off the more cakes or crisps we consume in a single day. This led to the development of the notion of 'diminishing marginal utility', with which we could then model how consumers can best optimize the enjoyment they receive from a given level of income. The analogous concept of 'diminishing marginal productivity' was developed, suggesting that a single business would obtain less and less additional output from each additional worker or machine. Profit maximization involved selecting the point at which this marginal productivity – the marginal benefit of production – was equal to the marginal cost. Beyond that point, each extra factor of production would be producing too little to cover its cost. In a world of scarcity, margins mattered. That was where all of the interesting action took place in terms of ensuring economic efficiency: hence the term 'marginal revolution'.

This individual-centred movement fitted neatly with the scientific turn that came with the Enlightenment. As science became all the rage, emotions were out and rationality was in. Society was making the shift away from seeing the world as driven by fate, magic and heavenly forces to recognizing life around us as the product of scientific laws – laws that were for intellectuals to uncover and subsequently harness for the betterment of mankind. Enviously observing developments in scientific disciplines like physics, including its ability to reduce aggregate phenomena to the behaviour of individual atoms, economics was on a quest to become ever more scientific. That seemed, after all, to be the route to earning respect as an academic discipline. Economists had previously tended to involve themselves in business and politics; now science seemed to be a whole new higher calibre of activity. The marginal revolution, which opened the door for the application of maths to economics, appeared to be the way forward.

## Conclusion

Since the marginal revolution, economics has held on tight to its focus on individuals. Not only was the development of microeconomics – the study of how consumers and producers make choices – the natural result, but macroeconomics – the big-picture questions surrounding the causes of economic growth and economic crises that had long interested economists – has since been rebuilt on micro-foundations of rational, self-interested, calculating individuals.

The marginal revolution is, however, the marmite of economics. Many economists see it as the beginning of modern economics, but there are others who, as we will see in the next chapter, consider it the point at which economics began to go awry. Both, however, miss the historical context, the two prongs that were the scientific Enlightenment, with its faith in our ability to reason, and the rights-based philosophy of Locke and his followers which, when embodied in economics, culminated in economists assuming that people are rational, self-interested and calculating agents. Taken together, these two developments – outside of economics – had created the case for individual freedom in an age in which capitalism was fast replacing an older system of production, one in which the state and religious authorities bossed us all around.

It was on the basis of claiming that we were all rational – that we could all reason – that philosophers were making the case for individual freedom. And it was by showing that any resultant individual selfish behaviour, unchecked by Church and state, would not lead to complete chaos, either in our ability to meet our basic needs or in wider society, that economists were able to support this case for individuals to be freed from the wrath of the Church and the state, whether at home or in the colonies. As Mark Pennington recently noted, 'For much of human history, the prevailing assumption has been that the social order can only be maintained by the exercise of deliberate authority. It has been the contribution of the classical liberal tradition to argue that this is not so.'[9]

However, if we can certainly understand the direction that economics took in the context of the time, the turn was, nevertheless, a mixed blessing. First, as we will see in chapter 9, it limited economists' ability to understand the world, something which economists are still reluctant to admit because of the way in which they perceive alternative insights as being 'too soft' and 'feminine'. Second, and as will be seen in chapter 10, whilst some harnessed individual freedom to push for equal rights and equality of opportunity for women,[10] others accepted patriarchy and chose to divide up the economy into a public 'male' sphere, one of markets and politics where rationality and self-interest were thought to apply, and a 'feminine' domestic sphere in which the very opposite assumptions were thought to apply – a supposed world of altruism, dependency and self-sacrifice.[11] It was the sphere that economists chose to ignore at their peril.[12]

# 9

# Humans Versus Robots: the Behavioural Revolution

In recent years, economics has faced a behavioural challenge. Neuroscientists and psychologists have questioned whether economists are correct to assume that we are financially motivated, 'selfish', rational and calculating. As we will see in this chapter, behavioural economics has a point: human beings are motivated by much more than money, and we are something other than rational and calculating. Only by admitting this real human behaviour can we start to answer properly many of the big questions that economists ask: why we veer from boom to bust; the causes of economic growth; and why poverty is difficult to escape. However, as we will conclude, economics has resisted the behavioural challenge for one rather foolish reason: the association of self-interested, rational and calculating behaviour with masculinity. As Jane Humphries notes, '[a]s long as masculinity is associated with superiority, the idea that economics could be improved by becoming more feminine makes little sense.'[1]

## What Motivates Us?

Does money really make the world go round? Many economists model the world as if money is the key thing that motivates us, and many economic policies certainly assume that's the case. But in 1970 Richard Titmuss published *The Gift Relationship*, noting that paying people for their blood donations, as in the US health-care system, actually reduces the quality and quantity of blood donated, whereas in the British system there is no payment, aside from a cup of tea and a biscuit. Titmuss argued that the British system was superior because it did not rely on monetary reward. For a long time, the hypothesis went untested until, in 2008, Mellström and Johannesson published the results of an experiment. The unsuspecting volunteers – undergraduate students from Gothenburg University – responded to an advertisement for participants in a study relating to 'attitudes to blood donation'. The results were telling. Of those to whom payment was not offered, 43 per cent agreed to become blood donors. When payment was offered, the donation rate was lower, at 33 per cent. However, when the researchers offered a payment option that was more flexible, allowing the money to be donated to charity, the donation rate jumped back up to 44 per cent.

What is interesting is that when analysed in terms of pure rationality, there should be no difference in the last two scenarios: if you receive payment, you can still donate to charity, whether or not you are directly presented with the option. Clearly, however, people were put off by the idea that they might be seen by others to be giving blood for financial benefit. Behavioural economists have therefore distinguished between intrinsic and extrinsic motivations, where intrinsic motivations represent our attitudes and internal goals and extrinsic motivations represent the incentives we are given from outside sources to do something we might not otherwise wish to do (such as financial payment for our time, or public gratitude for a good deed). They note that extrinsic motivations such as money can crowd out intrinsic ones, meaning that money is not always the best motivator.

In addition to being motivated by more than money, experiments have shown that human beings also have an inherent sense of fairness. Perhaps the most famous example is the ultimatum game, a 'game' played between two individuals. Each individual is anonymous in the sense that they are not able to see each other or interact. The intention is to remove any social influence on the outcome of the game in an effort to reveal how we behave as isolated individuals. One individual (the 'proposer') is given a set amount of money (say, US$100) and has responsibility for deciding how to split that money between themselves and the other individual (offering anything between US$1 and US$100 to the other party). This other individual (the 'responder') can then either accept the proposed split or reject it; if they reject it, neither person receives any money.

Now, if proposers act in a purely rational, money-driven way, they would propose a split in which they keep US$99 and give the other party a miserly US$1 (or whatever the minimum possible figure is). This is because, if you believe people are rational, self-interested and calculating, it would not be sensible for the responder to reject *any* positive pay off (no matter how small); something is always better than nothing. However, the most common offer is a split much closer to US$50:US$50, and offers of less than US$30 to the second party are regularly rejected when the game is played.[2] In other words, people are happy to reject low offers – to effectively accept a financial loss – in an effort to punish someone they think is behaving 'unfairly'. The implication is clear: people do not only value money; they value fairness, and they want to feel respected.

Another popular game – the public goods game – also serves to reveal that we are much less self-interested and more 'pro-social' than economists have assumed. Suppose five volunteers are each given an initial sum of US$10 and have the option of contributing to a common pool (think of it as being a pot in the centre of the table). As in the ultimatum game, the volunteers cannot see each other and do not know the decisions being made by anyone other than themselves. However, what they are told is that any money added to the common pool will be multiplied by three and then shared out equally five ways. Faced with this situation, how much would you decide to contribute to the common pool? Well, if you acted as an economist supposes, you would likely reason that for every US$1 you put in the pot, you will receive only US$3/5 (i.e. 60 cents). As a result, the rational and self-interested thing to do is to keep the initial US$10 and contribute nothing. Of course, if everyone donated the whole of their US$10 to the common pool, they would all leave with the maximum amount possible: US$30. However, on an individual level, it is not rational to donate your own money but instead to hope that others will do so. The result is a 'free-rider' problem, where no one contributes and everyone is worse off as a result. As it turns out, when the game is played, people regularly donate around half of their initial sum to the common pool.[3] Furthermore, if the game is played multiple times with the same people, and they are each given the option of punishing anyone who does not 'cooperate' – but at a cost to themselves – they regularly do so.[4] In other words, within human groups there seem to be strong incentives to cooperate – and to punish those who do not. We need to go beyond money if we are to understand human behaviour.

## How Rational and Calculating are We?

Economists' starting point is that we all know what is good for us and are capable of achieving it. We don't need a 'nanny state' to help us make decisions. If we overeat, under-save or partner up with the 'wrong' person, the problem is simply one of too little information. All the state needs to do is to make sure that we have the right information. By assuming that we can all behave in a rational and calculating way, there is no additional need for intervention; the state cannot possibly be expected to lead to better decisions than those which we can make on our own behalf.

Herbert Simon argued that in the real world people possess neither the full set of information nor the time required to make the 'best' choice.[5] Furthermore, the human brain is limited in terms of its ability to process and weigh up all available options. Rather than being fully rational, Simon proposes that we are 'boundedly rational'. In the words of one writer, we should '[t]hink of the human brain as a personal computer, with a very slow processor and a memory system that is both small and unreliable'.[6] As a result, people often fall back on 'rules of thumb', what are known as heuristics, which render all the decisions in our daily lives much less complicated and time-consuming. However, whilst these heuristics make our lives easier, they are often not perfect and can lead to fallible decisions. For example, rather than going through the mental effort of working out which is the best-value supermarket, visiting each one to weigh up the various offers, we tend to return to the same supermarket we visited last time. This rule of thumb creates what has become known as the 'status quo bias'. Other rules of thumb were revealed in a series of experiments conducted by Daniel Kahneman and Amos Tversky. These show our natural tendency to jump to conclusions, to place excessive weight on our own experiences and to look only for evidence which confirms our beliefs (ignoring evidence which does the opposite).[7] The implication of these biases – biases created by the mental shortcuts that are hard-wired into our brains – is that we tend to be resistant to change, overconfident and stubborn and, as such, make decisions and act in a way that is not always in our own best interests.

We all know that sometimes our 'heart' tells us one thing and our 'head' tells us another. Daniel Kahneman argues that our thinking processes involve two 'systems'.[8] System 1 in the limbic region of the brain performs the 'thinking fast' part of our activity; it is associated with emotional ('hot') activity – it is intuitive, happens with little or no consciousness and is effort-free. System 2 in the prefrontal cortex is the 'thinking slow' part of the brain, where conscious and calculating activity takes place. For most of the time, System 1 – and not System 2 – is in charge, which accounts for why we so often fail to behave in the way economists predict.

To see the everyday battle in action, neuroscientists like to scan our brains. One group of researchers wired up volunteers to examine how the brain reacted when faced with the choice of receiving a US\$20 voucher to spend today or a US\$30 voucher in two weeks' time.[9] The results were revealing. The offer of US\$20 today stimulated activity in the emotional part of the brain, but the option of US\$30 in two weeks' time stimulated action in the calculating part of the brain, leading to an internal conflict. One option delivers instant gratification, satisfying our 'emotions', but the other seems more sensible from the point of view of the calculating part of our brain.

Two important findings have resulted from this work. The first is that we sometimes make decisions automatically, without really thinking about them. The second is we are strongly influenced by our emotions. There are, however, times when automatic and emotional behaviour can be helpful.[10] Although our System 1 brain is responsible for many of our mistakes, it is also responsible for much of what we get right. After much experience, it can produce 'expert intuition' of the kind that is invaluable to medics and firefighters who need to react to complex situations with great speed. Making decisions automatically and with emotion can have benefits, which might explain why our brains have developed to work in this way. Many common psychiatric disorders, such as obsessive-compulsive disorder, arise when we employ too much careful calculation and deliberation. Furthermore, individuals who lack the emotional – relative to cognitive – input in decisions often find decision making more difficult and are not always very good at it. If we can't 'feel' an outcome, we can end up making decisions that we see in retrospect are wrong.

## Why Behavioural Economics Matters

Behavioural economics has become all the rage in policy circles and has resulted in a number of recent Nobel prizes in economics. Policy makers have also begun to adopt its policy implications, in terms of 'nudging' us out of behaviour that is bad for us. However, whilst such interest might lead one to think that economists' way of thinking about individual behaviour is being transformed, according to David Levine, Professor in Economics at Washington University, 'nothing could be further from the truth'. In fact, he has written a whole book on the matter, asking 'Is behavioural economics doomed?'[11] So why, despite all of the evidence, has mainstream economics not embraced a more realistic set of assumptions about human behaviour in an effort to build a better understanding of the economy?

The typical answer is that building models will always require some form of simplification. Assuming human beings are self-interested, rational and calculating might be a little far-fetched, but it at least captures some important aspects of human behaviour. To assume the opposite would seem foolish. As the Nobel prizewinning economist Milton Friedman once famously noted, if we want to formulate a model which helps us to explain the actions of a snooker player, we will arrive at the most accurate predictions if we build the model assuming that the snooker player has a good grasp of physics, meaning the ability to calculate the trajectory and speed needed for each shot. A more realistic assumption would likely lead to worse – not better – predictions about how the game would be played. What matters, in other words, is not whether a model has realistic *assumptions* but how accurate its *predictions* are relative to alternative models.

In the real world, emotions, irrationalities and fallibility certainly exist, as any economist will happily admit, it's just that they don't think that those elements of behaviour are particularly relevant to understanding the economy. Economists, after all, focus mostly on markets, and it's commonly thought that in markets there is no place for emotions, vulnerabilities and weaknesses – the market compels everyone to behave in a selfish, rational and calculating way; otherwise, they will be swept under – they will be bankrupt.

The ultimate test, therefore, of whether economics should embrace real human psychology is whether it would make a substantial enough difference to the way we think about the economy. As we will see below, it is in fact impossible to answer many of the big questions that economists face without relaxing the *homo economicus* assumptions.

## 1 The causes of economic growth

The market is where most economists begin when they seek to explain the creation of economic prosperity. Markets are argued to harness our self-interest, encouraging us to invest and invent. This works in the form of carrots and sticks: markets create potential customers and therefore a potential financial reward in the form of profit; the competition they bring pushes entrepreneurs to keep costs low and increase their productivity, meaning we get the best product at a reasonable price. Perhaps naturally, therefore, rational, calculating and self-interested behaviour has come to be seen as an important driver of economic prosperity.

Now, at the very centre of economic growth is technological change. Typically, we think of this as a response to the potential financial reward on offer in terms of higher profits or a valuable patent. However, as Joel Mokyr has pointed out, many of the technologies associated with the Industrial Revolution would not have taken place had inventors been purely driven by financial self-interest.[12] The patent system was expensive and cumbersome and few inventors actually profited from it. It was only in view of the fact that we overestimate our own chances of success that the system stimulated invention. It is not cool, calculating robotic behaviour that leads people to start new businesses and develop new technologies or new ideas; it is the (irrational) human element. As Keynes neatly summarized it, '[i]f human nature felt no temptation to take a chance, no satisfaction (profit apart) in constructing a factory, a railway, a mine or a farm, there might not be much investment merely as a result of cold calculation'.[13]

In fact, non-financial motives are just as important as financial ones. Technological change rests on improvements in science. Rather than private financial gain, scientific advances often have at their roots a desire to wipe out pain and suffering, simple curiosity, or the hope of recognition from colleagues. These motives can represent a much more powerful inducement and reward than money, bringing the social regard and 'warm glow' that would not have surprised Smith. The Enlightenment movement – commonly seen as giving birth to modern science – involved scientists coming together, cooperating to help make the world a better place, not for financial gain but for the public at large. Still today, this motivation drives the efforts of many scientists. Private-sector activity might rely on profit-driven self-interested behaviour, but it draws upon the ideas and innovations of scientists working with very different motives. Interestingly, as psychologist Teresa Amabile has shown, attempts to incentivize creativity and independent thought through financial rewards, regular evaluations and competition can in fact hinder rather than help.[14] Although conventional economics can teach us the importance of science and technology (and who would be surprised by that), its simple conception of human behaviour cannot explain it, or indeed help us to encourage it. That's a big problem, given that science and technology are so central to economic growth.

In addition to the sphere of production, there is another sphere which is equally as important for economic growth but which economists increasingly chose to ignore: reproduction.[15] Although economists regularly talk about the 'accumulation of capital', the accumulation of people – which combines with capital – also requires attention. In macro models, people need to be treated as an output as well as input, as in the pioneering feminist macro model constructed by Elissa Braunstein, Irene van Staveren and Daniele Tavani, which integrates unpaid work – that generates people – with the more usual paid work.[16] An economy can only thrive if it has a stock of well-functioning and productive individuals, historically the product of good parenting and women's reproductive and nurturing work, much of which takes place within the home. Here, money is not the driving force; rather, as Sabine O'Hara argues, it is care, altruism and love. By reducing human beings to robots, economists have ignored all of the work which goes on behind the scenes, outside of the market. They have taken for granted women's hard labour and devalued work within the home, where it is not carried out for financial reward.[17] As Folbre notes, whilst behavioural economists study norms of trust and reciprocity, they would do well to also look at norms of care and obligation.[18]

## 2   From boom to bust: explaining the business cycle

Most explanations of the business cycle revolve around the idea of 'shocks'. The assumption is that, left to its own devices and without interference from government, the economy will be more or less stable. Markets should clear, ensuring that everyone who wants a job has a job and that every firm is able to sell whatever it wishes to produce. If the economy goes into 'recession', it is assumed to be the result of an outside shock on either the demand or supply side – to the amount people spend or to what the economy is capable of producing. The best way of insulating our economy from boom and bust is, therefore, to make sure that markets are flexible so that they can adjust quickly to such shocks.

John Maynard Keynes, Cambridge's most famous economist, is also often associated with the 'shock' explanation, particularly demand-side shocks: changes in investment, consumer spending, export demand or government spending. His most significant idea was that economies can fall into recession as a result of a reduction in any of these components of demand. Since Keynes put forward his theory of the business cycle in his *General Theory of Employment, Interest and Money*, economists have turned his insights into a mathematical model. They have shown that so long as prices and wages are free to adjust, the economy should quickly return to 'equilibrium' following a shock to demand.

However, by turning Keynes's insights into a full-blown mathematical model, economists have left out what Keynes really thought about the economy. Rather than seeing the economy as naturally stable, Keynes instead thought that instability was inevitable. Whilst economists have modelled his insight with the notion of demand 'shocks' to an otherwise stable system, Keynes had something altogether different in mind: an 'unknowable' future that makes rational, self-interested and calculating behaviour of the kind economists assume very difficult, if not impossible.

Keynes made the point that when we decide how much to invest (or to spend), we have to try to predict the future: the likely path of our future earnings and the likely returns from our investments. But, because the future is unknowable, it is impossible to make accurate assessments. We are, at all times, walking into the unknown, making decisions based on little knowledge. The result is that we regularly simply assume things will carry on as 'normal' and follow the crowd. We jump on bandwagons, fearful of missing out on something, over-confident one moment and overcome by panic the next. The spirit of the group will regularly take hold – what Keynes called 'animal spirits' – leading to waves of optimism and pessimism that destabilize the economy. Human behaviour is both erratic and open to social influence. Psychology and sociology both matter.[19]

## 3   Personal finance, poverty and social mobility

Only by recognizing that humans are human can we start to understand many of the everyday challenges we face, challenges which have a major impact on our lives, on our personal finances, on our health and on our emotional well-being. Behavioural economics suggests that by uncovering the part of our human flaws that are systematic (that are 'predictably irrational'), policy makers can work out ways of 'nudging' us into making better decisions.[20]

Architects have always known that our surroundings can have a big effect on the choices we make. When designing office buildings, they will, for example, use an open-plan layout in places where human interaction aids the exchange of ideas and, where it does not, make sure that bathrooms are easily accessible so people do not waste time bumping into colleagues. Behavioural economics similarly argues that we can design 'choice environments' that make it easier for people to make the 'right' decision. Those responsible for positioning food items at the supermarket check-out desk and in school canteens can, for example, 'nudge' us to make 'better' choices. Furthermore, when it comes to saving schemes and pensions, rather than asking us whether we want to opt in, we should instead be asked whether we would like to 'opt out', the idea being that doing what is 'right' is much easier if it does not require action. Evidence suggests that opt-in schemes produce an enrolment rate of around 60 per cent but opt-out schemes lead to a much higher enrolment of 90–95 per cent.[21]

When employed by the state, in what Cass Sunstein and Richard Thaler have called 'libertarian paternalism',[22] this will not be costly to the taxpayer and will not involve limiting choice or prohibiting certain goods. In other words, it will not impinge on personal freedom and does not mean bigger government – just better government.

According to Sendhil Mullainathan and Eldar Shafir, self-control of the kind needed to maximize our long-term well-being becomes a particular problem when our minds are occupied with other things such as work deadlines or financial stress.[23] That can create vicious circles of deprivation. Many of the concerns we regularly face as human beings can easily come to dominate our lives. This can have an advantage – it can help the brain to work out a solution – but it also comes with a major negative: it deprives us of the mental energy needed for everything else. Our brains 'tunnel', ignoring things that are outside the problem at hand. The result is that we give in to temptation, snap at our children and become forgetful. This is a particular problem as so many of the decisions which have a positive effect on our long-term well-being require continual vigilance and self-control. Eating healthily, keeping fit, taking medication, keeping our skills up to date, nurturing our relationships and saving for the future are all cases in point, making them difficult to achieve when we are financially stressed. By contrast, many of the decisions that have a negative effect on our lives are one-offs; signing up to a costly loan is all too quick and easy and seems to provide an instant fix when our minds are dominated by a particular problem. Poverty 'taxes the brain', making digging ourselves out of it all the more difficult – and, one might therefore say, all the more important for governments to take it seriously.

Tackling poverty requires economists not only to pay attention to psychology but also to sociology. That includes what other people think of us. As I found out from my own experiences of living below the breadline, human dignity and respect are just as important as money – perhaps even more so when you are poor. Where claiming benefits is public, as was the case with free school meals in my own youth, people may go without in order to preserve what they see as their self-respect. The result can be long-term damage to health and well-being. And, where they are unable to access the financial resources they need, individuals find other ways of earning respect from their peers. Unable to participate in 'normal' society, they create their own, along with a sense of purpose and belonging. Respect is, of course, central to gang culture. George Akerlof and Rachel Kranton have researched the power of identity, noting that seemingly perverse behaviour – including behaviour that can cause us pain – can be explained by our desire to belong and to signal that we are part of a group.[24] The resultant social structures can, however, affect the ability of particular individuals to make the jump to 'normal' society, either because they become socialized to value whatever the gang values or because building life outside comes with severe punishment.

One way in which I saw the forces of psychology and society at work in my own local community was through a process that I will call *careless talk*.[25] Put yourself in the situation of being a young person from a working-class community who is thinking of applying to a top university. Just when you are building the confidence to make an application, someone scuppers it by saying, 'Why bother? You know you won't make it.' Of course, one such statement is not really a problem. But when it becomes frequent, that is a different matter. Careless talk succeeds in knocking the confidence of aspiring young people and making them imagine that even if they were to be successful, they would be excluded or laughed at. I can tell you that the only reason I ever felt 'left out' after leaving my home town was a result of paranoia – a paranoia brought about by others which took a while to shake off.

From my own experiences at least, it seems clear that young people with the ability to succeed can encounter everyday resistance from those around them, rather than from those at the top (with whom, to be honest, they rarely come into daily contact). However, the idea that communities can damage their own members might sound rather paradoxical: after all, why would a community want to discourage its most talented from succeeding? One possibility is that communities aim to keep their members grounded – to prevent them from becoming 'too big for their boots'. This chimes with the work of the anthropologist Richard Borshay Lee, who found that the hunters of the indigenous !Kung community he studied were subject to ridicule if they returned with a big kill.[26] This ridicule served to prevent arrogance, helping to preserve social harmony. Another possibility is that careless talk forms part of a self-defence mechanism – one that can help people who do not move 'upwards'. None of this is to say that communities are in any way malicious. However, what is perhaps true to say is that people can sometimes have a strong incentive to champion, propagate and magnify what they might not realize are 'untruths', with the unfortunate and entirely unintended effect of limiting social mobility.

In economics, it has become normal to blame poverty and the lack of social mobility on economic factors, such as the 'hourglassing' of the economy, the ability of richer families to give their children additional support and a lack of funding for schools or welfare. However, to truly understand such important issues, economists also need to rethink the assumptions they make about human behaviour.

## Conclusion

By leaving human reality in the cold, economists have not only over-simplified the world but have limited their ability to understand it. However, resistance to behavioural economics doesn't merely reflect the ghost of Milton Friedman's snooker player. Another ghost has been hanging over economics since its early days in the eighteenth and nineteenth centuries, when reason began to trump emotion and science began to trump the arts. It is the ghost of *macho man*.[27]

When economics set out its formal assumptions about economic behaviour at the time of the marginal revolution, society was developing rather set views about men and women. In the words of Lord Henry in Oscar Wilde's *The Picture of Dorian Gray*, '[m]y dear boy, no woman is a genius. Women are a decorative sex. They never have anything to say, but they say it charmingly. Women represent the triumph of matter over mind, just as men represent the triumph of mind over morals.' Emotions and irrationalities were (wrongly, of course) cast as female, and reason and calculation – so revered by the Enlightenment – as male.[28] Diversions from 'rational, self-interested and calculating' behaviour were therefore thought to be 'soft' and 'unrigorous'.[29] The idea of independence was glorified and associated with men; that of dependence was despised. The autonomous self became the ideal, not the connected and supposedly 'female' self.[30] Furthermore, since economics has been defined much more by its approach – by the application of its standard assumptions – than by its subject matter, it 'makes economists particularly reluctant to admit dissent which challenges their approach, for this would threaten a methodological unravelling that would leave them naked in the world'.[31]

Although economists aimed for a 'scientific approach', they were far from objective. When the subject was fast developing in the nineteenth century, it was against the backdrop of an economy in which the Industrial Revolution was pushing women out of the workplace and into the home.[32] With the gendered divide now erected between the market and the home, economists increasingly focused their attentions on the market. When it comes to the market, it is difficult to prize anything other than self-interested, calculating and rational behaviour, so such assumptions seemed entirely justifiable – that is until we realize that the sphere of market production is only one half of the story. The activities taking place outside the market, which also depend on care, love and altruism, are just as important for understanding economic success (and failure).

However, rather than incorporating non-market activity into economics, or questioning society's heavily gendered assumption that the home is female and paid work is male, many economists actively contributed to the growing sexism within society.[33] That includes leading economists associated with the marginal revolution: Alfred Marshall, who argued in favour of 'family wages' for men, and F. Y. Edgeworth, who argued that women and men should *not* be paid equally for equal work.[34] Through the support they gave to sexist practices, economists have actively contributed to gender inequalities. And they employed economic theory to back up their arguments. In the words of Michele Pujol, Marshall 'opposes employment for married women' and gave his support to the practice of paying women less than men for exactly the same work so as to keep them in the home 'to enhance the environment in which male workers and their children live, and to generate greater health, character and ability'.[35] Women's work, he argued, created a negative externality that must therefore be discouraged. A woman's individual freedom came second to what he thought was best for society as a whole. Needless to say, it serves to show the risks of ignoring individual freedom when judging what is best for society.[36]

Economics, to borrow the words of Jane Humphries, was 'not only made by gendered subjects but it made gendered subjects'.[37] It's time for the subject to free itself of its masculine biases.[38]

# 10

## Economics Meets Feminism

Behavioural economics has provided a powerful critique of economists' assumptions about individual behaviour: that we are rational, self-interested and calculating. It is, as we've seen, impossible to get to grips with big economic problems without relaxing these assumptions. However, as we saw in chapter 8, the assumptions were not made without justification. They grew out of two philosophical revolutions taking place in the nineteenth century: the idea that we could all 'reason' and a belief in individual rights. To model the economy as if people were *not* rational would have undermined the case for individual freedom. Given that the state and religion had shackled the masses for centuries, and that they were only just starting to break free and take control of their lives, that would have been a dangerous course. Although behavioural economics is, of course, right to point to the need for economists to adjust their assumptions, we should not lose sight of this deeper point – or of the fight for individual freedom that gave rise to those assumptions. One might argue that critiques of economics have gone too far, but in this chapter we will see that there is also a sense in which they haven't gone far enough. Economists need to pay more attention to three things in particular if they are to fully comprehend the causes of poverty and prosperity: the body, family and society.

### The Body

In the eighteenth century, Mary Wollstonecraft, who penned what is commonly seen as the first celebrated piece of feminist writing,

*A Vindication of the Rights of Woman*, wrote with passion in a letter to the former Bishop of Autun:

> Consider, I address you as a legislator, whether, when men contend for their freedom, and to be allowed to judge for themselves respecting their own happiness, it be not inconsistent and unjust to subjugate women, even though you firmly believe that you are acting in the manner best calculated to promote their happiness? Who made man the exclusive judge, if woman partake with him the gift of reason?[1]

At this time, women were assumed to be fragile, emotional and irrational creatures. According to Wollstonecraft, this impression was not only wrong, it had resulted from their unequal treatment. This unequal treatment meant that 'their minds are not in a healthy state'. In resisting the fight for votes for women, the anti-suffrage movement relied on propagating the idea that women were mentally incapable of rational and reasoned thought. They argued that women's 'natural' capabilities were in providing moral and emotional support for their families; that men and women had different but complementary abilities.[2] Women's political freedom thereby rested on making the case that women were rational self-interested beings 'just like men'.

But precisely because freedom was initially thought of in the context of men's lives, it was inevitable that something would be missing: women's bodies. In the words of Lucy Stone, a prominent US feminist of the mid-nineteenth century, '[i]t is very little to me to have the right to vote, to own property etc., if I may not keep my body, and its uses, in my absolute right.'[3]

Given its neglect in concepts of freedom, women's control over their fertility has always been controversial, even amongst economists like Malthus who highlighted the problem of excessive population growth.[4] Birth control pioneers, like Marie Stopes and Margaret Sanger, were viewed with suspicion and even faced the wrath of the law. The battle for a woman's right to control her own body has certainly not been easy, and it is still very much ongoing. In some countries the state's hold on women's bodies is so strong that even a miscarriage brings a risk of arrest. Rich countries are unfortunately not immune. Freedom to access technologies such as abortion continues to be restricted and, even where they have such freedom, women regularly face abuse for accessing them. Paradoxically, some of those most vehemently in favour of individual freedom are the very same people who move to deny women's bodily autonomy.

Economists tend to assume that we can each freely make choices and that we carefully think about every decision. That should be no different when it comes to having children. In fact, given the impact on our lives, it should be even more the case than when choosing a car or what to have for dinner. But, according to US data, amongst young unmarried women, 60 per cent of births are the result of unplanned pregnancies.[5] In the United Kingdom, for young women in the 20–24 age group, the proportion of all pregnancies that are planned is less than half, standing at around 40 per cent.[6] This means that the majority were either unplanned or fall into the mysterious category of 'ambivalence'. For women aged 16–19, the situation is even more worrying, as only 12 per cent of pregnancies are planned. Globally, the average is almost one in two.[7] Given the costs of raising children, which exceed £200,000 per child in the United Kingdom in modern money, each addition to the family makes a big difference, never mind an extra two, three, four or more children. If we are to make sure that women have control over their lives, much more needs to be done.

Comparing our lives today with those of our female ancestors shows just what is at stake.[8] When I was a child, my grandmother used to tell me stories about her own grandmother who, like me, was small, slight, had long hair and was good with numbers. As it turns out, although her mental arithmetic might have put her at the top of the class, she wasn't so astute when it came to choosing a husband. You could say that the man she married loved drink quite a lot more than he loved his family. My great-great-grandmother gave birth to more than ten children, including at least six boys and, so the story goes, she would regularly send two of them to wait outside the local pub to beg their father for money before he spent it all at the next pub. After years of abuse, she finally got her own back: when her husband tried to escape wartime conscription on the basis of what he claimed was a disability, she secretly told the conscription officers that they should wait for him outside the pub the next evening. Needless to say that he didn't remember to limp in the right way after an evening of alcohol. She was finally free – in one way at least.

Seeing your own children go without must be one of the most heartbreaking feelings any mother can experience. Without the benefit of modern-day contraception, women like my great-great-grandmother must have felt entirely out of control. Every time she missed a period, she must have realized that there would soon be an extra mouth to feed, meaning spreading her earnings ever more thinly and reducing the portion sizes for existing children.

We all have stories like these, and we all know what a difference the welfare state could have made. Child allowances, paid to the mother, free health care and maternity benefits could, I'm sure, have transformed her life along with those of many others. What such personal stories also reveal, however, is that there is another cause of poverty. In the case of my great-great-grandmother, it's easy to see that freedom to control her own fertility would have transformed her life just as much as the welfare state ever could. Feeding, clothing and nurturing two, three or even four children instead of ten or more would have made an immeasurable difference to the family's standard of living. Giving women the power to control their own fertility is not just about rights for women, it is also about giving families what they need to keep the wolf from the door, affecting the lives of the boys and girls of the next generation.

As we saw earlier, at the root of the West's economic riches was the way in which late marriage restricted fertility. The fact that female bodily freedom has been limited for most of history helps to explain why economic prosperity is so rare – and so recent. With women lacking control over their wombs, it's not that surprising that the human race was, until recently, condemned to a life of dearth and deprivation. We tend to assume that poverty reduction has been a result of – depending on whether you are right or left leaning – capitalism or the welfare state; from the point of view of women, control over their bodies must surely be near the top of the list. And, as we saw earlier in the book, the lack of freedom for women in poorer countries not only affects their home economies but also has serious adverse spillover effects on richer economies, including on their wages, inequality and economic growth.

If economists truly want to make the most of their *homo economicus* assumptions, they need to bring women's bodily autonomy into the picture. Rather than simply assuming individual agency, economists need to do much more to address the lack of it – and be cognisant of attempts to restrict it, even in rich countries.

## Family

Economists like to divide the world up in a very simple and straight-forward manner. It is a world consisting of twin spheres: the market and the state. It is a division that underpinned the great showdown between capitalism and communism and that led to the notion that to make the market work better we need to shrink the state.

Political thinkers and economists alike have been reluctant to delve beyond the public sphere, believing that life outside is personal rather than political.[9] As we have seen, economics developed at a time when the home and the market were becoming increasingly segregated along gender lines, which led it to prioritize the market and to fail to properly consider the important interactions between the two. However, as feminists know well, personal *is* political. It is fundamentally necessary to understand what happens in the private sphere if we are to understand what is happening in the economy overall.

In *A Treatise on the Family*, the economist Gary Becker decided to take a walk into this unknown territory, applying market concepts to the family.[10] He modelled the family as if it were a business – one in which people think about efficiency and make calculated decisions about whether to get married, how many children to have and whether to go out to work or stay at home. He argued that traditional gender roles – the idea that men go out to work and women remain in the home – were the result of an efficient process of specialization.

There is, however, a fundamental flaw with this Becker-led way of thinking about the family, an approach which has become known as New Home Economics: the assumption of altruism. Although economists assume self-interested behaviour in the public sphere – in markets and in politics – they are seemingly happy to assume completely the opposite in regard to the family: that the family works harmoniously as a unit to maximize 'household' utility.

The reality is that we cannot assume that family members are altruistic towards one another. Accepting that is key to understanding where poverty and inequality originate. As we saw in part I, for many of the world's poorest women – in the past and in the present – marriage is not a free choice. The resultant dynamics of family life are, therefore, highly unlikely to be altruistic. Instead, the family becomes the site in which inequalities are propagated and poverty is passed on from generation to generation. That's even the case when marriage is a free choice, when who is earning what can soon start to affect who in the household has the biggest say. Only by understanding this can we even begin to get to grips with the challenges faced by women and the way these interact with the wider economy. Little wonder, therefore, that economists' forays into the home have come under fire from feminist economists, including Nancy Folbre.[11]

Folbre has developed an alternative to Becker's altruistic model of family life.[12] In an article entitled 'Exploitation Comes Home', she applies Marxist thinking to the household. In contrast with Becker, Marxist feminism sees the family as a hotbed of conflict. Family harmony is not taken for granted, and decisions made by individual members cannot be automatically treated as 'efficient'. The relationship between the patriarch and other family members is seen as analogous to that between a capitalist and workers: imagine all family earnings and resources going into one pot, from which all members

receive just enough to subsist, with the 'surplus' accruing to the patriarch. Although this might seem far-fetched, it is not entirely amiss.

Take the example of my own grandparents. Their life was pretty typical of working-class families in the north of England. However, despite working full-time, my grandmother was solely responsible for all of the household chores and raising the children. In return, she received a weekly household allowance from my grandfather, as was fairly common in those days. This was topped up by my grandmother's own earnings and, where necessary, she would take on extra work, such as cleaning jobs in the evenings, to make ends meet. The rest of my grandfather's income was spent on himself, on things like cigarettes and bingo. Only when my grandmother accompanied him to a meeting to discuss his pension entitlement, for which he thought her mathematical eye might come in useful, did she realize the full extent of the discrepancy between what he had been earning and his 'housekeeping' contribution. Funnily enough, he was a lifelong socialist and yet, rather ironically, had been treating his own wife and children in the same way that he thought capitalists treated their workers.

Of course, not all families are the same. In fact, as we've seen, the way families work exhibits tremendous variety across the world.[13] That variety includes how new couples are formed in the first place – the extent to which it is the choice of the individuals or that of their families; whether marriages are expected to be within or outside the family; whether newly married couples are absorbed into an existing household or form their own household; whether assets change hands upon marriage, and women's status in regard to property; how children born outside of marriage are looked upon; whether there is an onus on younger generations to care for older generations within the home; and how inheritance is dealt with. All of this, however, matters deeply for the autonomy of women.

Gender equality and associated prosperity cannot be achieved when there are so many restrictions on women's freedom that come from within the home. The gender gap in the market will not close until it also closes within the home. But, it will not close within the home unless it closes within the market. Where there are fewer market opportunities for women, more demands will be placed on them within the family, and, where that's the case, the more restricted they become in terms of their ability to achieve their potential in the public sphere. In other words, gender inequalities within the home and the marketplace act to reinforce one another. That explains why gender inequality can be so difficult to beat and the prosperity that builds on equality so difficult to bring about. However, economic policy makers can make a difference, if only they open their eyes. Giving women more rights over household income has been shown to have a significant effect on the welfare of the wider family, leading to greater spending on basic facilities (such as toilets), health care and education.[14] Sadly, in the case of Britain, we seem to be moving in the opposite direction. The new benefits system is one that pays benefits into the bank account of the chief income earner (typically male), increasing rather than decreasing their bargaining power at the cost of their partner.[15] Economists still need to open up life within the home if they want to defeat inequality and poverty.

## From Family to Dependency

As we have seen, agency is central to economics. People are assumed to be free individuals, interacting anonymously through the marketplace. The notion of being a dependent is largely alien, and the phrase 'dependency' carries with it some rather negative connotations. However, whilst the majority of us spend a large portion of our lives directly contributing to the economy in a financial sense, from the time of our birth to the day of our death we each face numerous periods of dependency, from infancy and childhood to periods of study, pregnancy, illness, unemployment and old age. Dependency is as much a fact of life as death and taxes, and it leaves us vulnerable – a vulnerability with which women have, historically, been intimately familiar. In the words of Avner Offer, '[i]n these circumstances there may be no agency, no two feet to stand on, nothing to sell, no bargaining power, and restrained cognitive capacity.'[16]

In 'traditional' societies, dependency was dealt with by the family. The family was, in a sense, the original welfare state.[17] One of the major restrictions on women's freedom is a set of social norms premised on the idea that women exist for the care of others within the family. However, this reality is made invisible by economics. Whilst economists measure and model those who receive direct monetary reward for their work, they ignore unpaid labour, and it certainly hasn't been thought worth including in national economic accounts.[18] And, they model labour as an input into production, ignoring the fact that labour is itself an output of another production process, one involving reproductive and caring labour.[19]

According to Sabine O'Hara, 'care' is in fact central to all economic activity. The market and the world of business does not (and cannot) exist in a vacuum.[20] It depends intimately upon life outside of the market: on the care provided within families and communities (which, for example, serves to provide a healthy and well-functioning workforce); on the state of trust within society; and on our ability to sustain the natural environment. Economists' neglect of this dependency of markets upon non-market activity – and the human dependencies within it – has resulted in an undervaluation of the contribution of family, society and the environment to our economy. The problem is that care depends on all of those things that economists typically ignore: reciprocity, altruism and responsibility for others.[21] Economists cannot get to grips with care until they become more flexible in terms of the assumptions they make about human behaviour.

Only in recent decades, as more and more women have joined the labour market, have economic policy makers been forced to face the problem of dependency in terms of increasing demand for child and elderly care services. In the past, society burdened women with the responsibility of care by restricting their freedom outside the home.[22] The question it now confronts is where it wishes to go from here: how will we manage dependency? Assuming it away, or assuming that we can all cope with it privately by taking out insurance and pensions, fails to get to grips with a vital part of human existence and would likely leave women juggling both paid work and care. Given the big changes taking place in the economy, politics and society – the 'rise of the robots', the 'gig economy', the ageing population and restrictions on immigration – this is a question that is in fact becoming more, not less, pressing. And it's one that should be thought of as central to many of the problems we now face: stress; fertility falling to below population replacement levels; low wages in the care sector; the gender wage gap that results from the unequal distribution of care; and a slowdown in productivity and economic growth as the care economy expands.

Amongst feminist groups, there is an increasing call to treat care, including child care and elderly care, as part of the economic infrastructure that should be funded by the taxpayer. That's because children do not just represent a private benefit for their parents, they are also a public good, without which human life could not continue. That means whether or not we ourselves choose to have children, we all have a stake in – and a responsibility to contribute towards – the care of the next generation. Furthermore, if we ignore care, it will only serve to perpetuate gender inequalities within the home, inequalities that in turn erupt in the market, costing the economy. Realistically, leaving care to the market either means leaving care to women or leaving the 'needy' without support.[23] Finally, as Susan Himmelweit argues, we cannot just treat care like any other good or service. There are three features that distinguish care: it 'involves the development of a relationship'; 'caring responsibilities and needs are unequally distributed'; and 'social norms influence the allocation of care and caring responsibilities'.[24] All of this means that leaving care entirely to the market can only be expected to produce problems. One thing is for sure: the current approach to the provision of care is not working. Hence we are facing a 'crisis of care'.[25]

Having made the case for state intervention in the realm of care, we must also add a note of caution. Socialist societies from the time of Robert Owen have frequently aimed for the complete socialization of care. But the end point of this approach was the destruction of the family.[26] This drive to eliminate the family is visible throughout Soviet architecture. Housing designs included communal dining rooms and shared laundry facilities. According to Engels, the family is the last vestige of a bourgeois society; it directs our actions inwards, rather than outwards for the common good. It encourages us to pursue private property and to think in an individual-centred way. Socialists argued that the joys of sex were constrained by our concern for the consequences: the need to feed the resultant mouths. By socializing care, socialism promised a society free of individualism - and with freer sex.[27]

## Society

As far as economists are concerned, individuals are born into the world with their own well-developed tastes and preferences. We then engage with each other through the market, doing the best we can to achieve those exogenous needs and desires. However, feminist thinking highlights the fact that being human involves a process of socialization, of being socialized into the family and community.[28] Our preferences and desires are not, therefore, exogenous and independent; they are in part socially constructed. By assuming they are stable, economists accept rather than seek to explain gender differences: they attribute gender differences in pay, in the choice of occupations and in the gender division of domestic labour to the different 'tastes' of men and women.[29] And, by adopting a bargaining approach to explain economic outcomes such as pay, they ignore the difference between the actual value of work and its perceived value, with work that is labelled 'female' carrying lower rewards.[30] As Frances Woolley notes, if we are to fully explain women's disadvantage, we need to endogenize tastes by recognizing the role of society.[31]

From Mary Wollstonecraft and Simone de Beauvoir to more recent writers such as Nancy Folbre and Clare Chambers,[32] feminists have long pointed out that what men and women want from life is framed by a socially constructed view of gender roles: that, for example, men should earn and women should be carers. Wollstonecraft writes that 'men endeavour to ... render us alluring objects for a moment; and women, intoxicated by the adoration which men, under the influence of their senses, pay them, do not seek to obtain a durable interest in their hearts, or to become the friends of the fellow-creatures who find amusement in their society'.[33] Or, more simply in the famous words of de Beauvoir, 'one is not born, but rather becomes, a woman.'[34]

What such writers tell us is that our preferences and desires are created through our interaction with society. Importantly, they 'internalize' power and status structures. What we think we want in part reflects what society wants us to want, whether that is to be a domestic goddess or a high-earning financier. Cultural norms and values can affect and constrain our decisions in obvious ways, but they can also do it in these much more subtle ways: they can become internalized.

The idea of socialization suggests that a focus on individual agency and ensuring equality of opportunity is not sufficient for women's freedom. Women may feel that they are freely 'choosing' to do particular things – whether that be to choose concealing or revealing clothing, or to aspire to become a housewife or a page-three girl – when in a different world they may have chosen to do something else entirely. Where constraints are internalized rather than externalized, they can be all the more difficult to budge. Doing so requires more than giving individual women the freedom to choose; it is also necessary to tackle the big picture, the wider structures of society.

This, of course, helps explain why patriarchy can be slow to change. It also accounts for why when change does happen, it cannot be understood in terms of a 'rational, self-interested calculating' being. Naila Kabeer notes that collective action is necessary for 'social transformation'.[35] Alice Evans notes the importance of 'norm perceptions' – of what we think other people think is acceptable. Since most care work is undertaken behind closed doors, it can therefore be difficult to change the perception that care work is 'for women' (and is 'unmanly'). Visibility is therefore key to change.[36]

However, although it is easy to accept that society can have a powerful influence on our individual choices, the policy implications should not allow others to override the individual preferences of women. When taken to its extreme, the notion of socialization can be used as justification to force individuals to do something against their will – 'for their own good'. That includes western authorities banning women from wearing headscarves or western feminist groups campaigning against sex work. Here the assumptions of mainstream economics – that of 'rational, self-interested and calculating' beings

– can in fact help to rein in such thinking. People are, quite simply, assumed to know what is best for themselves. That might be missing something but so too is the opposing view, one which can lead us to incursions on women's individual freedom. Ultimately, we must walk a fine line between the two.

## Conclusion

In this chapter we have seen both the benefits of and limitations to women's freedom of economists' concept of individuals as rational, self-interested and calculating beings. From a feminist point of view, the problem with economists' assumptions is something other than that identified by behavioural economics: rather, it's the neglect of the body, the family and society.

The historically male concept of freedom has resulted in a neglect of women's bodily autonomy, including their freedom to control their own fertility. This neglect of fertility leads us to the second problem with economics: its neglect of family. In the words of Michelle Baddeley, '[t]he standard assumption in economics is that we all behave as if others do not actually exist as individuals'.[37] The private sphere of life has, sadly, been seen as entirely separate to the economy. In recent years, economists have, of course, tried to make some connection between the individual and society, developing the notion of 'social capital'. Furthermore, behavioural economics is increasingly noting the power of social influence, turning to sociology and not just psychology. However, the gender element has been largely ignored.

Once fertility, family and society are brought into the picture, we see the way in which our decisions are shaped by numerous tensions: between what we want and what society expects; between our own inner interests and those of the people we care about; between our need for autonomy but the reality of dependence; and between our hearts and our heads, or our brains versus our bodies. This means that to fully understand the economy, we need to think about *both* sets of polar extremes: individuality and relationships; independence and dependence; and reason and emotion.[38] Rather than opposing one another, the mainstream neoclassical economic model of human behaviour and the behavioural-cum-feminist one need to come together: it is by considering the life that goes on between the two, rather than at the extremes, that we will be able to build a better understanding of the economy, one that can help deliver equitable and sustainable prosperity.[39]

# Conclusion

Deep within the entrance hall of the Woolworth Building – one of New York's oldest skyscrapers and a living monument to American capitalism – is a golden mosaic. At the very centre can be found the goddess of commerce, flanked on each side by two men on bended knees presenting the goddess with the transport innovations that first enabled globalization: the ship and the railway. Although the mosaic might suggest that feminism and economics are natural bedfellows in the heavenly world of the gods, it is not the case here on earth. As we have seen throughout this book, when it comes to almost all of the big questions – from the causes of prosperity, boom and bust and inequality to debates about the state and the market – economists' neglect of sex and gender is severely limiting their ability to find the right answers, or to design and deliver appropriate policies.

As we saw in part I, where we looked at the causes of prosperity, the now popular story of how the West grew rich is largely one of male inventors and industrialists, with female liberation presented as a mere by-product. However, the truth is that women were equally important in the rise of the West; it's just that their role has gone relatively unnoticed. At a time when women's rights and freedoms are under attack in large parts of the world, the role of women in creating successful economies must now be recognized. If there is one key difference between the West and 'the rest' that can help explain their relative fortunes, it is women's freedom.

Advances in women's freedom were central to the story of how the West grew rich, feeding through to affect all the factors that drive economic prosperity: technology, savings, skills, entrepreneurism and even democracy. Until greater economic significance is placed on gender equality as the cause – not consequence – of economic success, women's freedom will not be given the importance it deserves, and gender inequalities will go unaddressed. That includes unequal access to markets and resources, the inadequate birth control and unequal distribution of care. If policy makers in poor countries want to identify the obstacles in the way of their own country's growth, they only need to look inside their own homes.

As we saw in part II, if we want to explain the conjunction of a slowdown in western economic growth, together with rising income inequality, we also need to bring women's freedom centre stage. It wasn't so long ago that the world was divided into two: in one half, women had at least a reasonable degree of equality and, with it, an economy on a relatively sound footing; in the other, women had, on average, far fewer rights, even bigger families to take care of, and both they and their economy paid the price. As the world has gone global, these two very different equilibria have been forced together, with the latter acting to undermine the high-wage equilibrium of the former. It is little wonder that western working-class wages have stagnated and income inequality has rocketed. In time, one would hope that women's freedoms would expand across all countries, meaning that we can all converge on the high-wage high-freedom equilibria, and then we can return to the virtuous circle that once existed between rising wages and rising productivity.

However, as we saw in chapter 3, we cannot assume that gender equality is on a naturally improving trend towards full equality. Gender inequality has risen as well as fallen throughout the course of history. Today, birth control is underfunded, leaving many of the world's poorest women without access to the vital supplies they need.[1] The UN Family Planning Agency faces a US$700 million funding gap.[2] Even in the West, women's freedoms – including their access to birth control – are under threat. So too is their liberty to dress as they wish – whether to fully cover or reveal – and, as we saw in chapter 5, their freedom to monetize their bodies in the same way that they can monetize their brains. We must not be complacent that women's freedoms will forever increase or that women always know what's best for other women. When it comes to policy, we must make sure that women are free to make their own choices, whether or not other women (or men) like the choices they make. The emphasis of policy should be on opening up options for women – not closing them down, such as by making access to birth control more difficult, banning clothes that are either too concealing or revealing, or criminalizing the buying (or selling) of sex.

Sex and gender equality are not only relevant for prosperity and inequality, they also have a bearing on perhaps the greatest challenge we face in the modern world: the depletion of our environment. Despite the fact that the world has been able to sustain an ever-expanding population for the past two centuries, there is a limit to how many people we can realistically fit on the planet without it costing the natural world. Given that it is the world's poorest women who bear the brunt of environmental damage, gender and the environment cannot be separated.[3] Indeed, feminist economists have drawn parallels between how the economy 'free-rides' on the 'free labour' provided by women within the home and how it behaves likewise in regard to the natural world. Addressing environmental issues is often seen in terms of wind farms and other such technologies. However, reproduction is just as, if not more, relevant. As we have seen throughout this book, where women have complete control over their own bodies, they make fertility decisions of their own choosing that, by happy coincidence, fit much more neatly with the ecological limits of the planet than when they have no such choice at all. Birth control is essential to saving the planet and yet, as I have already noted, remains significantly underfunded.

Throughout our discussions, we have seen both the virtuous and vicious dynamics that are at work when it comes to gender and the economy. The gender gap doesn't just reflect gender inequalities; it also feeds into them, making it more likely that women retreat into the home and men become the main income-earners. Equality within the home cannot be achieved until there is equality in the market; however, in turn, equality in the market is difficult to achieve when there is still so much inequality within the home. This serves to explain both why economies can seem trapped in situations of gender inequality but also why, once things start to change, positive feedback effects are created that serve to bring about relatively rapid improvement. And, once gender equality does improve, it places the economy on a stronger footing and, if properly channelled, in turn feeds back to further aid gender equality, creating a further virtuous circle. Trying to get the process started, as happened in north-western Europe in the centuries before the Industrial Revolution, is the tricky part. However, as we have seen throughout, markets that provide opportunities for women are a vital part of this story.

Access to markets is key to providing women with an escape from social practices that stand in the way of their freedom. We have seen the way in which opportunities to engage in paid labour brought about radical changes in family life in Britain, including in the elimination of early marriage, all of which culminated in the Industrial

Revolution. Access to markets, which in turn requires access to resources, education and training, is equally vital for women in poorer countries today. Evidence suggests that gender inequality is significantly lower in parts of China where more job opportunities have historically been available for women, such as in the cotton textile sector.[4]

This does not, however, mean that markets are perfect. To make the most of markets, we also need to be ready to question the laws, regulations and institutions that underpin them, all of which can themselves embody heavily gendered social norms. That includes revising property law, family law and employment law, and improving women's political representation so that the experiences of women do not fall under the radar. The expectation that unpaid care is 'women's work' remains a major problem in almost all rich economies, something which policy could do much more to address (or at least not perpetuate) through taxation and welfare systems. When ushering in change, we have, however, to be aware of 'unexpected consequences' if we are to ensure that policies to 'empower' women do not backfire. For example, changes in inheritance law have been shown to increase the murder rate of female family members,[5] greater access to reproductive technology (such as abortion) has resulted in women being put under pressure to abort baby girls,[6] whilst increasing labour market access can increase the total amount of work expected of women (giving them a 'double-shift' of paid as well as unpaid work) and has even been shown to increase domestic violence.[7] Many of these effects are precisely the opposite of those predicted by economic models. If such adverse effects of gender equality policies are to be avoided, complementary laws may need to be adopted, such as those tackling violence against women. However, men also need to be brought onboard, and social norms need to be tackled – and this may be best done through popular culture rather than by economic policy. The way men and women's 'roles' are represented in everything from soap operas to advertising can greatly affect what men and women expect of one another, creating a feeling of anxiety when their socially constructed identities are challenged.[8] To improve gender outcomes in poorer countries, a 'big push' is therefore required to target social norms at the same time as women's access to the market is enhanced, and the foundations of the market – its laws, regulations and institutions - are reformed to eliminate gender bias. This big push can help limit the backlash effects, leading to a total effect that is more than the sum of its parts. A half-hearted approach, tinkering here and there, cannot be expected to deliver material change.

As we saw in part III of the book, feminist thinking has a lot to contribute to debates about the state versus the market, highlighting both some under-appreciated downsides as well as some under-appreciated upsides. Feminism has a lot to offer, wherever you are on the political spectrum. Perhaps the single greatest contribution from feminist scholarship, relevant to rich as well as poorer countries, is to suggest the addition of a vital third sphere to our thinking about state and markets: the domestic sphere.[9] It is a sphere that dramatically changes the way we think about the trade-offs between markets and the state, suggesting that they can in fact be complementary rather than conflicted. Only by addressing the 'crisis of care' – the way in which the economy depends on 'free labour' within the home – can we achieve more equitable and sustainable growth outcomes. When the state cuts back on spending, as has been the case with structural reform in poorer countries and austerity in richer ones, it cannot keep expecting women to pick up the pieces. There is a lesson to be learned from chapter 7: a higher level of women's freedom helped the West to build relatively capable states, ones in which the state and the market worked with, rather than against, one another. Further such progress can still be made on this score today, both at home and abroad.

Altogether, if we want a more prosperous economy, and also one where that prosperity is sustainable and equitable, economists need to start recognizing the transformative power of women's freedom – and doing more to support it.

I first began studying economics because I wanted to answer big questions. I wanted to understand the sources of prosperity and poverty – including the economic decline and destitution which surrounded me when I was growing up. Having lived through my first experience of boom and bust in the late 1980s and early 1990s during a recession that hit my parents' small business particularly hard, I also wanted to discover whether instability was inevitable, or whether, having seen the human toll, there was anything more that policy makers could do about it. When studying for my A-levels between the ages of 16 and 18, I devoured the works of the classical economists on the bus back and forth to Oldham Sixth Form College. I remember exactly where I was on that bus the first time I opened my library copy of Adam Smith's *Wealth of Nations*. I was hooked. It led me on to an economics degree at the University of Cambridge. Before long, however, I realized that what I was being taught in lectures wasn't quite what I had been expecting. Where were the big debates? Where was the intermingling of society, politics, history and philosophy of the kind needed to truly understand economic outcomes? I spent most of my time applying maths to simplistic models of decidedly un-human behaviour – and increasingly so with every year.

At this time, in the late 1990s, feminism was not, however, at a high point. After all, we had all been brought up – thanks to the Spice Girls and their 'girl power'– to assume that we women had the same potential as the boys we studied alongside. However, as the years went by, and as shown throughout this book, I increasingly came to realize that to answer all of those big questions, it was necessary to think about both sex and gender – about both the biological and socially constructed differences between men and women. The more I began to confront the inequalities between men and women, the more I realized that feminism had passed economics by. It was as if the women's movement had never happened.

So why has economics failed to embrace feminism, and how, going forward, does it need to change if it is to become more open to feminist concerns? Well, let me present a humble manifesto for change, containing four simple and very achievable demands.

1   Re-centre economics on content rather than on approach. Economics might make more progress if, as is the case with almost every other academic subject, it was defined less by an approach – one that involves applying the assumptions of a rational, maximizing and self-interested economic agent to situations of scarcity – and more by its actual content. If this were the case, then the vast human activity that takes place outside the market, and yet is nevertheless essential to the economy, along with the broader connections between the public and private spheres, would in turn become an essential part of economics, rather than being either ignored or left for non-economists to consider. As things stand, they remain nowhere to be seen in the common core of material included in an economics degree.

2   Increasing interdisciplinarity. One cannot understand the workings of an economy – including what makes it poor or prosperous – without also knowing something about history, about society, about philosophy, and being cognizant not just of class but also of gender and race. This means that economics needs to become much more open and interdisciplinary, as the student-led groups Post-Crash Economics and Rethinking Economics have called for. Economics needs to stop seeing itself as 'the king of the social sciences'. It needs to refrain from its historic academic imperialism, from seeking to bring its insights to bear on every subject, without listening to and learning from what those other subjects have to offer in return. One study of bibliometrics data found that the top articles in politics and sociology reference economists between five and eight times more than the other way around.[10]

Economists' interactions with other academic disciplines need to be two-way; not one way. But that will only happen once economists come to respect other disciplines.

Rather than appearing dull and dry, as a branch of applied mathematics, economics could be much more exciting than it is at present, bringing together all of the many aspects of human life in order to think big thoughts about poverty and prosperity. Markets, the state and society are fundamentally linked. If we are to understand the multitude of connections between them, we need to see them in the round, rather than to separate them out and treat them as three different spheres of study, with concrete walls dividing them. Breaking down these walls would help us to appreciate, as I have tried to emphasize throughout, that the market is not an independent entity. The rules by which markets operate, and the agents within them, are the product of the state and society. Markets can be 'made', and they can also be made to work better for those involved. In the process of doing so, however, economists cannot escape difficult ethical and philosophical questions or social assumptions and taboos. Those include the notion that the sciences are superior to the arts, that the brain is superior to the body, that care is women's work, and that sex and women's bodies are sinful. The latter holds the key to tackling so many practices that curtail women's freedom, from restrictions on women's work and mobility that aim to preserve their sexual honour through to FGM, restricted birth control and clothing that is intended to disincentivize sex.

3 Economists, including feminist ones like myself, need to spend more time listening and less time talking, not just to policy makers and businesses, but also to those on the periphery of what we think of as 'formal' economic activity – immigrant labour, welfare claimants, workers in sweatshops overseas and sex workers. By listening, we can learn; we can learn things that can help us develop a much better understanding of poverty and prosperity, and what policy changes are needed to improve the lives of those who are, sadly, all too regularly ignored. And, in the vein of 'feminist standpoint epistemology' (of women speaking up), it can also help us to challenge the social order.[11]

Sometimes even small changes can make a big difference. Take the simple administrative mechanics of the welfare state, not something that economists would normally consider but which can affect poverty just as much as the size of benefits themselves. Whose account benefits are paid into – the main income earner or the caregiver – can, for example, have powerful effects on the lives of women.[12] How long it takes to receive benefits after making an application also has big effects on how 'risky' it is for an unemployed person to seek and accept work, work which increasingly comes without a long-term contract, or for an abused woman to leave her partner. When it comes to taxation, whether taxes are paid at the level of the household or by individuals can also make a big difference to women's lives. Where women are secondary as opposed to primary income earners, but taxation takes place at the household level, the effective marginal tax rate they pay is higher, as their partner's higher earnings take them beyond the lower tax threshold. This may help to equate incomes between families, but it acts to widen the gender gap within families.[13]

4   Economics needs to admit that it displays an aggressive form of masculinity – and so does economic policy. Macho biases are, as we saw in part IV, interwoven throughout the whole fabric that is economics, a fabric that is all too often assumed to be 'gender neutral'.[14] These macho biases deeply affect everything from what economists choose to measure and study to the assumptions they make when modelling the economy and the methods they most value. As we have seen in the course of the book, the most popular measure of all – GDP – ignores both the vital contribution made by care to the economy and the sustainability of the growth process. Taking these things on board isn't simply a matter of tinkering at the seams. Calculations suggest that unpaid work alone amounts to some 20–50 per cent of GDP,[15] and that, once we adjust for well-being and sustainability, the performance of the economy in the last few decades looks nowhere near as impressive. Economic change can bring a dark as well as a positive side and, unless we force ourselves to capture the former as well as the latter, we risk not only reducing rather than enhancing our standard of living but depleting the economic foundations on which future prosperity will be built. Rather than taking for granted existing economic measures, economists need to spend more time reflecting on how we choose to measure the economy.

When it comes to assumptions, economists have prized the autonomous independent agent, ignoring or downplaying the human connections between individuals, meaning that difficult questions – of great relevance to the economy – have been sidestepped. How, for example, should we deal with the situation of dependency that we all face at different stages of life? By failing to address the reality of dependence, we have been left with an escalating 'crisis of care' including not only the 'problem' of elderly and child care but health problems associated with juggling too many balls, fertility rates that have fallen below replacement levels in many western countries, and low pay for those working in the care sector. Many of today's economic problems – and its environmental ones – are rooted in a failure to deal with dependency.

In the words of Jane Humphries, 'Feminist economics requires the central character be changed from the autonomous, isolated agent who needs no social contacts to a socially and materially situated human being.'[16] By assuming away the connections involved in human life, economics has ignored many of the real-life economic challenges that face us all every day.

According to Paula England, economists have not only neglected dependency but have also placed 'the independent self' on a pedestal.[17] Caregivers are cast as detractors from economic activity and are regularly presented as a potential pool that can be tapped in an effort to push up GDP, ignoring the fact that they are already contributing to the economy.[18] Although the feminist project has often been interpreted as one in which women achieve the same degree of independence as men, a world in which we are all independent is impossible. Achieving gender equality should not be about 'making women like men', as if what is considered masculine is somehow better, but about both men and women meeting in the middle. As Nancy Fraser argues, that means we all need to contribute to care, not just women and not just mothers.[19] Without it, there will be no future generation. There will be no future economy.

The world of work can no longer continue to operate on the assumption that we all have someone at home to press our suits, do the dishes and look after the kids whilst we stay at our desk and work late. According to Fraser, it is not single mums who deserve to be cast as free riders, but the men who have for decades shirked their caring responsibilities, piling them onto their partners whilst they themselves relish the public glory and power that paid work brings. The same applies to the companies whose profits have been built on all of those same invisible behind-the-scenes women – the women who have given birth to the workforce and who have spent years turning out their partners clean, tidy and well fed every day. Policy needs to recognize the current conflicts between the workplace and the home, and the deeply ingrained gendered assumptions about work and care. Policy – including that of austerity – also needs to be aware of its own gendered consequences. As Diane Elson has argued, the domestic sector cannot be assumed to be a 'bottomless well' that can automatically pick up the slack when governments decide to cut back on spending. Unless it receives inputs from other sectors to match the outputs that it provides, care resources are depleted – and so too is the base for all other activity.[20]

By continuing along its current path, economics has succeeded in one way at least: in making itself much less relevant to people's lives than it truly deserves to be. If taken seriously, this four-point manifesto would give economics a renewed power, the power to become a more flexible, more human and more useful discipline. By feeding through to policy, it would not only improve the lives of women the world over, it would also serve to bring about more equitable and sustainable economic outcomes for us all.

Robert Solow, Nobel prizewinner for his work on the causes of prosperity, allegedly said that 'everything reminds Milton [Friedman, a fellow Nobel prizewinner] of the money supply. Well, everything reminds me of sex, but I keep it out of the paper.'[21] This is precisely why economics is failing. What economics needs is not the X-Factor. It is the 'Sex Factor'.

I fell in love with economics as a 16-year-old girl growing up in a deprived part of deindustrializing Manchester in the 1990s. I am still in love with it today, despite nearly falling out of love with it at university. Economics is my life – and always will be. I just wish that it loved me – as a feminist – back in the same way.

Perhaps one day it will be unnecessary for me to appear naked at the Royal Economic Society conference in an effort to draw attention to the elephant in the room: economics has a serious sex problem – a problem about which economists remain in denial, and which has restricted economic growth, increased inequality and damaged the planet. It has hurt us all.

Until economics faces up to its problem with sex, I will just have to keep on making the point in every way I know how – with and without words.

# Notes

## Introduction

1 Becker (1981); Grossbard (2006).
2 Fourcade, Ollion and Algan (2015).
3 Humphries (1995), p. xxvi–xxvii; Ferber and Lowry (1976).
4 Harding (1986); Bordo (1986); Nelson (1992); McCloskey (2008).
5 Ferber and Teiman (1981); Nelson (1992): 122; Pujol (1998), p. 2.
6 Summarized in Tankersley and Scheiber (2018).
7 Humphries (1995), p. xiv.
8 Ibid.; Nelson (1992).
9 Wang (2016); UNFPA (2017); Rodgers (2018).
10 Bearak et al. (2018).
11 UNFPA (2017).

## Part I Introduction

1 World Bank GDP per capita figures for 2017, available at https://data.worldbank.org/indicator/NY.GDP.PCAP.PP.CD
2 Milanovic (2015).
3 Wiesner-Hanks (2015), ch. 4.

## Chapter 1 Censored: How the West (Supposedly) Got Ahead

1 Fara (2010).
2 Ehret (2014).

3  Akyeampong et al. (2014), pp. 5–7.
4  Akyeampong et al. (2014), p. 7; Inikori (2014).
5  Bateman (2016b).
6  The Dependency School argues that the rise of the West and decline of the rest are part of the same process (Rodney 1972; Amin and Pearce 1976; Wallerstein 1976).
7  Bateman (2016b).
8  Stiglitz (2016).
9  Bateman (2016b); Van Bavel (2016); Spek, Leeuwen and Zanden (2013).
10  Contrary to Polanyi (1944) and Finley (1999).
11  Polanyi (1966); Van Bavel (2016); Inikori (2007); Akyeampong et al. (2014), pp. 8–10, and the chapters contained therein.
12  Bateman (2016b).
13  McCloskey (2010).
14  De Moor and Van Zanden (2010); Ogilvie (2011), pp. 91, 183, 187, 414; Howell (2010), pp. 100–1; Fontaine (2014), pp. 134, 146.
15  North and Thomas (1973); North (1981, 1990); Jones (1988); De Long and Schleifer (1993); Landes (1999); Hall and Jones (1999); Parente and Prescott (2002); Acemoglu, Johnson and Robinson (2001, 2002, 2005); Acemoglu and Robinson (2012); Engerman and Sokoloff (2002); Greif (2006). Along the way, there has been a significant debate amongst economists regarding the relative role of geography and institutions in prosperity creation. On geography, see Jones (1987), Diamond (1999), Gallup, Sachs and Mellinger (1999) and Olsson and Hibbs (2005). On how geography and institutions can interact, see Acemoglu, Johnson and Robinson (2001); Engerman and Sokoloff (2002); Easterly and Levine (2003); Rodrik, Subramanian and Trebbi (2004).
16  North and Weingast (1989); De Long and Schleifer (1993).
17  Van Zanden, Buringh and Bosker (2011).
18  Ghanem and Baten (2016), p. 221; Austin (2016); Broadberry (2016), p. 38.
19  Austin (2016).
20  Akyeampong et al. (2014), p. 10; Bates (2014); Reid (2014).
21  Glaeser et al. (2004).
22  Ogilvie and Carus (2014).
23  Examples of using culture to explain economic outcomes range from Weber (2016) to Wiener (1981) and Landes (1999), who writes 'If we learn anything from the history of economic development, it is that culture makes all the difference.'
24  Nunn (2012), Spolaore and Wacziarg (2009, 2013); Michalopoulos and Papaioannou (2011). Also Guiso, Sapienza and Zingales (2006); Bisin and Verdier (2000, 2001); McCloskey (2010, 2011, 2017); Alesina and Giuliano (2015); Tabellini (2008, 2010); Mokyr (2017); Rubin (2018).
25  Michalopoulos and Papaioannou (2010).
26  Tabellini (2008, 2010).
27  Kroeber and Kluckhohn (1952).
28  Richerson and Boyd, 2006, p. 5.

29 McCloskey (2010).
30 Michalopoulos and Xue (2017).
31 Rubin (2018) considers interactions between religion and political institutions.
32 Greif (1994, 2006); Alesina and Giuliano (2010); Platteau (2014); Rubin (2018).
33 Alesina and Giuliano (2010).
34 Bryson (2016).
35 Mokyr (2009, 2017).
36 The concept of the Industrious Revolution is relevant here. See de Vries (2008).
37 Mokyr (2017).
38 According to Bates (2014), p. 439, Africa's problem was a lack of verification and diffusion of knowledge, due to limited literacy and a desire to keep ideas 'secret'.
39 McCloskey (2010, 2011, 2017).
40 Austin (2016), p. 321; Mandala (1984).
41 Platteau (2014).
42 Platteau (2014); Wiesner-Hanks (2015), pp. 253–4.
43 Ibid, p. 268.
44 Ibid, pp. 66–9.
45 Ibid, p. 69.
46 McClintock (1995), pp. 22–7.
47 Williams (1994); Eltis and Engerman (2000); Fatah-Black and van Rossum (2014); Akyeampong et al. (2014); Beckert (2015).
48 Allen (2001, 2009, 2014). See Scheidel (2010) for ancient economies.
49 Stephenson (2018); Allen (2018).
50 See e.g. Geloso (2018). Also Gragnolati, Moschella and Pugliese (2011).
51 Humphries (2013); Humphries and Schneider (2018).
52 Acemoglu (2002) contains a model which shows that where the elasticity of substitution between factors of production is low, Allen's intuition is correct. Otherwise, technologies may focus more on the abundant rather than the scarce factors of production, as Humphries (2013) argues was the case in the cotton industry.
53 See e.g. Rodrik (1998) and Hausmann, Rodriguez and Wagner (2006). Also Broadberry and Wallis (2017).
54 See Jones (1988) on Asia, Ober (2015) on Greece, Fouquet and Broadberry (2015) on Italy and de Vries and van der Woude (1997) on Holland. More generally, Mokyr (1990) and Fara (2010).
55 Allen (2001); Broadberry (2016), pp. 35–6.
56 Inikori (2014).
57 Acemoglu, Johnson and Robinson (2002).
58 Pomeranz (2012) and Parthasarathi (1998) argue that China and India (respectively) were on a par with Europe until around 1800. Others date the divergence earlier: Ma (2016), p. 189; Broadberry (2016), p. 35.

59  Bertola and Ocampo (2016), p. 123.
60  Ashraf and Galor (2011).
61  Clark (2007) argues that the survival rate (the evolutionary advantage) was greatest for families who educated their children, leading to a gradual rise in the proportion of the population that was educated.
62  For a technical exposition of this unified growth theory, see Galor and Weil (2000); Galor (2011).
63  Galor and Mountford (2008).
64  For a summary of the various economic factors affecting fertility, including declining infant mortality and child labour, expanding capital markets, increasing demand for skills and a declining gender wage gap, see Galor (2005).
65  For example, it doesn't receive a single mention in Galor (2005). Cinnirella, Klemp and Weisdorf (2017) find some limited evidence of birth control in use, albeit clearly not to modern standards.
66  Rodgers (2018).
67  UNFPA (2017).
68  Diamond (1999); Campbell (2016).
69  Stern (2006).
70  Raworth (2018).
71  Hawken (2017).
72  Rai, Hoskyns and Thomas (2011).
73  Agarwal (1992): 120.
74  Nelson and Power (2018).
75  On social provisioning, see Nelson (1993) and Power (2004). On social reproduction, see Rai, Hoskyns and Thomas (2011).
76  Coyle (2014).
77  Bjørnholt and McKay (2014); Berik (2018).
78  Agarwal (1992): 150.
79  Habtezion (2013), pp. 2–3.
80  Akyeampong et al. (2014), p. 7.
81  Akyeampong et al. (2014), pp. 14–20.
82  Acemoglu, Johnson and Robinson (2002); Engerman and Sokoloff (2002).
83  Steckel and Prince (2001).
84  This body of research is summarized, with references, in Akyeampong et al. (2014), pp. 15–20.
85  Ibid., p. 19. Also see Bates (2014), p. 437.
86  Akyeampong et al. (2014), p. 20.
87  As Mokyr (2006) writes: '[t]hroughout history, the wealth resulting from economic growth has tended to attract predators and parasites the way jam attracts houseflies.'
88  Acemoglu and Robinson (2000).
89  Also see Parente and Prescott (1999).
90  Mokyr (2006); Mokyr and Nye (2007): 67–8.
91  Elbaum and Lazonick (1984); Mokyr and Nye (2007); Glaeser et al. (2004).

## Chapter 2    Uncensored: The Secret Recipe of Economic Success

1   Foreword, p. xiii. Note that this international agenda has certainly not been without feminist critique. See, for example, Prügl (2016), who argues that it is neoliberalism but with a feminist face.

2   Sometimes referred to as modernization theory. See Inglehart and Norris (2003), pp. 7–10; Dilli, Rijpma and Carmichael (2015). For an outline of the links in both directions, see Duflo (2012).

3   On the former, see Kabeer and Natali (2013); Morrison, Dhushyanth and Sinha (2007); Duflo (2012). On the latter, see Mies (1986).

4   Studies which find a link include Klasen (1999, 2002); Klasen and Lamanna (2009); Barsh and Yee (2011); Woetzel et al. (2015). On the opposing side, see Seguino (2000a,b, 2011). For a summary, Prügl (2016).

5   Morrison, Dhushyanth and Sinha (2007), abstract and p. 37. Bandiera and Natraj (2013). Also see Duflo (2012) and Prügl (2016). However, Kabeer and Natali (2013) argue that there is a relatively stronger link from gender equality to growth than there is in the opposite direction.

6   Sen (1999).

7   For a feminist reinterpretation, see Hirschmann (2007).

8   Nussbaum (2013).

9   Prügl (2016): 45.

10   For a full discussion, see the 2016 *Feminist Economics* 22(1) special issue on 'Voice and Agency'.

11   Van Zanden, Rijpma and Kok (2017).

12   Carmichael, de Pleijt and van Zanden (2016).

13   Ibid.

14   For a comparison of European with other family systems, see Burguiere et al. (1996); Das Gupta (1999); Therborn (2004); Kok (2017); and the references contained therein.

15   Das Gupta (1999): 173.

16   Engels and Hunt (2010).

17   Lévi-Strauss (1956, 1970. For a discussion, see Rubin (1975).

18   Within Asia, for example, South India and South-east Asia had more bilateral kinship systems than elsewhere in the region (such as North India and China), which was relatively more favourable for women (Das Gupta et al. 2003: 9). To quote Kok (2017), '[t]he family systems of Sri Lanka and of most regions in Southeast Asia seem to have offered women more "leeway" than they could enjoy in India, China or Japan.' As Kok notes, here were also differences between southern China and elsewhere in China, whilst in Japan women were in a more favourable position – at least until the eleventh century.

19   Howell (2010), pp. 116–17; Wiesner-Hanks (2015).

20   Edlund and Lagerlöf (2006); Edlund (2006): 622.

21   Edlund and Lagerlöf (2006): 304–7.

22  Das Gupta (1999): 178.
23  Das Gupta et al. (2003).
24  Agarwal (1998).
25  See Eswaran (2014), ch. 5.
26  Kok (2017).
27  Kok (2017); Therborn (2004).
28  Van den Heuvel (2007); De Moor and Van Zanden (2010); Ogilvie (2011), pp. 91, 183, 187, 414; Howell (2010), pp. 100–1; Fontaine (2014), pp. 134, 146.
29  Howell (2010), pp. 100–1, 110, 140; Fontaine (2014), pp. 142–3.
30  Fontaine (2014), p. 138.
31  Howell (2010), p. 100. Also Fontaine (2014), pp. 135, 147.
32  Kok (2017); Coquery-Vidrovitch (1997).
33  Kok (2017); Robertson (1988): 446.
34  Kok (2017); Sheldon (2017); Berger and White (2008); Mandala (1984): 142; Coquery-Vidrovitch (1997): 'it was mainly women who farmed.'
35  Berger and White (2008), p. 6; Robertson (1988): 'Sub-Saharan African women have borne and now bear the major social recognised responsibility for providing substance for themselves and their children.'
36  Austin (2016).
37  On the economic causes of polygamy, see Boserup (1970) and Becker (1981).
38  Robertson (1988): 441.
39  Coquery-Vidrovitch (1997): p. 10.
40  Robertson (1988).
41  Platteau (2014).
42  Robertson (1988).
43  Anderson (2007); Eswaran (2014), p. 224. On the causes of both, see Eswaran (2014), ch. 7.
44  Botticini and Siow (2003).
45  Rao (1993, 2007).
46  Wrigley and Schofield (1981); de Moor and van Zanden (2010); Clark (2007), table 4.2, p. 76.
47  Kok (2017).
48  For a discussion of child marriage in India, see Kok (2017). Some parts of Asia, such as in Sri Lanka and Southeast Asia, where the family system was less adverse to women's freedom, the age of marriage was higher than in India or China.
49  Wiesner-Hanks (2015), p. 148.
50  Ibid., pp. 103, 176, 199.
51  Ibid., pp. 105, 107. See Humphries and Weisdorf (2015) for more detail, which shows strong longer-term fluctuations.
52  Kok (2017).
53  Van den Heuvel (2007); de Moor and van Zanden (2010; Ogilvie (2011), pp. 91, 183, 187, 414; Howell (2010), pp. 100–1; Fontaine (2014), pp. 134, 146.

54 Wiesner-Hanks (2015), p. 77.
55 Wiesner-Hanks (2015).
56 Ibid.
57 McClintock (1995); Morgan (2004); Campbell, Miers and Miller (2008); Hartman (2016).
58 Kok (2017).
59 Alesina and Giuliano (2010).
60 De Moor and van Zanden (2010).
61 Ogilvie and Carus (2014). Fontaine (2014) notes how women have historically relied more on informal markets due to discriminatory practices in those commonly used by men.
62 Dyer (2009), p. 218.
63 Foreman-Peck (2011); Bateman (2016e).
64 Bateman (2016c).
65 Hajnal (1982).
66 There has been some debate. See Dennison and Ogilvie (2014) and Carmichael et al. (2015).
67 White et al. (1988).
68 Tertilt (2005).
69 Humphries and Weisdorf (2015) have disputed the extent to which women's wages rose with the Black Death, but it is still likely that they were greatly in demand (perhaps more so).
70 De Moor and van Zanden (2010): 22.
71 Black, Grönqvist and Öckert (2017); Humphries (2012), Table 2. For modern-day evidence on the higher poverty rates for larger families: 'Growing Unequal? Income Distribution and Poverty in OECD countries,' OECD (2008), p. 138.
72 Humphries (2012), p. 22.
73 Also see Klemp and Weisdorf (2018).
74 De Moor and van Zanden (2010): 24.
75 Fontaine (2014), p. 150.
76 See McCloskey (2010) for a detailed discussion and critique.
77 Lambrecht (2013).
78 On sex as a powerful economic force, see Adshade (2013).
79 Laslett (1988).
80 Greif (1994, 2006); Alesina and Giuliano (2010, 2011).
81 Todd (1988, 2011).
82 Alesina and Giuliano (2011) find that in the modern day, stronger kinship ties are associated with less political participation.
83 Eswaran (2014), pp. 322–5.
84 Van Bavel and Rijpma (2015); Alesina and Giuliano (2010) note that preferences for redistribution are stronger amongst women.
85 Esping-Andersen (2000); Offer (1997); Alesina and Giuliano (2010).
86 Smith (1986), pp. 205–6; Wrigley (1988), pp. 118–22; Solar (1997). This view has been tempered by Hindle (2004), pp. 398–405, 410.
87 Lambrecht (2013).

88 Alesina et al.(2015) find that stronger kinship ties are associated with lower mobility of labour (as the emotional costs of moving are greater), and with it there is a greater desire to regulate local labour markets.
89 Lambrecht (2013), p. 28.
90 Roberts (2016).
91 Most notably Boserup (1970).

## Chapter 3 When Did Sexism Begin?

1 World Economic Forum (2017).
2 Goldin (1990), pp. 59–63. On the United Kingdom, see Humphries and Weisdorf (2015).
3 World Bank (2011); Duflo (2012).
4 Konner (2015). Also see Dyble et al. (2015).
5 Engels (2010) with an introduction by T. Hunt.
6 Also see Hartmann (1976).
7 Alesina, Giuliano and Nunn (2013).
8 Smuts (1995).
9 Giuliano (2017).
10 Scott (2018).
11 Carmichael, de Pleijt and van Zanden (2016).
12 De Moor and van Zanden (2010). There is some debate about precisely when the change in family structure occurred, with evidence of change either side of the Black Death. See Edwards and Ogilvie (2018).
13 Voigtländer and Voth (2013).
14 Wiesner-Hanks (2015).
15 Ogilvie and Carus (2014), p. 467.
16 Horrell and Humphries (1995).
17 Burnette (2008).
18 Ibid. Also in the United States (Goldin 1990).
19 Wrigley and Schofield (1981).
20 Bowden (1925), pp. 229, 342; Richards (1974): 340, fn. 16; 341, fn. 18.
21 Pinchbek (1930), pp. 306, 375.
22 Richards (1974): 347; Checkland (1964), p. 216.
23 Folbre (1991); Kessler-Harris (2001). On the implications for government policy, Pateman (1988); Pedersen (1995, 2018); Kessler-Harris (2001); Esping-Andersen (2013); Cooke (2011).
24 Amott and Matthaei (1991), esp. pp. 321–4.
25 Ibid., p. 322.
26 Ibid., pp. 4–5.
27 Wheeler and Thompson (1825). Quoted in Bryson (2016), p. 28.
28 Perlmann and Margo (2001).
29 Amott and Matthaei (1991); Bryson (2016), pp. 75–6.
30 Bryson (20016), pp. 82–91.

31 Goldin (2018).
32 Esping-Andersen (2009); Goldin (2018).
33 Xue (2016) finds greater gender equality today in parts of China in which cotton production developed, offering women great labour market opportunities.
34 Amott and Matthaei (1991), pp. 319–20.
35 Goldin (1990).
36 Ibid., ch. 6; Amott and Matthaei (1991), pp. 315–16, 320.
37 Goldin (1990), pp. 4–5; Goldin and Katz (2008).
38 Fox (2018).
39 Wajcman (2010).
40 Acemoglu (2002).
41 Wajcman (2010).
42 Ibid.: 151.
43 Pujol (1984, 1998); Folbre (1991, 2009).

# Chapter 4   Income Inequality: What Does Sex Have to Do with It?

1 Piketty (2014).
2 Milanovic (2016); Scheidel (2018).
3 Kuznets (1955).
4 Piketty (2014); IMF (2017).
5 Roser (2016).
6 Hammar and Waldenström (2017).
7 Roser (2016).
8 Roser and Ortiz-Ospina (2018).
9 Ibid.
10 UNU-WIDER, World Income Inequality Database; Coontz (2014).
11 Milanovic (2013), p. 11 (Fig. 4).
12 See Wood (2018) for a summary of the literature and debate.
13 Acemoglu et al. (2016); Autor, Dorn, and Hanson (2013, 2016); Pierce and Schott (2016).
14 Ibid.
15 Acemoglu et al. (2016).
16 Milanovic (2013).
17 Wood (2018); Helpman (2017). Though increased use of technology may be a response to greater international competition (Wood 2018: 8).
18 Acemoglu (2002): 781–2.
19 Goldin and Katz (2008). Also see Chetty and Hendren (2018a,b); Chetty et al. (2016); Chetty et al. (2014).
20 Goldin and Katz (2008), p. 325.
21 Frey and Osborne (2017).
22 Bukodi et al. (2014).

23 Atkinson (2001). Rodrik (1997) argued that globalization made it ever more difficult to tax the rich.
24 Stiglitz (2015).
25 Lindert (2017), pp. 1, 4.
26 Piketty (2014).
27 Geier et al. (2014).
28 Quoted in Geier et al. (2014).
29 Haskins, Isaacs and Sawhill (2008), see esp. ch. 5.
30 Woolley (1993): 487; Haddad and Kanbur (1990).
31 Freund and Oliver (2014). For historic trends in the United States, see Edlund and Kopczuk (2009) and Boushey, de Long and Steinbaum (2017), pp. 381–3 (tables 4 and 5).
32 Chant (2008).
33 Kramer et al. (2016).
34 https://www.one.org/us/take-action/poverty-is-sexist/
35 Harris (2017).
36 Strober (1984); Goldin (1990), ch. 3; Hegewisch and Hartmann (2014); Humphries (1995), p. xxxiii.
37 Kessler-Harris (2001, p. 6, 2015). On the earnings penalty in care, see Budig and Misra (2010). More generally, Sen (1987); Folbre (2004); Gammage, Kabeer and van der Meulen Rodgers (2016).
38 Ferrant, Pesando and Nowacka (2014); Bryson (2016), pp. 264–7 provides a summary of the 'care and capitalism' literature.
39 ILO (2018).
40 Bearak et al. (2018).
41 For more discussion, a good place to start is the 2015 inequality special issue of the journal *Gender and Development*. See e.g. Kabeer (2015).
42 Even once we take on board the increasing tendency for richer men to marry richer partners, without changes in women's earnings, inequality would still have grown 37.8 per cent faster (Duke 2015). Coontz (2014).
43 Greenwood et al. (2014).
44 Sawhill (2014).
45 Ibid.
46 Ibid.; Rodgers (2018).
47 Kramer et al. (2016).
48 See, for example, Chetty and Hendren (2018a,b), Chetty et al. (2016), Chetty et al. (2014).
49 Lewis (2009); O'Connor, Orloff and Shaver (2009); Elson and Cagatay (2000); Daly (2005); Balakrishnan, Heintz and Elson (2016).
50 Wiesner-Hanks (2015); Folbre (1991); Kessler-Harris (2001), pp. 7–11.
51 This section largely draws on Bateman (2016d).
52 Nangle (2015), pp. 5–6; Goodhart, Pradhan and Pardeshi (2015).
53 Allen (2009).
54 Goodhart, Pradhan and Pardeshi (2015).
55 UNICEF (2014).
56 Ibid.

57  Ibid.
58  Wang (2016); UNFPA (2017); Rodgers (2018).
59  Bearak et al. (2018).
60  World Bank data.
61  Goodhart and Erfurth (2014); Lu and Teulings (2016).
62  Siegel (2013).
63  In some western countries, fertility has fallen to well below replacement level, something which has been connected to the burden of unpaid care placed on women.
64  Lucas (2004).
65  See, for example, Stiglitz (2015); Semuels (2016); IMF (2017).
66  Humphries and Weisdorf (2015).
67  Goldin (2008).
68  Amott and Matthaei (1991), pp. 319–20, 346.
69  Pateman (1988); Amott and Matthaei (1991), p. 354; Pedersen (1995, 2018); Kessler-Harris (2001); Esping-Andersen (2013); Cooke (2011).
70  In Geier et al. (2014).
71  A point best noted within the intersectional literature. See Hill Collins and Bilge (2016) and Amott and Matthaei (1991).
72  Fraser (2013b).

## Chapter 5   Sex Sells: the Body Versus the Brain

1  For more on the variation in policy, and for a similar conclusion, see Bettio, della Giusta and di Tommaso (2017).
2  Bateman (2014).
3  Walter (2011); Banyard (2016).
4  Phipps (2014).
5  Bindel (2017a,b).
6  Sprinkle (2009), p. 10.
7  Taylor (1992); Strossen (2000); McElroy (2002). Also, on pornography, Cornell (2007).
8  Lee (2014).
9  Birks (2018).
10  Bettio, Della Giusta and Di Tommaso (2017) point to a continuum of agency.
11  The Nordic model recommends the criminalization of the purchase of sex; on the End Banking for Human Traffickers Act, see Hatch (2018a, 2018b); FOSTA/SESTA legislation in the United States has severely affected sex workers ability to advertise online, and Sarah Champion, MP, has proposed that similar policies be adopted in the United Kingdom. See Hatch (2018b).
12  Quoted in Daggers and Neal (2006), p. 48.
13  MacKinnon (1987), p. 188.
14  Dworkin (1993): 9–10.
15  Nordic Model Now (2016).

16 Lewis (2009); O'Connor, Orloff and Shaver (2009); Fraser (2013b); Balakrishnan, Heintz and Elson (2016).
17 Lu and Teulings (2016).
18 Bettio, Della Giusta and Di Tommaso (2017).
19 Lister (2018).
20 Quoted in Clarkson (1939): 296.
21 Ibid.: 300.
22 Edlund and Korn (2002).
23 Cogoni, Carnaghi, and Silani (2018).
24 Bettio, Della Giusta and Di Tommaso (2017).
25 Della Giusta, di Tommaso and Jewell (2017).
26 Gupta (2015).
27 Laverte (2017).
28 For a summary of research, see Bettio, Della Giusta and Di Tommaso (2017).
29 Lee (2015).
30 Corvid (2015).
31 McClintock (1995).
32 Bettio, Della Giusta and Di Tommaso (2017).
33 McClintock (1995).
34 Hakim (2011).
35 Dworkin (1993): 5–6.
36 Schrijvers (1991).
37 Gomes and Boesch (2009).
38 Bateman (2017).

## Part III   Introduction

1 Cudd and Holmstrom (2011).
2 Mauro et al. (2015).
3 Data from OECD (figures for 2008).
4 Mazzucato (2011); Stiglitz (2016); Thaler and Sunstein (2008).
5 Allison (2018); Kleiner and Krueger (2013); Furman (2016).
6 Bateman (2016a).
7 The literature is extensive. For a start, see Mies (1986); Fraser (2013b); Federici (2004); McClintock (1995).
8 McElroy (1991); Taylor (1992); Abbey (2014); Nussbaum (2013). For a feminist interpretation of Ayn Rand, see Gladstein and Sciabarra (1999).

## Chapter 6   Marx Versus Markets

1 Stiglitz (2016).
2 Hartmann (1979).
3 Federici (2004).
4 Dowling (2015). Also see Dowling and Harvie (2014).

5 For a historical perspective, Amott and Matthaei (1991) and McClintock (1995).
6 Fraser (2009).
7 Seguino (2000a,b). Also Blecker and Seguino (2002); Ertürk and Cagatay (1995); Standing (1999). On the subsequent debate, see Seguino (2011).
8 Humphries (2012, 2013).
9 Royal Commission on Employment of Children in Factories (1833). See, in particular, section D2, p. 37 and p. 54.
10 Kabeer (2003), p. xix. Also see Kabeer and Natali (2013), p. 36.
11 Agarwal (1992).
12 Fontaine (2014); Polanyi (1944); Thompson (1991).
13 Rubinstein (1981).
14 Ibid.
15 Mokyr and Nye (2007): 67.
16 Mill (1859), ch. 1.
17 De Moor and van Zanden (2010).
18 Froide (2017).
19 Xue (2016).
20 Swedberg (2011).
21 Hickel and Khan (2012).
22 Hayek (1944); Friedman and Friedman (1982).
23 Quoted in Postell and Watson (2011), p. 65.
24 Hignett et al. (2018).
25 Leeson and Russ (2017); Hester (2014); Sollée (2017).
26 Chang (2011); Marshall (2014).
27 Steinberg (2016).
28 Prügl (2016); Htun and Weldon (2017).
29 Offer (2012); Mosini (2012).
30 Medema (2009).
31 Pujol (1998).
32 Fraser (2013b); Faria (2018).
33 Gibson-Graham (2006a,b).
34 Prügl (2016).
35 Agarwal (1992).
36 See Prügl (2016) on the associated agenda of the World Bank.
37 Eswaran (2014), pp. 365–8.
38 Fraser (2013a), ch. 8, esp. pp. 196–7.
39 Fraser (2013b), p. 132; Faria (2018).
40 Hayek (1979); Faria (2018).

# Chapter 7  Why Women Make Better States

1 Ortiz-Ospina and Roser (2018).
2 Ma and Rubin (2017).

3   Johnson and Koyama (2017).
4   Acemoglu et al. (2014).
5   Acemoglu, Moscona and Robinson (2016).
6   Elson (1998); Rai, Hoskyns, and Thomas (2011).
7   Duflo (2012).
8   Friedman and Schwartz (1963).
9   Lu, Luan and Sng (2016).
10  Fraser (2013b), ch. 8.
11  McCulloch (1848), p. 156.
12  Pennington (2011), p. 42.
13  Pateman (1988); Pedersen (1995).
14  Kessler-Harris (2001). See p. 300 (fn. 36–38) of the latter for further references on gender and the US welfare system. Also see Goldin (1990), including for a detailed discussion of marriage bars and sex segregation.
15  Cooke (2011). Also see Esping-Andersen (2013) and, on the United States, Kessler-Harris (2001).
16  Pedersen (2018). Also see Kessler-Harris (2001, p. 5), for the same point in regard to the United States.
17  Benería, Berik and Floro (2016), ch. 2; Elson (2012); Hozic and True (2016); Rubery (2015).
18  Htun and Weldon (2017), p. 159.
19  Ibid., p. 160.
20  Ibid., table 6.1, p. 164.
21  Stiglitz (2016).
22  Dahlerup (2018).
23  Offer (2002).
24  Johnson and Koyama (2017).
25  Besley and Persson (2009).
26  Skarbek (2014).
27  Scott (2018).
28  Scheidel (2017).
29  Blaydes and Chaney (2013).
30  Klein and Ogilvie (2017).
31  Epstein (2000).
32  Besley and Persson (2009).
33  Tilly (1975); Dincecco, Fenske and Onorato (2014); Koyama, Moriguchi and Sng (2017).
34  On East Anglia, Oosthuizen (2017).
35  Karaman and Pamuk (2013); O'Brien (2010).
36  Rubin (2018), pp. 17, 202–4.
37  For a feminist perspective, Hirschmann (2007).
38  Rubin (2018), pp. 206–7.
39  Aghion et al. (2010).
40  Johnson and Koyama (2017). Also Tabellini (2008); Guiso, Sapienza and Zingales (2016); Xue and Koyama (2018).
41  Alesina and Giuliano (2015).

42 Johnson and Koyama (2017).
43 Carmichael, de Pleijt and van Zanden (2016).
44 Todd (1988, 2011); Mill (1859, 1869); Okin (1989); Carmichael (2016), p. 32.
45 Kok (2017).
46 Bryson (2016).
47 Greif (2006).
48 Greif (1994).
49 Van Bavel and Rijpma (2015).
50 Johnson and Koyama (2017).
51 Laslett (1988).
52 Bateman (2016b).
53 Roberts (2016).
54 See Collins and Teele (2017) for a discussion and empirical critique.
55 For a summary, see Eswaran (2014), pp. 322–5.
56 Lott and Kenny (1999).
57 Funk and Gathmann (2014).
58 Kabeer (1997); Duflo (2003).
59 Agarwal (1992).

# Chapter 8  Me, Myself and I: A History of the Individual

1 Sandelin, Trautwein and Wundrak (2008), pp. 1, 3.
2 For a historical perspective and feminist critique of the separate versus connected self, see England (1989): 15–17.
3 Backhouse (2002), ch. 6.
4 Ibid., pp. 114–15.
5 Smith (1776).
6 Meek (1962), p. 70.
7 Dasgupta (1987), ch. 6.
8 Jevons (1888), ch. 3.
9 Pennington (2011).
10 Taylor (1992); McElroy (2001); Hirschmann (2007).
11 Kessler-Harris (2001), p. 7.
12 Picchio (1992); Ferber and Nelson (1993); Nelson (2018); Folbre (1991, 2009); Folbre and Hartmann (1988).

# Chapter 9  Humans Versus Robots: the Behavioural Revolution

1 Humphries (1995), p. xvi.
2 Roth et al. (1991).
3 Ledyard (1995).
4 Fehr and Gächter (2000).

5   Simon (1957).
6   Thaler (1992), ch. 1.
7   Tversky and Kahneman (1974).
8   Kahneman (2011).
9   McClure et al. (2004).
10  Damasio (1994); Gigerenzer (2008). Cohen (2005) notes the power of emotions in a primitive setting and how reason and control developed once the environment changed.
11  Levine (2012).
12  Mokyr (2009).
13  Keynes (1936).
14  Amabile (1998).
15  Picchio (1992).
16  Braunstein, van Staveren and Tavani (2011).
17  Waring (1988); O'Hara (2013).
18  Folbre (2009), p. 316.
19  Baddeley (2018); Shiller (1984); Baddeley (2017), ch. 8.
20  Ariely (2008).
21  Thaler and Sunstein (2008).
22  Thaler and Sunstein (2008).
23  Mullainathan and Shafir (2013).
24  Akerlof and Kranton (2011). For more on how the social nature of human beings affects our behaviour, see Baddeley (2017): a short intro, ch. 3.
25  Bateman (2015a).
26  Borshay Lee (1969).
27  Nelson (1992); McCloskey (2008).
28  Bryson (2016), p. 151; Nelson (1992).
29  Nelson (1995), p. 132; McCloskey (2008); Marçal (2015).
30  England (1989): 15–17. For a more general discussion, also see Harding (1986) and Bordo (1986).
31  Ibid.
32  Folbre (1991); Pujol (1984).
33  Pujol (1984). J. S. Mill is one of the few exceptions, though see Pujol (1998) for a more nuanced discussion.
34  Pujol (1984); Edgeworth (1923): esp. 493.
35  Pujol (1984): 217.
36  In a similar vein, Nussbaum (2013), ch. 2, argues that we need more *not less* individualism if we are to take note of feminist concerns.
37  Humphries (1995), p. xviii.
38  Ferber and Nelson (1993).

## Chapter 10   Economics Meets Feminism

1   Wollstonecraft (1792).
2   Bryson (2016), p. 14.

3   Quoted in Samuels (1992), p. 97.
4   Folbre (2009), pp. 117–20.
5   Sawhill (2014).
6   Wellings et al. (2013).
7   Bearak et al. (2018).
8   This short section draws on Bateman (2015b).
9   Bryson (2016), pp. 148–9.
10  Becker (1981); Grossbard (2006).
11  Folbre and Hartmann (1988); Bergmann (1995); Woolley (1996).
12  Folbre (1982). Also see Agarwal (1997) and Basu (2006).
13  Zanden, Rijpma and Kok , (2017), ch. 2.
14  Kabeer (1997); Duflo (2003).
15  Howard (2018).
16  Offer (2017).
17  De Moor and van Zanden (2010).
18  Waring (1988); Folbre (1991).
19  Folbre (2009), pp. 124–5, 130.
20  See Bryson (2016), ch. 11, pp. 254–5 and pp. 264–7 for further discussion.
21  O'Hara (2013); Himmelweit (2006).
22  Folbre (2001).
23  Ibid..
24  Himmelweit (2006).
25  Bateman (2017b); Fraser (2016).
26  Bryson (2016), pp. 24, 61,199.
27  Bryson (2016), pp. 24, 61.
28  England (1989): 23; Folbre (2004). Also Sen (1977, 1987).
29  Woolley (1993); Humphries (1995), p. xxxiii.
30  Sen (1987); Folbre (2004); Gammage, Kabeer and van der Meulen Rodgers (2016).
31  Woolley (1993): 496.
32  Folbre (2004); Chambers (2008).
33  Wollstonecraft (1792).
34  De Beauvoir  (1973), p. 301.
35  Kabeer (2003).
36  Evans (2016).
37  Baddeley (2017), p. 19.
38  Nelson (1995), p. 136; Bryson (2016), p. 152.
39  England (1989) suggests that the dichotomization is itself mistaken – that rationality and emotions should not, for example, be separated.

## Conclusion

1   Wang (2016); Rodgers (2018); UNFPA (2017).
2   Ahmed (2018).

3  Agarwal (1992).
4  Xue (2016).
5  Eswaran (2014), pp. 365–8.
6  Jha et al. (2011).
7  Paul (2016); Eswaran (2014), pp. 234–6.
8  Jensen and Oster (2009).
9  Rai (2013).
10  Fourcade, Ollion and Algan (2015).
11  Harding (1986); Humphries (1995), p. xiii.
12  Howard (2018).
13  Bateman (2016e).
14  Nelson (1992).
15  OECD (2011), ch. 1.
16  Humphries (1995), p. xvi.
17  England (1989).
18  See, for example, Woetzel et al. (2015).
19  Fraser (2013b).
20  Elson (1998); Rai, Hoskyns and Thomas (2011).
21  Edlund (2006): 622.

# References

Abbey, R. (2014). *The Return of Feminist Liberalism*. Abingdon: Routledge.

Acemoglu, D. (2002). Directed Technical Change. *Review of Economic Studies* 69(4): 781–809.

Acemoglu, D. and Robinson, J. (2000). Political Losers as a Barrier to Economic Development. *American Economic Review* 90(2): 126–30.

Acemoglu, D. and Robinson, J. (2012). *Why Nations Fail*. New York: Crown.

Acemoglu, D., Johnson, S. and Robinson, J. (2001). The Colonial Origins of Comparative Development: An Empirical Investigation. *American Economic Review* 91(5): 1369–1401.

Acemoglu, D., Johnson, S. and Robinson, J. (2002). Reversal of Fortune: Geography and Institutions in the Making of the Modern World Income Distribution. *The Quarterly Journal of Economics* 117(4): 1231–94.

Acemoglu, D., Johnson, S. and Robinson, J. (2005). Institutions as a Fundamental Cause of Long-Run Growth, in P. Aghion and S. Durlauf (eds), *Handbook of Economic Growth*. Amsterdam: Elsevier, pp. 385–472.

Acemoglu, D., Moscona, J. and Robinson, J. (2016). State Capacity and American Technology: Evidence from the Nineteenth Century. *American Economic Review* 106(5): 61–7.

Acemoglu, D., Autor, D., Dorn, D., Hanson, G. and Price, B. (2016). Import Competition and the Great US Employment Sag of the 2000s. *Journal of Labor Economics* 34(S1): S141–S198.

Acemoglu, D., Chaves, I., Osafo-Kwaako, P. and Robinson, J. (2014). *Indirect Rule and State Weakness in Africa: Sierra Leone in Comparative Perspective*. NBER Working Paper.

Adshade, M. (2013). *Dollars and Sex*. San Francisco: Chronicle Books.

Agarwal, B. (1992). The Gender and Environment Debate: Lessons from India. *Feminist Studies* 18(1): 119–58.

Agarwal, B. (1997). 'Bargaining' and Gender Relations: Within and Beyond the Household. *Feminist Economics* 3(1): 1–51.

Agarwal, B. (1998). *Field of One's Own*. Cambridge: Cambridge University Press.

Aghion, P., Algan, Y., Cahuc, P. and Shleifer, A. (2010). Regulation and Distrust. *Quarterly Journal of Economics* 125(3): 1015–49.

Ahmed, M. (2018). Access to Contraception is a Global Development Issue. *Centre for Global Development*. Available at: https://www.cgdev.org/blog/access-contraception-global-development-issue

Akerlof, G. and Kranton, R. (2011). *Identity Economics*. Princeton, NJ: Princeton University Press.

Akyeampong, E., Bates, R., Nunn, N. and Robinson, J. (2014). *Africa's Development in Historical Perspective*. Cambridge: Cambridge University Press.

Alesina, A. and Giuliano, P. (2010). The Power of the Family. *Journal of Economic Growth* 15(2): 93–125.

Alesina, A. and Giuliano, P. (2011). Family Ties and Political Participation. *Journal of the European Economic Association* 9(5): 817–39.

Alesina, A. and Giuliano, P. (2015). Culture and Institutions. *Journal of Economic Literature* 53(4): 898–944.

Alesina, A., Giuliano, P. and Nunn, N. (2013). On the Origins of Gender Roles: Women and the Plough. *The Quarterly Journal of Economics* 128(2): 469–530.

Alesina, A., Algan, Y., Cahuc, P. and Giuliano, P. (2015). Family Values and the Regulation of Labor. *Journal of the European Economic Association* 13(4): 599–630.

Allen, R. (2001). The Great Divergence in European Wages and Prices from the Middle Ages to the First World War. *Explorations in Economic History* 38(4): 411–47.

Allen, R. (2009). *The British Industrial Revolution in Global Perspective*. Cambridge: Cambridge University Press.

Allen, R. (2014). The High Wage Economy and the Industrial Revolution: A Restatement. *The Economic History Review* 68(1): 1–22.

Allen, R. (2018). Real Wages Once More: A Response to Judy Stephenson. *The Economic History Review*. DOI: 10.1111/ehr.12663.

Allison, J. (2018). *Financial Crisis and the Free Market Cure*. New York: McGraw-Hill Education.

Amabile, T. (1998). How to Kill Creativity. *Harvard Business Review* 76(5): 76–87.

Amin, S. and Pearce, B. (1976). *Unequal Development*. Monthly Review Press.

Amott, T. and Matthaei, J. (1991). *Race, Gender and Work: A Multi-cultural Economic History of Women in the United States*. Quebec: Black Rose Books.

Anderson, S. (2007). The Economics of Dowry and Brideprice. *Journal of Economic Perspectives* 21(4): 151–74.

Ariely, D. (2008). *Predictably Irrational*. London: Harper.

Ashraf, Q. and Galor, O. (2011). Dynamics and Stagnation in the Malthusian Epoch. *American Economic Review* 101(5): 2003–41.

Atkinson, A. (2001). A Critique of the Transatlantic Consensus on Rising Income Inequality. *The World Economy* 24(4): 433–52.

Austin, G. (2016). Sub-Saharan Africa, in J. Baten (ed.), *A History of the Global Economy: 1500 to the Present*. Cambridge: Cambridge University Press, pp. 316–50.

Autor, D., Dorn, D. and Hanson, G. (2013). The China Syndrome: Local Labor Market Effects of Import Competition in the United States. *American Economic Review* 103(6): 2121–68.

Autor, D., Dorn, D. and Hanson, G. (2016). The China Shock: Learning from Labor-Market Adjustment to Large Changes in Trade. *Annual Review of Economics* 8(1): 205–40.

Backhouse, R. (2002). *The Penguin History of Economics*. London: Penguin.

Baddeley, M. (2017). *Behavioural Economics*. Oxford: Oxford University Press.

Baddeley, M. (2018). *Copycats and Contrarians*. New Haven, CT: Yale University Press.

Balakrishnan, R., Heintz, J. and Elson, D. (2016). *Rethinking Economic Policy for Social Justice*. Abingdon: Routledge.

Bandiera, O. and Natraj, A. (2013). Does Gender Inequality Hinder Development and Economic Growth? Evidence and Policy Implications. *The World Bank Research Observer* 28(1): 2–21.

Banyard, K. (2016). *Pimp State*. London: Faber & Faber.

Barsh, J. and Yee, L. (2011). *Unlocking the Full Potential of Women in the US Economy*. New York: McKinsey Global Institute.

Basu, K. (2006). Gender and Say: A Model of Household Behaviour with Endogenously Determined Balance of Power. *The Economic Journal* 116(511): 558–80.

Bateman, V. (2014). Why I Posed Naked and Natural. *The Guardian*. 16 May.

Bateman, V. (2015a). Social Mobility: What Really Holds People Back? *Times Higher Education*, 11 August.

Bateman, V. (2015b). Reducing Poverty the Female Way. *CapX*, 17 November.

Bateman, V. (2016a). Classical Liberalism: The Foundation for a New Economics? *Critical Review* 28(3–4): 440–60.

Bateman, V. (2016b). *Markets and Growth in Early Modern Europe*. London: Routledge.

Bateman, V. (2016c). Tax Policy is Widening the Gender Gap. *Bloomberg View*, 14 April.

Bateman, V. (2016d). The World has a Sex Problem: It's Hurting Growth. *Bloomberg View*, 9 September.

Bateman, V. (2016e). *Women, Fertility and Economic Growth*. Economic History Society Annual Conference Paper.

Bateman, V. (2017a). Economics Must Embrace the Sex Industry. *Times Higher Education*, 30 March.

Bateman, V. (2017b). Capitalism is Suffering a Crisis of Care. *Unherd*, 21 November.

Bates, R. (2014). The Imperial Peace, in E. Akyeampong, R. Bates, N. Nunn and J. Robinson (ed.), *Africa's Development in Historical Perspective*. Cambridge: Cambridge University Press, pp. 424–44.

Bearak, J., Popinchalk, A., Alkema, L. and Sedgh, G. (2018). Global, Regional, and Subregional Trends in Unintended Pregnancy and its Outcomes from 1990 to 2014: Estimates from a Bayesian Hierarchical Model. *The Lancet Global Health* 6(4): e380–e389.

Beauvoir, S. de (1973). *The Second Sex.* New York: Vintage.

Becker, G. (1981). *A Treatise on the Family.* Cambridge, MA: Harvard University Press.

Beckert, S. (2015). *Empire of Cotton: A New History of Global Capitalism.* London: Penguin.

Benería, L., Berik, G. and Floro, M. (2016). *Gender, Development and Globalization.* Abingdon: Routledge.

Berger, I. and White, E. (2008). *Women in Sub-Saharan Africa.* Bloomington, IN: Indiana University Press.

Bergmann, B. (1995). Becker's Theory of the Family: Preposterous Conclusions. *Feminist Economics* 1(1): 141–50.

Berik, G. (2018). *Toward More Inclusive Measures of Economic Well-being: Debates and Practices.* Geneva: ILO.

Bertola, L. and Ocampo, J. (2016). Latin America, in J. Baten (ed.), *A History of the Global Economy.* Cambridge: Cambridge University Press.

Besley, T. and Persson, T. (2009). The Origins of State Capacity: Property Rights, Taxation, and Politics. *American Economic Review* 99(4): 1218–44.

Bettio, F., Della Giusta, M. and Di Tommaso, M. (2017). Sex Work and Trafficking: Moving Beyond Dichotomies. *Feminist Economics* 23(3): 1–22.

Bindel, J. (2017a). Why Prostitution Should Never Be Legalised. *The Guardian*, 11 October.

Bindel, J. (2017b). *The Pimping of Prostitution: Abolishing the Sex Work Myth.* London: Palgrave Macmillan.

Birks, K. (2018). Grid Girls and Puritans. *Quillette*, 9 February.

Bisin, A. and Verdier, T. (2000). 'Beyond the Melting Pot': Cultural Transmission, Marriage, and the Evolution of Ethnic and Religious Traits. *Quarterly Journal of Economics* 115(3): 955–88.

Bisin, A. and Verdier, T. (2001). The Economics of Cultural Transmission and the Dynamics of Preferences. *Journal of Economic Theory* 97(2): 298–319.

Bjørnholt, M. and McKay, A. (2014). *Counting on Marilyn Waring: New Advances in Feminist Economics.* Bradford, ON: Demeter Press.

Black, S., Grönqvist, E. and Öckert, B. (2017). Born to Lead? The Effect of Birth Order on Noncognitive Abilities. *Review of Economics and Statistics* 100(2): 274–86.

Blaydes, L. and Chaney, E. (2013). The Feudal Revolution and Europe's Rise: Political Divergence of the Christian West and the Muslim World before 1500 CE. *American Political Science Review* 107(1): 16–34.

Blecker, R. and Seguino, S. (2002). Macroeconomic Effects of Reducing Gender Wage Inequality in an Export-Oriented, Semi-Industrialized Economy. *Review of Development Economics* 6(1): 103–19.

Bordo, S. (1986). The Cartesian Masculinization of Thought. *Signs: Journal of Women in Culture and Society* 11(3): 439–56.

Borshay Lee, R. (1969). Eating Christmas in the Kalahari. *Natural History* (December): 60–4.

Boserup, E. (1970). *Woman's Role in Economic Development*. London: Allen & Unwin.

Botticini, M. and Siow, A. (2003). Why Dowries? *American Economic Review* 93: 1385–98.

Bourguignon, F. and Morrisson, C. (2002). Inequality among World Citizens: 1820–1992. *American Economic Review* 92(4): 727–44.

Boushey, H., de Long, J. and Steinbaum, M. (2017). *After Piketty*. Cambridge, MA: Harvard University Press.

Bowden, W. (1925). *Industrial Society in England*. New York: Macmillan.

Braunstein, E., van Staveren, I. and Tavani, D. (2011). Embedding Care and Unpaid Work in Macroeconomic Modeling: A Structuralist Approach. *Feminist Economics* 17(4): 5–31.

Broadberry, S. (2016). The Great Divergence in the World Economy: Long-Run Trends of Real Income, in J. Baten (ed.), *A History of the Global Economy: 1500 to the Present*. Cambridge: Cambridge University Press, pp. 35–9.

Broadberry, S. and Wallis, J. (2017). *Growing, Shrinking, and Long-Run Economic Performance: Historical Perspectives on Economic Development*. NBER Working Paper 23343.

Bryson, V. (2016). *Feminist Political Theory*. London: Palgrave.

Budig, M. and Misra, J. (2010). How Care-work Employment Shapes Earnings in Cross-National Perspective. *International Labour Review* 149(4): 441–60.

Bukodi, E., Goldthorpe, J., Waller, L. and Kuha, J. (2014). The Mobility Problem in Britain: New Findings from the Analysis of Birth Cohort Data. *The British Journal of Sociology* 66(1): 93–117.

Burguiere, A., Klapisch-Zuber, C., Segalen, M., Lévi-Strauss, C. and Tenison, S. (1996). *History of the Family*. Cambridge: Polity Press.

Burnette, J. (2008). Women Workers in the British Industrial Revolution, ed. Robert Whaples. *EH.Net Encyclopedia*.

Campbell, B. (2016). *The Great Transition*. Cambridge: Cambridge University Press.

Campbell, G., Miers, S. and Miller, J. (2008). *Women and Slavery*. Athens, OH: Ohio University Press.

Carmichael, S. (2016). *Marriage, Family and Gender Inequality*. PhD. Utrecht.

Carmichael, S., de Pleijt, A. and van Zanden, J. (2016). *Gender Relations and Economic Development: Hypotheses about the Reversal of Fortune in EurAsia*. CGEH Working Paper. Utrecht University.

Carmichael, S., de Pleijt, A., van Zanden, J. and de Moor, T. (2015). *Reply to Tracy Dennison and Sheilagh Ogilvie: The European Marriage Pattern and the Little Divergence*. CGEH Working Paper. Utrecht University.

Chambers, C. (2008). *Sex, Culture, and Justice*. University Park, PA: Pennsylvania State University Press.

Chang, H. (2011). *23 Things They Don't Tell You about Capitalism*. London: Bloomsbury.

Chant, S. (2008). The 'Feminisation of Poverty' and the 'Feminisation' of Anti-Poverty Programmes: Room for Revision? *The Journal of Development Studies* 44(2): 165–97.

Checkland, S. (1964). *The Rise of Industrial Society in England, 1815–1885*. London: Longmans.

Chetty, R. and Hendren, N. (2018a). The Impacts of Neighborhoods on Intergenerational Mobility I: Childhood Exposure Effects. *The Quarterly Journal of Economics* 133(3): 1107–62.

Chetty, R. and Hendren, N. (2018b). The Impacts of Neighborhoods on Intergenerational Mobility II: County-Level Estimates. *The Quarterly Journal of Economics* 133(3): 1163–228.

Chetty, R., Hendren, N., Kline, P. and Saez, E. (2014). Where is the Land of Opportunity? The Geography of Intergenerational Mobility in the United States. *The Quarterly Journal of Economics* 129(4): 1553–623.

Chetty, R., Hendren, N., Lin, F., Majerovitz, J. and Scuderi, B. (2016). Childhood Environment and Gender Gaps in Adulthood. *American Economic Review* 106(5): 282–8.

Cinnirella, F., Klemp, M. and Weisdorf, J. (2017). Malthus in the Bedroom: Birth Spacing as Birth Control in Pre-Transition England. *Demography* 54(2): 413–36.

Clark, G. (2007). *A Farewell to Alms*. Princeton, NJ: Princeton University Press.

Clarkson, F. (1939). History of Prostitution. *The Canadian Medical Association Journal* 41(3): 296–301.

Cogoni, C., Carnaghi, A. and Silani, G. (2018). Reduced Empathic Responses for Sexually Objectified Women: An fMRI Investigation. *Cortex* 99: 258–72.

Cohen, J. (2005). The Vulcanization of the Human Brain: A Neural Perspective on Interactions between Cognition and Emotion. *Journal of Economic Perspectives* 19(4): 3–24.

Collins, M. and Teele, D. (2017). *Revisiting the Gender Voting Gap in the Era of Women's Suffrage*. Unpublished paper.

Cooke, L. (2011). *Gender–Class Equality in Political Economies*. New York: Routledge.

Coontz, S. (2014). The New Instability. *The New York Times, Sunday Review*, 26 July.

Coquery-Vidrovitch, C. (1997). *African Women: A Modern History*. New York: Perseus.

Cornell, D. (2007). *Feminism and Pornography*. Oxford: Oxford University Press.

Corvid, M. (2015). Should it be Illegal to Pay for Sex? We have a Right to Profit from our Sexual Labour. *The Guardian*, 24 March.

Coyle, D. (2014). *GDP: A Brief and Affectionate History*. Princeton, NJ: Princeton University Press.

Cudd, A. and Holmstrom, N. (2011). *Capitalism, for and against*. Cambridge: Cambridge University Press.

Daggers, J. and Neal, D. (2006). *Sex, Gender, and Religion*. New York: Peter Lang.

Dahlerup, D. (2018). *Has Democracy Failed Women?* Cambridge: Polity Press.

Daly, M. (2005). Changing Family Life in Europe: Significance for State and Society. *European Societies* 7(3): 379–98.

Damasio, A. (1994). Descartes' Error and the Future of Human Life. *Scientific American* 271(4): 144.

Das Gupta, M. (1999). Lifeboat versus Corporate Ethic: Social and demographic Implications of Stem and Joint Families. *Social Science & Medicine* 49(2): 173–84.

Das Gupta, M., Zhenghua, J., Bohua, L., Zhenming, X., Chung, W. and Hwa-Ok, B. (2003). Why is Son Preference So Persistent in East and South Asia? A Cross-Country Study of China, India and the Republic of Korea. *Journal of Development Studies* 40(2): 153–87.

Dasgupta, A. (1987). *Epochs of Economic Theory*. Oxford: Basil Blackwell.

De Long, J. and Shleifer, A. (1993). Princes and Merchants: European City Growth before the Industrial Revolution. *The Journal of Law and Economics* 36(2): 671–702.

De Moor, T. and van Zanden, J. (2010). Girl Power: The European Marriage Pattern and Labour Markets in the North Sea Region in the Late Medieval and Early Modern Period. *The Economic History Review* 63(1): 1–33.

De Vries, J. (2008). *The Industrious Revolution*. Cambridge: Cambridge University Press.

De Vries, J. and van der Woude, A. (1997). *The First Modern Economy*. Cambridge: Cambridge University Press.

Della Giusta, M., di Tommaso, M. and Jewell, S. (2017). Stigma and Risky Behaviors among Male Clients of Sex Workers in the UK. *Feminist Economics* 23(3): 23–48.

Dennison, T. and Ogilvie, S. (2014). Does the European Marriage Pattern Explain Economic Growth? *The Journal of Economic History* 74(3): 651–93.

Diamond, J. (1999). *Guns, Germs, and Steel*. New York: W. W. Norton.

Dilli, S., Rijpma, A. and Carmichael, S. (2015). Achieving Gender Equality: Development versus Historical Legacies. *Economic Studies* 61(1): 301–34.

Dincecco, M., Fenske, J. and Onorato, M. (2014). Is Africa Different? Historical Conflict and State Development. *SSRN Electronic Journal*, 15 December.

Dowling, E. (2015). Retrieving the Heart of the Market? *Just World Institute*, University of Edinburgh, 28 July.

Dowling, E. and Harvie, D. (2014). Harnessing the Social: State, Crisis and (Big) Society. *Sociology* 48(5): 869–86.

Duflo, E. (2003). Grandmothers and Granddaughters: Old-Age Pensions and Intrahousehold Allocation in South Africa. *The World Bank Economic Review* 17(1): 1–25.

Duflo, E. (2012). Women Empowerment and Economic Development. *Journal of Economic Literature* 50(4): 1051–79.

Duke, B. (2015). How Married Women's Rising Earnings Have Reduced Inequality. *Center for American Progress*, 29 September.

Dworkin, A. (1993). Prostitution and Male Supremacy. *Michigan Journal of Gender and Law* 1(1): 1–12.

Dyble, M., Salali, G., Chaudhary, N., et al. (2015). Sex Equality Can Explain the Unique Social Structure of Hunter-Gatherer Bands. *Science* 348(6236): 796–8.

Dyer, C. (2009). *An Age of Transition?* Oxford: Clarendon Press.

Easterly, W. and Levine, R. (2003). Tropics, Germs, and Crops: How Endowments Influence Economic Development. *Journal of Monetary Economics* 50(1): 3–39.

Edgeworth, F. (1923). Women's Wages in Relation to Economic Welfare. *The Economic Journal* 33(132): 487.

Edlund, L. (2006). Marriage: Past, Present, Future? *Economic Studies* 52(4): 621–39.

Edlund, L. and Kopczuk, W. (2009). Women, Wealth, and Mobility. *American Economic Review* 99(1): 146–78.

Edlund, L. and Korn, E. (2002). A Theory of Prostitution. *Journal of Political Economy* 110(1): 181–214.

Edlund, L. and Lagerlöf, N. (2006). Individual Versus Parental Consent in Marriage: Implications for Intra-Household Resource Allocation and Growth. *American Economic Review* 96(2): 304–7.

Edwards, J. and Ogilvie, S. (2018). *Did the Black Death Cause Economic Development by 'Inventing' Fertility Restriction?* 7 May, CESifo Working Paper Series No. 7016. Munich: Center for Economic Studies and Ifo Institute.

Ehret, C. (2014). Africa in World History Before ca. 1440, in E. Akyeampong, R. Bates, N. Nunn and J. Robinson (eds), *Africa's Development in Historical Perspective*. Cambridge: Cambridge University Press.

Elbaum, B. and Lazonick, W. (1984). The Decline of the British Economy: An Institutional Perspective. *The Journal of Economic History* 44(2): 567–83.

Elson, D. (1998). The Economic, the Political and the Domestic: Businesses, States and Households in the Organization of Production. *New Political Economy* 3(2): 189–208.

Elson, D. (2012). The Reduction of the UK Budget Deficit: A Human Rights Perspective. *International Review of Applied Economics* 26(2): 177–90.

Elson, D. and Cagatay, N. (2000). The Social Content of Macroeconomic Policies. *World Development* 28(7): 1347–64.

Eltis, D. and Engerman, S. (2000). The Importance of Slavery and the Slave Trade to Industrializing Britain. *The Journal of Economic History* 60(1): 123–44.

Engels, F. and Hunt, T. (2010). *The Origin of the Family, Private Property, and the State*. London: Penguin Classics.

Engerman, S. and Sokoloff, K. (2002). Factor Endowments, Inequality, and Paths of Development among New World Economies. *Economía* 3(1): 41–109.

England, P. (1989). A Feminist Critique of Rational-Choice Theories: Implications for Sociology. *The American Sociologist* 20(1): 14–28.

Epstein, S. (2000). *Freedom and Growth*. New York: Routledge.

Ertürk, K. and Cagatay, N. (1995). Macroeconomic Consequences of Cyclical and Secular Changes in Feminization: An Experiment at Gendered Macromodeling. *World Development* 23(11): 1969–77.

Esping-Andersen, G. (2000). *Social Foundations of Postindustrial Economies*. Oxford: Oxford University Press.

Esping-Andersen, G. (2009). *The Incomplete Revolution*. Cambridge: Polity Press.

Esping-Andersen, G. (2013). *The Three Worlds of Welfare Capitalism*. Cambridge: Polity Press.

Eswaran, M. (2014). *Why Gender Matters in Economics*. Princeton, NJ: Princeton University Press.

Evans, A. (2016). The Decline of the Male Breadwinner and Persistence of the Female Carer: Exposure, Interests, and Micro–Macro Interactions. *Annals of the American Association of Geographers* 106(5): 1135–51.

Fara, P. (2010). *A Four Thousand Year History*. Oxford: Oxford University Press.

Faria, F. (2018). The Double Movement in Polanyi and Hayek. *Ethics, Politics & Society* 1: 22.

Fatah-Black, K. and van Rossum, M. (2014). Beyond Profitability: The Dutch Transatlantic Slave Trade and its Economic Impact. *Slavery & Abolition* 36(1): 63–83.

Federici, S. (2004). *Caliban and the Witch*. New York: Autonomedia.

Fehr, E. and Gächter, S. (2000). Cooperation and Punishment in Public Goods Experiments. *American Economic Review* 90(4): 980–94.

Ferber, M. and Lowry, H. (1976). The Sex Differential in Earnings: A Reappraisal. *Industry and Labour Relations Review* 29(3): 377–87.

Ferber, M. and Nelson, J. (1993). *Beyond Economic Man*. Chicago, IL: University of Chicago Press.

Ferber, M. and Teiman, M. (1981). The Oldest, the Most Established, and the Most Quantitative of the Social Sciences – and the Most Dominated by Men: The Impact of Feminism on Economics, in D. Spender (ed.), *Men's Studies Modified: The Impact of Feminism on the Academic Disciplines*. New York: Pergamon Press, pp. 125–39.

Ferrant, G., Pesando, L. and Nowacka, K. (2014). *Unpaid Care Work: The Missing Link in the Analysis of Gender Gaps in Labour Outcomes*. Paris: OECD Development Centre.

Finley, M. (1999). *The Ancient Economy*. Berkeley, CA: University of California Press.

Folbre, N. (1982). Exploitation Comes Home: A Critique of the Marxian Theory of Family Labour. *Cambridge Journal of Economics* 6(4): 317–29.

Folbre, N. (1991). The Unproductive Housewife: Her Evolution in Nineteenth-Century Economic Thought. *Signs: Journal of Women in Culture and Society* 16(3): 463–84.

Folbre, N. (2001). *The Invisible Heart*. New York: The New Press.

Folbre, N. (2004). *Who Pays for the Kids?* Hoboken: Taylor and Francis.

Folbre, N. (2009). *Greed, Lust and Gender*. Oxford: Oxford University Press.

Folbre, N. and Hartmann, H. (1988). The Rhetoric of Self-Interest: Ideology and Gender in Economic Theory, in R. Solow, A. Klamer and D. McCloskey (eds), *The Consequences of Economic Rhetoric*. Cambridge: Cambridge University Press, pp. 184–207.

Fontaine, L. (2014). *The Moral Economy*. New York: Cambridge University Press.

Foreman-Peck, J. (2011). The Western European Marriage Pattern and Economic Development. *Explorations in Economic History* 48(2): 292–309.

Fouquet, R. and Broadberry, S. (2015). Seven Centuries of European Economic Growth and Decline. *Journal of Economic Perspectives* 29(4): 227–44.

Fourcade, M., Ollion, E. and Algan, Y. (2015). The Superiority of Economists. *Journal of Economic Perspectives* 29(1): 89–114.

Fox, J. (2018). Women are Taking Over the Fastest-Growing Jobs. *Bloomberg View*, 20 February.

Fraser, N. (2009). Feminism, Capitalism and the Cunning of History. *New Left Review* 56: 97–117.

Fraser, N. (2013a). A Triple Movement? *New Left Review* 81 (May/June).

Fraser, N. (2013b). *Fortunes of Feminism*. Brooklyn, NY: Verso Books.

Fraser, N. (2016). Contradictions of Capital and Care. *New Left Review* 100.

Freund, C. and Oliver, S. (2014). The Missing Women in the Inequality Discussion. *Peterson Institute for International Economics*, 5 August.

Frey, C. and Osborne, M. (2017). The Future of Employment: How Susceptible are Jobs to Computerisation?. *Technological Forecasting and Social Change* 114: 254–80.

Friedman, M. and Friedman, R. (1982). *Capitalism and Freedom*. Chicago, IL: University of Chicago Press.

Friedman, M. and Schwartz, A. (1963). *A Monetary History of the United States, 1867–1960*. Princeton, NJ: Princeton University Press.

Froide, A. (2017). *Silent Partners*. Oxford: Oxford University Press.

Funk, P. and Gathmann, C. (2014). Gender Gaps in Policy Making: Evidence from Direct Democracy in Switzerland. *Economic Policy* 30(81): 141–81.

Furman, J. (2016). Forms and Sources of Inequality in the United States. *Vox*, 17 March.

Gallup, J., Sachs, J. and Mellinger, A. (1999). Geography and Economic Development. *International Regional Science Review* 22(2): 179–232.

Galor, O. (2005). From Stagnation to Growth: Unified Growth Theory, in P. Aghion and S. Durlauf (eds), *Handbook of Economic Growth*. Amsterdam: Elsevier.

Galor, O. (2011). *Unified Growth Theory*. Princeton, NJ: Princeton University Press.

Galor, O. and Mountford, A. (2008). Trading Population for Productivity: Theory and Evidence. *Review of Economic Studies* 75(4): 1143–79.

Galor, O. and Weil, D. (2000). Population, Technology, and Growth: From Malthusian Stagnation to the Demographic Transition and Beyond. *American Economic Review* 90(4): 806–28.

Gammage, S., Kabeer, N. and van der Meulen Rodgers, Y. (2016). Voice and Agency: Where are We Now? *Feminist Economics* 22(1): 1–29.

Geier, K., Bahn, K., Gamble, J., Eisenstein, Z. and Boushey, H. (2014). How Gender Changes Piketty's 'Capital in the Twenty-First Century'. *The Nation*, 6 August.

Geloso, V. (2018). Were Wages That Low? Real Wages in the Strasbourg Region before 1775. *The Journal of Interdisciplinary History* 48(4): 511–22.

Ghanem, R. and Baten, J. (2016). Middle East, North Africa and Central Asia, in J. Baten, (ed.), *A History of the Global Economy: 1500 to the Present*. Cambridge University Press, pp. 208–39.

Gibson-Graham, J. (2006a). *A Postcapitalist Politics*. Minneapolis: University of Minnesota Press.

Gibson-Graham, J. (2006b). *The End of Capitalism (as We Knew it)*. Minneapolis: University of Minnesota Press.

Gigerenzer, G. (2008). *Gut Feelings*. London: Penguin.

Giuliano, P. (2017). *Gender: An Historical Perspective*. NBER Working Paper. NBER.

Gladstein, M. and Sciabarra, C. (1999). *Feminist Interpretations of Ayn Rand*. University Park, PA: Pennsylvania State University Press.

Glaeser, E., La Porta, R., Lopez-de-Silanes, F. and Shleifer, A. (2004). Do Institutions Cause Growth? *Journal of Economic Growth* 9(3): 271–303.

Goldin, C. (1990). *Understanding the Gender Gap*. Oxford: Oxford University Press.

Goldin, C. (2018). The U-Shaped Female Labor Force Function in Economic Development and Economic History, in T. Schultz (ed.), *Investment in Women's Human Capital and Economic Development*. Chicago, IL: University of Chicago Press, pp. 61–90.

Goldin C. and Katz, L. F. (2008). *The Race between Education and Technology*. Cambridge, MA: Belknap Press of Harvard University Press.

Gomes, C. and Boesch, C. (2009). Wild Chimpanzees Exchange Meat for Sex on a Long-Term Basis. *PLoS ONE* 4(4): e5116.

Goodhart, C. and Erfurth, P. (2014). Demography and Economics: Look Past the Past. VoxEU, 4 November.

Goodhart, C., Pradhan, M. and Pardeshi, P. (2015). *Could Demographics Reverse Three Multi-Decade Trends? Technical report, Global Issues*. London: Morgan Stanley.

Gragnolati, U., Moschella, D. and Pugliese, E. (2011). The Spinning Jenny and the Industrial Revolution: A Reappraisal. *The Journal of Economic History* 71(2): 455–60.

Greenwood, J., Guner, N., Kocharkov, G. and Santos, C. (2014). Marry Your Like: Assortative Mating and Income Inequality. *American Economic Review* 104(5): 348–53.

Greif, A. (1994). Cultural Beliefs and the Organization of Society: A Historical and Theoretical Reflection on Collectivist and Individualist Societies. *Journal of Political Economy* 102(5): 912–50.

Greif, A. (2006). *Institutions and the Path to the Modern Economy*. Cambridge: Cambridge University Press.

Grossbard, S. (2006). The New Home Economics at Columbia and Chicago, in S. Grossbard (ed.), *Jacob Mincer: A Pioneer of Modern Labor Economics*. New York: Springer, pp. 37–53.

Guiso, L., Sapienza, P. and Zingales, L. (2006). Does Culture Affect Economic Outcomes? *Journal of Economic Perspectives* 20(2): 23–48.

Guiso, L., Sapienza, P. and Zingales, L. (2016). Long-Term Persistence. *Journal of the European Economic Association* 14(6): 1401–36.

Gupta, R. (2015). Should it be Illegal to Pay for Sex? Reduced Demand Will Act as a Brake on Trafficking. *The Guardian*, 24 March.

Habtezion, S. (2013). *Overview of Linkages between Gender and Climate Change. Policy Brief (Asian and the Pacific)*. New York: United Nations Development Programme.

Haddad, L. and Kanbur, R. (1990). How Serious is the Neglect of Intra-Household Inequality? *The Economic Journal* 100(402): 866–81.

Hajnal, J. (1982). Two Kinds of Preindustrial Household Formation System. *Population and Development Review* 8(3): 449–94.

Hakim, C. (2011). *Erotic Capital*. New York: Basic Books.

Hall, R. and Jones, C. (1999). Why Do Some Countries Produce So Much More Output Per Worker than Others? *The Quarterly Journal of Economics* 114(1): 83–116.

Hammar, O. and Waldenström, D. (2017). Global Earnings Inequality, 1970–2015. *CEPR Discussion Paper*.

Harding, S. (1986). *The Science Question in Feminism*. Ithaca: Cornell University Press.

Harris, B. (2017). What the Pay Gap between Men and Women Really Looks Like. *World Economic Forum Agenda*, 6 November.

Hartman, S. (2016). The Belly of the World: A Note on Black Women's Labors. *Souls* 18(1): 166–73.

Hartmann, H. (1976). Capitalism, Patriarchy, and Job Segregation by Sex. *Signs: Journal of Women in Culture and Society* 1(3, Part 2): 137–69.

Hartmann, H. (1979). The Unhappy Marriage of Marxism and Feminism: Towards a More Progressive Union. *Capital & Class* 3(2): 1–33.

Haskins, R., Isaacs, J. and Sawhill, I. (2008). *Getting Ahead or Losing Ground: Economic Mobility in America*. Brookings Economic Mobility Project. Brookings Institution.

Hatch, J. (2018a). British Sex Workers Protest Proposal that Would Shut Down Their Websites. *Huffington Post*.

Hatch, J. (2018b). First Congress Took Sex Workers' Websites. Now It's Coming for Their Bank Accounts. *Huffington Post*.

Hausmann, R., Rodriguez, F. and Wagner, R. (2006). *Growth Collapses. CID Working Paper*. Cambridge, MA: Harvard University.

Hawken, P. (2017). *Drawdown*. New York: Penguin Books.

Hayek, F. (1944). *The Road to Serfdom*. London: Routledge.

Hayek, F. (1979). *Law, Legislation and Liberty, Volume 3*. Chicago, IL: University of Chicago Press.

Hegewisch, A. and Hartmann, H. (2014). *Occupational Segregation and the Gender Wage Gap: A Job Half Done*. Washington, DC: Institute for Women's Policy Research.

Helpman, E. (2017). Globalisation and Wage Inequality. *Journal of the British Academy* 5: 125–62.

Hester, M. (2014). *Lewd Women and Wicked Witches*. London and New York: Routledge.

Hickel, J. and Khan, A. (2012). The Culture of Capitalism and the Crisis of Critique. *Anthropological Quarterly* 85(1): 203–27.

Hignett, K., Ilic, M., Leinarte, D. and Snitar, C. (2018). *Women's Experiences of Repression in the Soviet Union and Eastern Europe*. London: Routledge.

Hill Collins, P. and Bilge, S. (2016). *Intersectionality*. Cambridge: Polity Press.

Himmelweit, S. (2006). The Prospects for Caring: Economic Theory and Policy Analysis. *Cambridge Journal of Economics* 31(4): 581–99.

Hindle, S. (2004). *On the Parish?* Oxford: Clarendon Press.

Hirschmann, N. (2007). *Gender, Class, and Freedom in Modern Political Theory*. Princeton, NJ: Princeton University Press.

Horrell, S. and Humphries, J. (1995). Women's Labour Force Participation and the Transition to the Male-Breadwinner Family, 1790–1865. *The Economic History Review* 48(1): 89–117.

Howard, M. (2018). *Universal Credit and Financial Abuse: Exploring the Links*. Women's Budget Group. Available at: https://www.endviolenceagainstwomen.org.uk/wp-content/uploads/FINAL-full-report-financial-abuse-and-uc.pdf

Howell, M. (2010). *Commerce before Capitalism in Europe, 1300–1600*. New York: Cambridge University Press.

Hozic, A. and True, J. (2016). *Scandalous Economics*. Oxford: Oxford University Press.

Htun, M. and Weldon, S. (2017). States and Gender Justice, in K. Morgan and A. Orloff (eds), *The Many Hands of the State*. Cambridge: Cambridge University Press.

Humphries, J. (ed.). (1995). *Gender and Economics*. Aldershot: Edward Elgar.

Humphries, J. (2012). Childhood and Child Labour in the British Industrial Revolution. *Economic History Review* 66(2): 395–418.

Humphries, J. (2013). The Lure of Aggregates and the Pitfalls of the Patriarchal Perspective: A Critique of the High Wage Economy Interpretation of the British Industrial Revolution. *The Economic History Review* 66(3): 693–714.

Humphries, J. and Schneider, B. (2018). Spinning the Industrial Revolution. *The Economic History Review* (May).

Humphries, J. and Weisdorf, J. (2015). The Wages of Women in England, 1260–1850. *The Journal of Economic History* 75(2): 405–47.

ILO (International Labour Office) (2018). *Care Work and Care Jobs for the Future of Decent Work*. Geneva: International Labour Office.

IMF (International Monetary Fund) (2017). *Tackling Inequality*. IMF Fiscal Monitor. Available at: http://www.imf.org/en/Publications/FM/Issues/2017/10/05/fiscal-monitor-october-2017

Inglehart, R. and Norris, P. (2003). *Rising Tide*. Cambridge: Cambridge University Press.

Inikori, J. (2007). Africa and the Globalization Process: Western Africa, 1450–1850. *Journal of Global History* 2(1): 63–86.

Inikori, J. (2014). Reversal of Fortune and Socioeconomic Development in the Atlantic World: A Comparative Examination of West Africa and the Americas, 1400–1850, in E. Akyeampong, R. Bates, N. Nunn and J. Robinson (eds), *Africa's Development in Historical Perspective*. Cambridge: Cambridge University Press, pp. 56–86.

Jensen, R. and Oster, E. (2009). The Power of TV: Cable Television and Women's Status in India. *Quarterly Journal of Economics* 123(3): 1057–94.

Jevons, W. (1888). *The Theory of Political Economy*. London: Macmillan.

Jha, P., Kesler, M., Kumar, R., et al. (2011). Trends in Selective Abortions of Girls in India: Analysis of Nationally Representative Birth Histories from 1990 to 2005 and Census Data from 1991 to 2011. *The Lancet* 377(9781): 1921–8.

Johnson, N. and Koyama, M. (2017). States and Economic Growth: Capacity and Constraints. *Explorations in Economic History* 64: 1–20.

Jones, E. (1987). *The European Miracle*. Cambridge: Cambridge University Press.

Jones, E. (1988). *Growth Recurring*. Oxford: Oxford University Press.

Kabeer, N. (1997). Women, Wages and Intra-household Power Relations in Urban Bangladesh. *Development and Change* 28(2): 261–302.

Kabeer, N. (2003). *Gender Mainstreaming in Poverty Eradication and the Millennium Development Goals*. London: Commonwealth Secretariat.

Kabeer, N. (2015). Gender, Poverty, and Inequality: A Brief History of Feminist Contributions in the Field of International Development. *Gender & Development* 23(2): 189–205.

Kabeer, N. and Natali, L. (2013). *Gender Equality and Economic Growth: Is there a Win–Win? IDS Working Paper*. Brighton: Institute of Development Studies.

Kahneman, D. (2011). *Thinking, Fast and Slow*. London: Penguin Books.

Karaman K. and Pamuk, Ş. (2013). Different Paths to the Modern State in Europe: The Interaction between Warfare, Economic Structure, and Political Regime. *American Political Science Review* 107(3): 603–26.

Kessler-Harris, A. (2001). *In Pursuit of Equity*. Oxford: Oxford University Press.

Kessler-Harris, A. (2015). *A Woman's Wage*. Lexington: The University Press of Kentucky.

Keynes, J. (1936). *The General Theory of Employment Interest and Money*. London: Macmillan.

Klasen, S. (1999). *Does Gender Inequality Reduce Growth and Development? Evidence from Cross-Country Regressions*. Policy Research Report on Gender and Development Working Paper Series. World Bank.

Klasen, S. (2002). Low Schooling for Girls, Slower Growth for All? Cross-Country Evidence on the Effect of Gender Inequality in Education on Economic Development. *The World Bank Economic Review* 16(3): 345–73.

Klasen, S. and Lamanna, F. (2009). The Impact of Gender Inequality in Education and Employment on Economic Growth: New Evidence for a Panel of Countries. *Feminist Economics* 15(3): 91–132.

Klein, A. and Ogilvie, S. (2017). *Was Domar Right? Serfdom and Factor Endowments in Bohemia. CEPR Working Paper.* London: CEPR.

Kleiner, M. and Krueger, A. (2013). Analyzing the Extent and Influence of Occupational Licensing on the Labor Market. *Journal of Labor Economics* 31(S1): S173–S202.

Klemp, M. and Weisdorf, J. (2018). Fecundity, Fertility and the Formation of Human Capital. *The Economic Journal*.

Kok, J. (2017). Women's Agency in Historical Family Systems, in J. van Zanden, A. Rijpma and J. Kok (eds), *Agency, Gender and Economic Development in the World Economy 1850–2000.* Abingdon: Routledge.

Konner, M. (2015). *Women After All: Sex, Evolution and the End of Male Supremacy.* New York: W. W. Norton & Company.

Koyama, M., Moriguchi, C. and Sng, T. (2017). *Geopolitics and Asia's Little Divergence: State Building in China and Japan after 1850.* Technical Report. Tokyo: Hitotsubashi Institute for Advanced Study.

Kramer, K., Myhra, L., Zuiker, V. and Bauer, J. (2016). Comparison of Poverty and Income Disparity of Single Mothers and Fathers across Three Decades: 1990–2010. *Gender Issues* 33(1): 22–41.

Kroeber, A. and Kluckhohn, C. (1952). Culture: A Critical Review of Concepts and Definitions. Papers of the Peabody Museum, Harvard University, Vol, XLVII, No. 1. Cambridge, MA: Peabody Museum.

Kuznets, S. (1955). Economic Growth and Income Inequality. *American Economic Review*, 45(1): 1–28.

Lambrecht, T. (2013). *The Welfare Paradox: Poor Relief and Economic Development in England in a European Perspective, c. 1600–c.1800.* EHS Annual Conference Paper. Available at: http://www.ehs.org.uk/dotAsset/b9f9c97f-f983-4693-91f6-2306983337ae.pdf

Landes, D. (1999). *Wealth and Poverty of Nations.* New York: Abacus.

Laslett, P. (1988). The European Family and Early Industrialization, in J. Baechler, J. Hall and M. Mann (eds), *Europe and the Rise of Capitalism.* Oxford: Basil Blackwell.

Laverte, M. (2017). Sexual Violence and Prostitution: The Problem is Your Image of Us. *Die Tageszeitung.* Available at: https://researchprojectgermany.wordpress.com/2017/12/29/sexual-violence-and-prostitution-the-problem-is-your-image-of-us/

Ledyard, O. (1995). Public Goods: Some Experimental Results, in J. Kagel and A. Roth (eds), *Handbook of Experimental Economics.* Princeton, NJ: Princeton University Press.

Lee, L. (2014). Sex Workers Want Rights – Not Rescue. *Ravishly*, 8 September.

Lee, L. (2015). Should It be Illegal to Pay for Sex? This Legislation Would Force Us to Work Alone. *The Guardian*, 24 March.

Leeson, P. and Russ, J. (2017). Witch Trials. *The Economic Journal* 128(613): 2066–105.

Lévi-Strauss, C. (1956). The Family, in H. Shapiro (ed.), *Man, Culture, and Society*. New York: Oxford University Press.

Lévi-Strauss, C. (1970). *The Elementary Structure of Kinship*. London: Eyre & Spottiswoode.

Levine, D. (2012). *Is Behavioural Economics Doomed? The Ordinary versus the Extraordinary*. Cambridge: Open Book Publishers.

Lewis, J. (2009). *Work–Family Balance, Gender and Policy*. Northampton: Edward Elgar Publishing.

Lindert, P. (2017). *The Rise and Future of Progressive Redistribution*. Commitment to Equity Institute Working Paper. Tulane University.

Lister, K. (2018). A Scheme to Support Sex Workers was Successful in Victorian Times – and It Can Work Today. *iNews*, 11 January.

Lott, Jr., J. and Kenny, L. (1999). Did Women's Suffrage Change the Size and Scope of Government? *Journal of Political Economy* 107(6): 1163–98.

Lu, J. and Teulings, C. (2016). Secular Stagnation, Bubbles, Fiscal Policy, and the Introduction of the Contraceptive Pill. *Centre for Economic Policy Research Policy Insight* 86. Available at: https://voxeu.org/article/secular-stagnation-bubbles-fiscal-policy-and-introduction-contraceptive-pill

Lu, Y., Luan, M. and Sng, T. (2016). The Effect of State Capacity under Different Economic Systems. *SSRN Electronic Journal*, 7 April.

Lucas, R. E. (2004). The Industrial Revolution: Past and Future. Annual Report, Federal Reserve Bank of Minneapolis, pp. 5–20.

Ma, D. (2016). China, in J. Baten (ed.), *A History of the Global Economy*. Cambridge: Cambridge University Press, pp. 188–201.

Ma, D. and Rubin, J. (2017). The Paradox of Power: Understanding Fiscal Capacity in Imperial China and Absolutist Regimes. *SSRN Electronic Journal*, 7 November.

MacKinnon, C. (1987). *Feminism Unmodified*. Cambridge, MA: Harvard University.

Mandala, E. (1984). Capitalism, Kinship and Gender in the Lower Tchiri (Shire) Valley of Malawi, 1860–1960: An Alternative Theoretical Framework. *African Economic History* 13: 137.

Marçal, K. (2015). *Who Cooked Adam Smith's Dinner?* London: Portobello Books.

Marshall, A. (2014). *Surprising Design of Market Economies*. Austin: University of Texas Press.

Mauro, P., Romeu, R., Binder, A. and Zaman, A. (2015). A Modern History of Fiscal Prudence and Profligacy. *Journal of Monetary Economics* 76: 55–70.

Mazzucato, M. (2011). *The Entrepreneurial State*. London: Demos.

McClintock, A. (1995). *Imperial Leather*. New York: Routledge.

McCloskey, D. (2008). Mr Max and the Substantial Errors of Manly Economics. *Economic Journal Watch* 5(2): 199–203.

McCloskey, D. (2010). *The Bourgeois Virtues*. Chicago, IL: University of Chicago Press.

McCloskey, D. (2011). *Bourgeois Dignity*. Chicago, IL: University of Chicago Press.

McCloskey, D. (2017). *Bourgeois Equality*. Chicago: University of Chicago Press.

McClure, S., Laibson, D. I., Loewenstein, G. and Cohen, J. D. (2004). Separate Neural Systems Value Immediate and Delayed Monetary Rewards. *Science* 306(5695): 503–7.

McCulloch, J. (1848). *A Treatise on the Succession to Property Vacant by Death*. London: Longman, Brown, Green, and Longmans.

McElroy, W. (1991). *Freedom, Feminism, and the State*. New York: Holmes & Meier.

McElroy, W. (2001). *Individualist Feminism of the Nineteenth Century*. Jefferson, NC: McFarland.

McElroy, W. (2002). *Liberty for Women: Freedom and Feminism in the 21st Century*. Chicago, IL: Ivan R. Dee.

Medema, S. (2009). *The Hesistant Hand: Taming Self-Interest in the History of Economic Ideas*. Princeton, NJ: Princeton University Press.

Meek, R. (1962). *The Economics of Physiocracy*. London: Allen & Unwin.

Michalopoulos, S. and Papaioannou, E. (2011). Divide and Rule or the Rule of the Divided? Evidence from Africa. NBER Working Paper 17184.

Michalopoulos, S. and Xue, M. (2017). *Folklore*. Working Paper. Available at: https://econ.uconn.edu/wp-content/uploads/sites/681/2018/01/draftOct30th_folklore_final.pdf

Mies, M. (1986). *Patriarchy and Accumulation on a World Scale*. London: Zed Books.

Milanovic, B. (2013). Global Income Inequality in Numbers: in History and Now. *Global Policy* 4(2): 198–208.

Milanovic, B. (2015). Global Inequality of Opportunity: How Much of Our Income Is Determined by Where We Live? *Review of Economics and Statistics* 97(2): 452–60.

Milanovic, B. (2016). *Global Inequality*. Cambridge, MA: Harvard University Press.

Mill, J. (1859). *On Liberty*. London: John W. Parker and Son.

Mill, J. (1869). *The Subjection of Women*. London: Longmans, Green, Reader & Dyer.

Mokyr, J. (1990). *The Lever of Riches*. New York: Oxford University Press.

Mokyr, J. (2006). Mercantilism, the Enlightenment, and the Industrial Revolution, in R. Findley (ed.), *Eli F. Heckscher (1879–1952): A Celebratory Symposium*. Cambridge, MA: MIT Press, pp. 269–303.

Mokyr, J. (2009). *The Enlightened Economy*. New Haven, CT: Yale University Press.

Mokyr, J. (2017). *A Culture of Growth*. Princeton, NJ: Princeton University Press.

Mokyr, J. and Nye, J. (2007). Distributional Coalitions, the Industrial Revolution, and the Origins of Economic Growth in Britain. *Southern Economic Journal* 74(1): 50–70.

Morgan, J. (2004). *Labouring Women: Reproduction and Gender in New World Slavery*. Philadelphia, PA: University of Pennsylvania Press.

Morrison, A., Dhushyanth, R. and Sinha, N. (2007). *Gender Equality, Poverty and Economic Growth*. Policy Research Working Paper. World Bank.

Mosini, V. (2012). *Reassessing the Paradigm of Economics*. Abingdon: Routledge.

Mullainathan, S. and Shafir, E. (2013). *Scarcity*. London: Allen Lane.

Nangle, T. (2015). *Labour Power Sets the Neutral Real Rate*. VoxEU.

Nelson, J. (1992). Gender, Metaphor, and the Definition of Economics. *Economics and Philosophy* 8(1): 103–25.

Nelson, J. (1993). The Study of Choice or the Study of Provisioning? Gender and the Definition of Economics, in M. Ferber and J. Nelson (eds), *Beyond Economic Man*. Chicago, IL: Chicago University Press, pp. 23–36.

Nelson, J. (1995). *Feminism, Objectivity and Economics*. London: Routledge.

Nelson, J. (2018). *Economics for Humans*. Chicago, IL: University of Chicago Press.

Nelson, J. and Power, M. (2018). Ecology, Sustainability, and Care: Developments in the Field. *Feminist Economics* 24(3): 80–8.

Nordic Model Now! (2016). Joint Submission to the Liberal Democrats 'Sex Work' policy Consultation. Available at: https://nordicmodelnow.org/2016/10/28/submission-to-the-liberal-democrats-sex-work-policy-consultation/

North, D. (1981). *Structure and Change in Economic History*. New York: W. W. Norton.

North, D. (1990). *Institutions, Institutional Change and Economic Performance*. Cambridge: Cambridge University Press.

North, D. and Thomas, R. (1973). *The Rise of the Western World*. London: Cambridge University Press.

North, D. and Weingast, B. (1989). Constitutions and Commitment: The Evolution of Institutions Governing Public Choice in Seventeenth-Century England. *The Journal of Economic History* 49(4): 803–32.

Nunn, N. (2012). Culture and the Historical Process. *Economic History of Developing Regions* 27 (suppl1.): S108–S126.

Nussbaum, M. (2013). *Sex and Social Justice*. Oxford and New York: Oxford University Press.

Ober, J. (2015). *The Rise and Fall of Classical Greece*. Princeton, NJ: Princeton University Press.

O'Brien, P. (2010). The Nature and Historical Evolution of an Exceptional Fiscal State and its Possible Significance for the Precocious Commercialization and Industrialization of the British Economy from Cromwell to Nelson. *The Economic History Review* 64(2): 408–46.

O'Connor, J., Orloff, A. and Shaver, S. (2009). *States, Markets, Families*. Cambridge: Cambridge University Press.

OECD (2008). *Growing Unequal? Income Distribution and Poverty in OECD Countries*. Paris: OECD Publishing.

OECD (2011). *Society at a Glance 2011*. Paris: OECD Publishing.

Offer, A. (1997). Between the Gift and the Market: The Economy of Regard. *The Economic History Review* 50(3): 450–76.

Offer, A. (2002). *Why Has the Public Sector Grown So Large in Market Societies? The Political Economy of Prudence in the UK, c. 1870–2000*. Discussion Papers in Economic and Social History. University of Oxford.

Offer, A. (2012). Self-Interest, Sympathy, and the Invisible Hand: From Adam Smith to Market Liberalism. *Economic Thought* 1(2): 1–14.

Offer, A. (2017). The Market Turn: From Social Democracy to Market Liberalism. *The Economic History Review* 70(4): 1051–71.

Ogilvie, S. (2011). *Institutions and European Trade*. Cambridge: Cambridge University Press.

Ogilvie, S. and Carus, A. (2014). *Institutions and Economic Growth in Historical Perspective*. CESifo Working Paper Series. Available at: https://ssrn.com/abstract=2463598

O'Hara, S. (2013). Everything Needs Care: Toward a Relevant Contextual View of the Economy, in M. Bjørnholt and A. McKay (eds), *Counting on Marilyn Waring: New Advances in Feminist Economics*. Bradford, ON: Demeter Press.

Okin, S. (1989). *Justice, Gender and the Family*. New York: Basic Books.

Olson, M. (2008). *The Rise and Decline of Nations*. New Haven, CT: Yale University Press.

Olsson, O. and Hibbs, D. (2005). Biogeography and Long-Run Economic Development. *European Economic Review* 49(4): 909–38.

Oosthuizen, S. (2017). *The Anglo-Saxon Fenland*. Oxford: Windgather Press.

Ortiz-Ospina, E. and Roser, M. (2018). Public Spending. Our World in Data. Available at: https://ourworldindata.org/public-spending

Parente, S. and Prescott, E. (1999). Monopoly Rights: A Barrier to Riches. *American Economic Review* 89(5): 1216–33.

Parente, S. and Prescott, E. (2002). *Barriers to Riches*. Cambridge, MA: MIT.

Parthasarathi, P. (1998). Rethinking Wages and Competitiveness in the Eighteenth Century: Britain and South India. *Past & Present* (158): 79–109.

Pateman, C. (1988). The Patriarchal Welfare State, in A. Gutman (ed.), *Democracy and the Welfare State*. Princeton, NJ: Princeton University Press.

Paul, S. (2016). Women's Labour Force Participation and Domestic Violence. *Journal of South Asian Development* 11(2): 224–50.

Pearlstein, S. (2013). Is Capitalism Moral? *The Washington Post*, 15 March.

Pedersen, S. (1995). *Family, Dependence and the Origins of the Welfare State*. Cambridge: Cambridge University Press.

Pedersen, S. (2018). One-Man Ministry, Review of *Bread for All: The Origins of the Welfare State* by Chris Renwick. *London Review of Books* 40(3): 3–6.

Pennington, M. (2011). *Robust Political Economy*. Cheltenham: E. Elgar.

Perlmann, J. and Margo, R. A. (2001). *American Schoolteachers, 1650–1920*. Chicago: Chicago University Press.

Phipps, A. (2014). *The Politics of the Body*. Cambridge: Polity Press.

Picchio, A. (1992). *Social Reproduction*. Cambridge: Cambridge University Press.

Pierce, J. and Schott, P. (2016). The Surprisingly Swift Decline of US Manufacturing Employment. *American Economic Review* 106(7): 1632–62.

Piketty, T. (2014). *Capital in the Twenty-First Century*. Cambridge, MA: Harvard University Press.

Pinchbeck, I. (1930). *Women Workers and the Industrial Revolution, 1750–1850*. London: G. Routledge & Sons.

Platteau, J. (2014). Redistributive Pressures in Sub-Saharan Africa: Causes, Consequences, and Coping Strategies, in E. Akyeampong, R. Bates, N. Nunn and J. Robinson (eds), *Africa's Development in Historical Perspective*. Cambridge: Cambridge University Press.

Polanyi, K. (1944). *The Great Transformation*. New York: Rinehart.

Polanyi, K. (1966). *Dahomey and the Slave Trade*. Washington, DC: Washington University Press.

Pomeranz, K. (2012). *The Great Divergence*. Princeton, NJ: Princeton University Press.

Postell, J. and Watson, B. (2011). *Rediscovering Political Economy*. Lanham, MD: Lexington Books.

Power, M. (2004). Social Provisioning as a Starting Point for Feminist Economics. *Feminist Economics* 10(3): 3–19.

Prügl, E. (2016). Neoliberalism with a Feminist Face: Crafting a New Hegemony at the World Bank. *Feminist Economics* 23(1): 30–53.

Pujol, M. (1984). Gender and Class in Marshall's Principles of Economics. *Cambridge Journal of Economics* 8(3): 217–34.

Pujol, M. (1998). *Feminism and Anti-feminism in Early Economic Thought*. Cheltenham: E. Elgar.

Rai, S. (2013). Gender and (International) Political Economy, in G. Waylen, K. Celis, J. Kantola and L. Weldon (eds), *The Oxford Handbook of Gender and Politics*. New York: Oxford University Press.

Rai, S., Hoskyns, C. and Thomas, D. (2011). *Depletion and Social Reproduction. Centre for the Study of Globalisation and Regionalisation Department of Politics and International Studies*. Warwick: University of Warwick.

Rao, V. (1993). The Rising Price of Husbands: A Hedonic Analysis of Dowry Increases in Rural India. *Journal of Political Economy* 101(4): 666–77.

Rao, V. (2007). The Economics of Dowries in India, in K. Basu (ed.), *Oxford Companion to Economics in India*. Oxford: Oxford University Press.

Raworth, K. (2018). *Doughnut Economics*: London: Chelsea Green.

Reid, R. (2014). The Fragile Revolution: Rethinking War and Development in Africa's Violent Nineteenth Century, in E. Akyeampong, R. Bates, N. Nunn and J. Robinson (eds), *Africa's Development in Historical Perspective*, Cambridge: Cambridge University Press, pp. 393–423.

Richards, E. (1974). Women in the British Economy since about 1700: An Interpretation. *History* 59(197): 337–57.

Richerson, P. and Boyd, R. (2006). *Not by Genes Alone*. Chicago, IL: University of Chicago Press.

Roberts, A. (2016). *Gendered States of Punishment and Welfare*. Abingdon: Routledge.

Robertson, C. (1988). Never Underestimate the Power of Women. *Women's Studies International Forum* 11(5): 439–53.

Rodgers, Y. (2018). *The Global Gag Rule and Women's Reproductive Health*. Oxford: Oxford University Press.

Rodney, W. (1972). *How Europe Underdeveloped Africa*. London: Bogle-L'Ouverture Publications.

Rodrik, D. (1997). *Has Globalization Gone Too Far?* Washington, DC: Institute for International Economics.

Rodrik, D. (1998). *Where Did All the Growth Go? External Shocks, Social Conflict, and Growth Collapses*. NBER Working Paper. NBER.

Rodrik, D., Subramanian, A. and Trebbi, F. (2004). Institutions Rule: The Primacy of Institutions over Geography and Integration in Economic Development. *Journal of Economic Growth* 9(2): 131–65.

Roser, M. (2016). Global Economic Inequality. *Our World in Data*. Available at: https://ourworldindata.org/global-economic-inequality

Roser, M. and Ortiz-Ospina, E. (2018). Global Extreme Poverty. *Our World in Data*. Available at: https://ourworldindata.org/extreme-poverty

Roth, A., Prasnikar, V., Okuno-Fujiwara, M. and Zamir, S. (1991). Bargaining and Market Behaviour in Jerusalem, Ljubljana, Pittsburgh and Tokyo: An Experimental Study. *American Economic Review* 81(5): 1068–95.

Royal Commission on Employment of Children in Factories (1833). Second Report, Minutes of Evidence. London: House of Commons Papers.

Rubery, J. (2015). Austerity and the Future for Gender Equality in Europe. *ILR Review*, 68(4): 715–41.

Rubin, G. (1975). The Traffic in Women: Notes on the 'Political Economy' of Sex, in R. Reiter (ed.), *Toward an Anthropology of Women*. New York: Monthly Review Press.

Rubin, J. (2018). *Rulers, Religion and Riches*. Cambridge: Cambridge University Press.

Rubinstein, W. (1981). *Men of Property*. London: Croom Helm.

Samuels, S. (1992). *The Culture of Sentiment: Race, Gender and Sentimentality in Nineteenth-Century America*. New York: Oxford University Press.

Sandberg, S. (2013). *Lean In: Women, Work, and the Will to Lead*. New York: Alfred A. Knopf.

Sandelin, B., Trautwein, H. and Wundrak, R. (2008). *A Short History of Economic Thought*. London: Routledge.

Sawhill, I. (2014). *Generation Unbound*. Washington, DC: Brookings Institution Press.

Scheidel, W. (2010). Real Wages in Early Economies: Evidence for Living Standards from 1800 BCE to 1300 CE. *Journal of the Economic and Social History of the Orient* 53(3): 425–62.

Scheidel, W. (2017). From Plains to Chains: How the State Was Born. *Financial Times*, 5 October.

Scheidel, W. (2018). *The Great Leveler*. Princeton, NJ: Princeton University Press.

Schrijvers, J. (1991). *Women's Autonomy: From Research to Policy*. Amsterdam: Institute for Development Research.

Scott, J. (2018). *Against the Grain*. New Haven, CT: Yale University Press.

Seguino, S. (2000a). Accounting for Gender in Asian Economic Growth. *Feminist Economics* 6(3): 27–58.

Seguino, S. (2000b). Gender Inequality and Economic Growth: A Cross-Country Analysis. *World Development* 28(7): 1211–30.

Seguino, S. (2011). Gender Inequality and Economic Growth: A Reply to Schober and Winter-Ebmer. *World Development* 39(8): 1485–7.

Semuels, A. (2016). Severe Inequality Is Incompatible with the American Dream. *The Atlantic*, 10 December.

Sen, A. (1977). Rational Fools: A Critique of the Behavioral Foundations of Economic Theory. *Philosophy & Public Affairs* 6(4): 317–44.

Sen, A. (1987). *Gender and Cooperative Conflicts*. Helsinki: World Institute for Development Economics Research.

Sen, A. (1999). *Development as Freedom*. Oxford: Oxford University Press.

Sheldon, K. (2017). *African Women: Early History to the 21st Century*. Bloomington, IN: Indiana University Press.

Shiller, R. (1984). Stock Prices and Social Dynamics. *Brookings Papers on Economic Activity* 1984(2): 457–98.

Siegel, H. (2013). *Why the Choice to be Childless is Bad for America*. Newsweek, 19 February.

Simon, H. (1957). *Models of Man: Social and Rational*. New York: John Wiley and Sons.

Skarbek, D. (2014). *The Social Order of the Underworld*. Oxford: Oxford University Press.

Smith, A. (1759). *Theory of Moral Sentiments*. Edinburgh: Kincaid and Bell.

Smith, A. (1776). *An Inquiry into the Nature and Causes of Wealth of Nations*. London: William Strahan and Thomas Cadell.

Smith, R. (1986). Transfer Incomes, Risk and Security: The Roles of the Family and the Collectivity in Recent Theories of Fertility Change, in D. Coleman and R. Schofield (eds), *The State of Population Theory Forward from Malthus*. Oxford: Basil Blackwell, pp. 188–211.

Smuts, B. (1995). The Evolutionary Origins of Patriarchy. *Human Nature* 6(1): 1–32.

Solar, P. (1997). Poor Relief and English Economic Development before the Industrial Revolution. *The Economic History Review* 48(1): 1–22.

Sollée, K. (2017). *Witches, Sluts, Feminists*. Berkeley, CA: ThreeL Media.

Spek, R., Leeuwen, B. and Zanden, J. (2015). *A History of Market Performance*. Abingdon: Routledge.

Spolaore, E. and Wacziarg, R. (2009). The Diffusion of Development. *Quarterly Journal of Economics* 124(2): 469–529.

Spolaore, E. and Wacziarg, R. (2013). How Deep Are the Roots of Economic Development? *Journal of Economic Literature* 51(2): 325–69.

Sprinkle, A. (2009). 40 Reasons Why Whores are My Heroes, in D. Sterry (ed.), *Hos, Hookers, Call Girls, and Rent Boys*. New York: Soft Skull Press, pp. 10–11.

Standing, G. (1999). Global Feminization Through Flexible Labor: A Theme Revisited. *World Development* 27(3): 583–602.

Steckel, R. and Prince, J. (2001). Tallest in the World: Native Americans of the Great Plains in the Nineteenth Century. *American Economic Review* 91(1): 287–94.

Steinberg, M. (2016). *England's Great Transformation*. Chicago, IL: University of Chicago Press.

Stephenson, J. (2018). 'Real' Wages? Contractors, Workers, and Pay in London Building Trades, 1650–1800. *The Economic History Review* 71(1): 106–32.

Stern, N. (2006). *Stern Review: The Economics of Climate Change*. Her Majesty's Treasury of the UK Government.

Stiglitz, J. (2015). *The Great Divide*. London: Allen Lane.

Stiglitz, J. (2016). The State, the Market, and Development. *UNU WIDER Working Paper*.

Strober, M. (1984). Towards a General Theory of Occupational Sex Segregation, in B. Reskin (ed.), *Sex Segregation in the Workplace*. Washington, DC: The National Academies Press.

Strossen, N. (2000). *Defending Pornography*. New York: New York University Press.

Swedburg, R. (2011). *The Household Economy: A Complement or Alternative to the Market Economy?* Center for the Study of Economy and Society Working Paper Series. Cornell University.

Tabellini, G. (2008). Institutions and Culture. *Journal of the European Economic Association* 6(2–3): 255–94.

Tabellini, G. (2010). Culture and Institutions: Economic Development in the Regions of Europe. *Journal of the European Economic Association* 8(4): 677–716.

Tankersley, J. and Scheiber, N. (2018). Wielding Data, Women Force a Reckoning Over Bias in the Economics Field. *New York Times*, 10 January.

Taylor, J. (1992). *Reclaiming the Mainstream*. Buffalo, NY: Prometheus Books.

Tertilt, M. (2005). Polygyny, Fertility, and Savings. *Journal of Political Economy* 113(6): 1341–71.

Thaler, R. (1992). *The Winner's Curse*. New York: Free Press.

Thaler, R. and Sunstein, C. (2008). *Nudge: Improving Decisions about Health, Wealth and Happiness*. New Haven, CT: Yale University Press.

Therborn, G. (2004). *Between Sex and Power: Family in the World 1900–2000*. London: Routledge.

Thompson, E. (1991). *Customs in Common*. London: Merlin Press.

Tilly, C. (1975). Reflections on the History of European State-Making, in C. Tilly (ed.), *The Formation of Nation States in Western Europe*. Princeton, NJ: Princeton University Press, pp. 3–84.

Titmuss, R. (1970). *The Gift Relationship: From Human Blood to Social Policy*. London: Allen and Unwin.

Todd, E. (1988). *The Explanation of Ideology*. Oxford: Basil Blackwell.

Todd, E. (2011). *L'origine des systèmes familiaux*. Paris: Gallimard.

Tversky, A. and Kahneman, D. (1974). Judgment under Uncertainty: Heuristics and Biases. *Science* 185(4157): 1124–31.

UNFPA (2017). *UNFPA Supplies Annual Report*. New York: United Nations.

UNICEF (2014). *Ending Child Marriage: Progress and Prospects*. New York: UNICEF.

Van Bavel, B. (2016). *The Invisible Hand?* Oxford: Oxford University Press.

Van Bavel, B. and Rijpma, A. (2015). How Important Were Formalized Charity and Social Spending before the Rise of the Welfare State? A Long-Run Analysis of Selected Western European Cases, 1400–1850. *The Economic History Review* 69(1): 159–87.

Van den Heuvel, D. (2007). *Women and Entrepreneurship*. Amsterdam: Aksant.

Van Zanden, J., Buringh, E. and Bosker, M. (2011). The Rise and Decline of European Parliaments, 1188–1789. *The Economic History Review* 65(3): 835–61.

Van Zanden, J., Rijpma, A. and Kok, J. (2017). *Agency, Gender, and Economic Development in the World Economy 1850–2000*. Abingdon: Routledge.

Voigtländer, N. and Voth, H. (2013). How the West 'Invented' Fertility Restriction. *American Economic Review* 103(6): 2227–64.

Wajcman, J. (2010). Feminist Theories of Technology. *Cambridge Journal of Economics* 34(1): 143–52.

Wallerstein, I. (1976). *The Modern World System*. New York and London: Academic Press.

Walter, N. (2011). *Living Dolls*. Frankfurt: Fischer-Taschenbuch-Verlag.

Wang, G. (2016). *Reproductive Health and Gender Equality*. London: Routledge.

Waring, M. (1988). *If Women Counted*. San Francisco: Harper.

Weber, M. (2016). *The Protestant Ethic and the Spirit of Capitalism*. Lanham: Dancing Unicorn Books.

Wellings, K., Jones, K., Mercer, C., et al. (2013). The Prevalence of Unplanned Pregnancy and Associated Factors in Britain: Findings from the Third National Survey of Sexual Attitudes and Lifestyles (Natsal-3). *The Lancet* 382(9907): 1807–16.

Wheeler, A. and Thompson, W. (1825). *Appeal of One Half of the Human Race, Women, Against the Pretensions of the Other Half, Men*. London: Longman, Hurst, Rees, Orme, Brown and Green.

White, D., Betzig, L., Mulder, M., et al. (1988). Rethinking Polygyny: Co-Wives, Codes, and Cultural Systems [and Comments and Reply]. *Current Anthropology* 29(4): 529–72.

Wiener, M. (1981). *English Culture and the Decline of the Industrial Spirit, 1850–1980*. Cambridge University Press.

Wiesner-Hanks, M. (2015). *Women and Gender in Early Modern Europe*. Cambridge: Cambridge University Press.

Williams, E. (1994). *Capitalism and Slavery*. Chapel Hill, NC: University of North Carolina Press.

Woetzel, J., Madgavkar, A., Ellingrud, K., et al. (2015). *The Power of Parity: How Advancing Women's Equality Can Add $12 Trillion to Global Growth*. New York: McKinsey Global Institute.

Wollstonecraft, M. (1792). *A Vindication of the Rights of Woman*. London: J. Johnson.

Wood, A. (2018). The 1990s Trade and Wages Debate in Retrospect. *The World Economy* 41(4): 975–99.

Woolley, F. (1993). The Feminist Challenge to Neoclassical Economics. *Cambridge Journal of Economics* 17(4): 485–500.

Woolley, F. (1996). Getting the Better of Becker. *Feminist Economics* 2(1): 114–20.

World Bank (2011). *World Development Report 2012: Gender Equality and Development*. Washington, DC: World Bank Group.

World Economic Forum (2017). *The Global Gender Gap Report*. Switzerland: World Economic Forum.

Wrigley, E. (1988). *Continuity, Chance and Change*. Cambridge: Cambridge University Press.

Wrigley, E. and Schofield, R. (1981). *The Population History of England, 1541–1871*. London: Edward Arnold for the Cambridge Group for the History of Population and Social Structure.

Xue, M. (2016). *High-Value Work and the Rise of Women: The Cotton Revolution and Gender Equality in China*. SSRN, 1 November.

Xue, M. and Koyama, M. (2018). *Autocratic Rule and Social Capital: Evidence from Imperial China*. MPRA Working Paper.

# Index